The
West of
England

The
West of
England

AN ARTIST'S JOURNEY THROUGH ENGLISH LANDSCAPES

SYDNEY R. JONES

SENATE

The West of England

First published in 1950 as *England South* by
The Studio Publications, London & New York

This edition published in 1998 by Senate,
an imprint of Tiger Books International PLC,
26A York Street, Twickenham,
Middlesex TW1 3LJ, United Kingdom

1 3 5 7 9 10 8 6 4 2

ISBN 1 85958 527 2

Printed and bound in the UK by
Cox & Wyman, Reading, England

CONTENTS

1. INTRODUCTION

NORTH OF THE THAMES TO THE ROMAN WALL

The kind reception given to my previous records of England, both at home and abroad, has encouraged me to complete this volume. It follows *England—South* and thus makes the second in a set of three books. These are planned to indicate characteristic features throughout the whole country by presenting selections of my drawings and notes collected from many places on occasions both recent and distant. The present pages concern the western half of England, bounded in the south by the course of the Thames and Gloucestershire, and in the north by Cumberland and the Roman Wall. Over this area the harvest of beauty, incident, and story is big and rich. My powers and paper supplies are limited. No more than a general pattern and picture has been attempted from too much known wealth available for use. Notable omissions will be found abundant. For these and other sins I beg a little forgiveness while performing my part as showman of drawings accompanied by words.

My humble offering from the West chiefly concerns old things: portions of the English heritage that are related in one way or another to mankind's acts in hatching chapters, paragraphs, and postscripts of the English tale. The sundry bits and details on view in these pages, as a bagman's samples might be, have been gleaned from the supplies that even to-day seem almost inexhaustible. They come from town and country, from busy highways and quiet places made and developed during the course of past life and history. Although the ancient prophet's idea of "the everlasting hills" is getting somewhat worn and out of date with the advent of bulldozers and similar destructive appliances, some of the originals of my subjects might be considered more or less permanent. The Pennine Chain, for instance, and landscapes of hills and valleys belong to this category; many though not all of the fields are likely to remain intact for some time yet. Other objects shown and described exist on more shaky and perilous tenures. Representatives of presents that have passed away or bloomed anew, they include cathedrals and churches, castles, big houses and small houses, towns, villages and hamlets, and such incidental items as windows once brightened by medieval, Elizabethan, and Georgian suns, chimneys that kept home fires burning for ages, and pubs old in the fame of time-honoured home-brews. Needless to state, a number of the buildings illustrated have been mauled and a few of them no longer are visible.

My subjects, with thousands more to be seen in every part of England, are present witnesses of the nation's passage through its centuries of peace and plenty, trouble and strife, and the ordinary bread-and-butter years sometimes garnished with cake. And as the deeds of individuals and nations generally mean more than their words, these works constructed by men and women and the natural scenes known and fashioned by them constitute infallible indicators of human thought, action, and ideals now and again aimed at. These accumulations of past years, manifestations of humanity's problems, capers, and exploits in living, doing, and dying, could not help being allied to the debatable subject usually termed art. This was inevitable, for it is a truism that art, in common with arms, legs, cooking, and other necessities, is an absolute part of the life of all persons and periods. Whether the general expression is considered good, bad, pretty, or ugly may depend on the spirit of the age that produces it and also what people happen to think of the results a long time afterwards. Art certainly differs in kind. Some of it is thought to have beauty, though what and where that quality is constantly arouses speculations and differences of opinion. Even at this moment sections of the public declare that the present age is one of battle between beauty and the beasts, though the wisest among them disagree on where the beauty lies and whether the fierce animals have lairs in the neighbourhood of Whitehall or elsewhere. This type of warfare did not always develop on the grand scale because the skilled practitioners far outnumbered the mere talkers and writers on art. Existing evidence proves that once upon a time abundant beauty thrived, blossomed, and ripened throughout England as men and women cherished and tended the earth, built homes, towns and villages, created wonders for worship, pomp, and circumstance, and gave to the things for daily use their inborn touch of artistry. An artistic race of the elevated sort evidently then peopled the land. The way of life bred fine artists in tune with the times, prompted truly national and great architecture, and made loveliness shine through the arts and the crafts. Everybody had a hand in the process, kings, nobles, churchmen, big bugs, little bugs, and the rank and file of the Joneses, Browns, Smiths, and Robinsons. Channels of thought and traditions flowed down from the developed culture of the Saxons, absorbed the Norman influence, bounded from strength to strength in the golden Gothic time, and streamed on melodiously through the early and late Renaissance years until the Industrial Revolution and its developments stemmed the current. Widespread beauty, once the common possession and inspiration, sank in shallows and in miseries. The bequest of a thousand years was engulfed in an era of new enlightenment. Truly might a present John Jones (descendant of the Joneses aforesaid) burst into poetic eloquence through his pressed-steel window and shout over the prefabricated party fence to John Smith (descendant of the Smiths aforesaid), "Oh, what a fall was there, my countrymen!"

Still, there is much to be thankful for. Amongst the host of amusing and material conveniences now available it is grateful and comforting to have mass-produced motor cars, charabancs, and bicycles for running everybody all over England to view the relics of beauty formed by the people of long ago. If Henry VIII, Cromwellians, and various ancients and moderns had never been born these relics might be even more plentiful, to furnish "the glittering plains" that William Morris often dreamed of. But the remains yet on view mean more than rosemary for remembrance of old life and times. They still can please and charm. They help to demonstrate that good art, beauty, and life flowed together harmoniously and they signify no reasons why a similar state of affairs may not happen again.

Hazlitt, we know, considered "One of the pleasantest things in the world is going a journey." I certainly agree with him and therefore ask the kind reader of this page to join me in journeys through parts of western England that have continued pleasant since Hazlitt spent his early years on our route at Wem and in 1798 heard Coleridge preach at Shrewsbury. The method of progress is as you wish, by mechanical wheels, in an armchair, or any other way favoured for perambulation or sitting down. My journeys over this area have been going on for some time, either on feet, bicycles, motors, railways, in a pony-trap, and even with a boat, a sketchbook always being handy and something to eat and drink in my bag in case of emergencies. Following the example of showmen who offer programmes to indicate what may be expected or endured, it seems best to begin with a brief outline of our ways and destinations. For present purposes my England of the west is divided from the east with an imaginary line formed by the Pennine Chain from Cumberland to the Peak; thus no more than the western regions of the large county of Yorkshire are included. The line then continues south along the eastern county boundaries of Derbyshire, Staffordshire, Warwickshire, and Oxfordshire.

The southern Chiltern country, the exodus of operations, crosses the narrow leg of Oxfordshire which points to the Thames, with Thame at the knee-joint and Henley and Reading at the foot. Chalk hills sweep in curves to the dips and "bottoms," the quietest and loveliest in the whole line of these heights. Grand beech woods clothe the slopes and juniper-trees stand darkly over the more open places. Villages are scattered and generally small. Farm and cottage walls of flint bonded with brickwork indicate location better than signposts. The Icknield Way, primitive and green in parts, winds an antique course from Cleeve to Chinnor. Escarpments above it, rising to more than 800 feet at Beacon and Bald Hills, offer extensive panoramas ending in distant haze and show where we are to go (23). Little rises and valleys over the near plain mark homelands of quaint and out-of-the-way villages, such as Wheatfield, Newington, and Berrick Salome, clustered round Chalgrove battlefield. The Thame stream divides them from higher ground with spy-points at Stanton St. John and

COTSWOLD STONE. *Tetbury.*

MIDLAND BLACK AND WHITE—*Weobley.*

NORTHERN STONE. *Burnsall in Wharfedale.*

PENNINE TOWN. *Alston, England's highest.*

Elsfield for distant views of Oxford (34-35). The Roman way, with legions of blackberry bushes at Ot Moor, points a straight line to Bicester and Newton of the Purcells. Across the vale the Cherwell flows down; ever winding and never hurrying, it sings a battle-song of 1644 at Cropredy Bridge, smiles at Banbury's fine lady, meanders past pretty borderlands, steeples, towers, and parks, and ends in measured paces at Addison's Walk, Magdalen bridge, and the Thames.

The chalk is no more. Stone reigns in its stead, the oolite stone coloured by nature in lovely tints, yielded at Hornton and a score of quarries, and beautifully worked by man. The land begins to rise in an arc from the Norman tower of Broughton Poggs, Witney butter cross, Woodstock's palace, and Adderbury's choice church and spire. Clear rivers, homes of the trout, sparkle along. The Coln winds through Coln Rogers, Bibury, and Fairford; the Windrush shoots under Bourton's little bridges and Burford's four arches; the Evenlode sweeps round Wychwood Forest. They hasten down from the wolds, for the real Cotswold country lies before us. We reach the uplands, airy and sometimes bleak on the tops and cosy in the valleys, wooded and flowered. Scenes everywhere are gracious with stone. It makes the field boundaries (which Cobbett thought ugly!). Stone walls and roofs, homes of lichen and stonecrop, beautify manor-houses, villagers' quarters, and miles of streets in country towns. Spread out far and wide are the places and spaces of the old wool trade and sheep flocks. Churches show proudly from Chipping Campden in the north to Wootton-under-Edge in the south. Their tall towers, mostly in the Perpendicular fashion, particularly commemorate the woolstaplers and clothmen who worshipped in sanctuaries created and paid for with gains made from wool. The Fosse Way crosses the hills, bearing a burden of history in its immemorial course from the Humber to the Exe. It mounts and dips and leads from Moreton-in-the-Marsh (actually over 400 feet up) to Stow-on-the-Wold, Northleach (43), Cirencester, and just misses rare old Tetbury. (9). Cirencester shoots a straight Roman arm to Birdlip and Gloucester; and at Birdlip Hill we have arrived at the high and final escarpments of the Cotswolds. The wooded and bold lines of the hills jut in and out, stand like cliffs over green oceans of land and the silvery windings of the Severn. Camps crown Cleeve, Haresfield, Uley, and height after height. Broadway Tower, a late addition of 1800, commands the north, and the south has its own tall monument at North Nibley to William Tyndale and the Bible. Every high point shows miles and miles of panoramas over the Severn vale, the Forest of Dean, and away to Abergavenny's Sugar Loaf, prospects fit to bring joy to every heart not made of oolite or any other stone (64).

Down in the fertile vale our routes point onward, past Cheltenham's pump room, terraces, and stucco, and the high fretted tower of Gloucester poised over old streets and an ancient New Inn (88, 89). For the present no more than a thought can be sent to Saxon Deerhurst or Berkeley's castle pile in which a

Plantagenet king was murdered, nor can loiterings yet be made to study the feats of the Severn school of masons from Bristol to Tewkesbury. Across the river the pretty way leads by the orchards of Westbury and the old inn of Newnham to Chepstow and the estuary. Stretches of water and sand, the vale and the Cotswolds combine in wide landscape effects and delicate colourings. The land mounts up from these lowly levels and we find the 5, 6, and 700-feet elevations of the Forest of Dean. Pleasant Stile, near Little Dean, gives the close details of the famous Severn bend, already traced from afar on the Cotswold heights. It turns from Epney's eel grounds, circles in a majestic sweep from Pimlico Sands to Bullo Pill, and winds round The Noose sandbank opposite Awre church. The silvery gleam of water, trees proudly massed, and the accent of roofs at Newnham afford a memorable sight of England. The Forest spreads for miles to the north, the south, and westward almost to Monmouth. Here at all times are dense woodlands clothed in the finery of every season, glorious stretches of oaks, the beech trees, shy ponds, scattered hamlets, and inns under greenwood trees. Ruardean Hill and many a point show where our tracks will be for reaching the winding Usk, Abergavenny, and Llanthony's ruined priory in the Honddu dip between the steep and lonely slopes of the Black Mountains (70). Staunton's 700-feet eminence presents another great and famous river bend, the victorious four-mile V made by the Wye on its way down from Symond's Yat to the bank of Offa's Dyke below Redbrook. The nearness of the significant Dyke denotes that we have gained the border country of earthworks, camps, and castles, to recall the dangerous days, nights, and years of the Marches.

With Geoffrey of Monmouth, Henry V, and Rolls the companion of Royce, Monmouth offers good names to illuminate various historical periods. But as we cannot stop at present to pry into the *Historia*, a royal birth, and Gordon-Bennett races, the fact that the town has two bridges is of premier importance (69). The bridges mean a meeting of waters; and when these happen to be the Wye and the Monnow, with the River Usk not far away, a trio of glorious scenic rivers await exploration. Here are scenes of world renown, the subjects painted by Turner and hosts of artists. Waters trace remarkable windings and beautiful curves. Hills and woods mass in grand vistas to far distances. Crags and heights give viewpoints for wide panoramas (81). Vales expand between Monmouth, Abergavenny, and Usk. It is a land of castles. Raglan (75), Chepstow, and others of fame, castles less well known at Grosmont, Skenfrith, White, Caldicot, and elsewhere, add the spice of romance to nature's store of loveliness. Enchantment ever triumphs at the popular Tintern ruins. St. Pierre with a gatehouse is but one of the gabled homes that suggest how peace and quiet indoors needed defence from without in the good old days. Stone walls at Caerwent, or the traditional landing-place for the conquest of Siluria near the Severn Tunnel at Sudbrook, bring a tinge of Roman hours to present days.

An approximate 40 miles upstream from Turner's "Junction of the Severn and the Wye" brings us to Tewkesbury, another meeting of waters. The Avon, "the soft-flowing Avon," joins its greater brother, the Severn, where the bells of the Norman abbey chime benedictions of peace over the meadows, grave-yards of the last hopes and petals of the Red Roses in the battle of 1471. Across the vale the Malvern Hills screen Herefordshire from the Worcestershire plain and Warwickshire, and the Avon, turning a slow movement from Watling Street near Rugby, glides sweetly through these two Midland counties spelt with the capital W. It waters quiet scenes of nature's beauty beautified by man; it shows England's true rural heart while leading across the centre of England.

Thatched roofs, timbered walls, and big chimney-stacks indicate our arrival

in Warwickshire. The Central Plain, extending beyond Birmingham, Coventry's spires, and Atherstone, holds the characteristic old homes of the district, often moated and framed in oak, as at Grimshaw (95) and Baddesley Clinton. North and south in the county rise stately mansions, such as Stoneleigh Abbey (96) and Compton Wynyates (115), to recall bygone times when a peer of the realm was a king in his own little kingdom. Warwick stands for a real castle that is lived in, but at Kenilworth no more than ruins and ghosts will welcome our footsteps in treading the halls of John of Gaunt and Queen Elizabeth's Leicester (112). Beyond the Vale of the Red Horse and the Fosse Way we discern one more battle point, Edge Hill, in command of rich landscapes and long distances patterned with the Midland fields and hedgerows. The Avon ever calls, flowing between leafy borders through the vale. It skirts Dunsmore Heath, where the Gunpowder Plotters hoped to proclaim a new queen but didn't, washes the otter's lairs at pretty Bubbenhall, divides Leamington from Warwick, winds through the Lucys' park at Charlecote, leaps the weir at Stratford church (107) bound for Bidford bridge and Worcestershire. Near and far stand the oaks and reminders of the Forest of Arden—Hampton-in-Arden, Henley-in-Arden, gnarled trunks in Packington Park, the Shakespeare oak in Stoneleigh Deer Park. These place-names of course tell that we are right in the heart of Shakespeare's England, a smiling countryside in which "the lark at heaven's gate sings" when the weather is warm and decent. At and round Stratford, in towns, villages, and fields that Shakespeare knew and loved, we can join with people of all nations and pay homage to the immortal name.

Elms, hundreds of them lined on the hedgerows and gathered in massy clusters, meet and greet us in Worcestershire. No county is richer in these noble trees. Like gallant soldiers on the march they stride across the plain which spreads out luxuriantly from Bredon Hill and the Clent Hills to Wyre Forest, Woodbury Hill, and the Malverns (132). On a downward course out of Warwickshire the Avon bends and curves a 25-mile sweep in sight of Bredon Hill and meanwhile graces an English fairyland of present comeliness and past memories. Here are villages to show pictorial combinations of oak timbering against white, thatched roofs, mingled colourings of old bricks and grey stone everywhere embowered in greenery. Cleeve (116), Cropthorne, Elmley Castle, Throckmorton, Birlingham, and a dozen more homely places will tempt any wanderer from hastening on. Evesham names its own vale, one that will offer wonderful sights when nature weaves films of snowy whiteness over the orchards in plum-blossom time. The good earth, praised for fruitfulness in the twelfth century by William of Malmesbury, continues to yield as if by magic. Evesham's ruins and standing buildings, including the Bell Tower (114), mark the sad ending of a mighty abbey, and fresh grass on Green Hill hides red stains where de Montfort fell in 1265. One more abbey relic a few miles away at Pershore and the Norman splendour of Tewkesbury further downstream complete this trio of abbeys, fragments of once great institutions that suggest how alluring the Avon must have been for monks dedicated to the quiet life with fish on Fridays.

The long course of the Severn continues. Passing between the woods of Wyre Forest and Areley, Layamon's dwelling-place "upon the Severn's bank," the river waters the fertile plain bounded by the hills of Abberley and then enters Worcester (108–109). Cathedral and stream unite in the memorable scene that has been responsible for pictures by the hundred before and since B. W. Leader put it on canvas. The great tower, the early Perpendicular masterpiece, stands nobly over the place of Cromwell's crowning victory and Charles's flight of

1651. Another hurrying can be traced from Alcester to Huddington, Hanbury, Burcot, Hagley, and Stourbridge, part of the route galloped hell for leather by the Gunpowder Plotters in November 1605. Huddington Court (124), home of Winter the Plotter, in but one of many timbered and moated houses standing in our tracks through the county. In fact, timbering is on view all the way from Birtsmorton in the south to Chaddesley Corbett in the north, shown by farms, cottages, and manor-houses, Dormston and other dovecotes framed in timber, and a timbered church tower here and there to partner the one at Pirton. In country and town the Midland brickwork appears, of Georgian and earlier dates. Though big castles and very great houses may not be found, such parks and places as Hagley, Westwood, and Croome visibly represent the aristocratic grandeur of a bygone classic age.

On the summit of Malvern Hills a mere step will take us out of Worcestershire into Herefordshire. The bird's-eye view is over one of England's fairest counties. We look towards the birthplaces of William Langland, John Abel the carpenter, Nell Gwyn, David Garrick, John Masefield. The slopes meet the wide vale broken by hills. Brockhampton, Dinmore, Wormsley, Haugh, and more miles of high woods, sportsmen's paradises all, are rarest among the rare in rich colourings and patterned shadows. Offa's Dyke and the Roman way from Leintwardine (*Bravonium*) to Kenchester (*Magna*) mark old boundaries. Beyond Abbey Dore, the Golden Valley, and ruined castles in the Marches, the hills mount up to join the heights of Wales. With many a graceful curve the Wye leads on from de Clifford's Castle of Clifford, bound for Hereford bridge (130–131) and Ross (137). The pretty Lugg river joins it after a long wandering from the woods of Aymestrey and Edward IV's battlefield at Mortimer's Cross. Cattle grazing in the meadows tell that we are among the Herefordshires. Orchard trees, growing hops, and pointed kilns promise cider, perry, and ale to lubricate happy wanderers in snug towns like Leominster, Bromyard, and Ledbury. The cathedral tower of Hereford stands for a centre-piece of the ball-flower ornament displayed in the churches. Nobody can fail to see the black-and-white, the oak and plaster, brave, dazzling effects in town and country scenes.

Leaving reminders of once live strongholds bunched together at Richard's Castle, Wigmore, and Brampton Bryan (149), we cross into Shropshire to find more and more castles standing in various stages of dilapidation from Clun (150) to Oswestry and Whittington (175). These, with camps and ditches on high points, may prompt sentimental romancing on Llewelyn ap Gruffydd, Owen Glyndwr, Roger de Montgomery, and earlier legendary giants who once enlivened the Marches with rows and raids until retirement in the numerous tumuli ended their expressions of brotherly love. The country, here rugged and mountainous, certainly has a warlike aspect. The great Dyke of Offa, worn and weary sentinel, presents its best section from Llanvair Hill into Montgomery-shire. Solitude reigns about the earthen rampart. The air is bracing, landscapes are fine, and slopes and woodlands of exceptional grandeur, almost untrodden by man, lead on through Clun Forest to the Black Mountain. The Stiperstones, the Long Mynd, and Caradoc (158) call us away from the borders of Wales into the wild Shropshire of *The Golden Arrow* and Mary Webb. The River Clun hastens from the mountains. Rippling, it sings a Housman song through "Clunton and Clunbury, Clungunford, and Clun," then swells the waters of

LVDLOW

the Teme. The stream meets Ludlow, perfect in situation and contents, and still haunted by Milton's *Comus*. Corve Dale opens out between Brown Clee Hill and Wenlock Edge. It promises a little world of natural and man-made beauty from Stokesay Castle (149) to Much Wenlock abbey. We meet the Severn once more, see it flowing by woods and ruins in the memorable view of Buildwas Abbey. Downstream, Bridgnorth castle and rebuilt church top the hillside town (163). Higher up, the river touches Wroxeter and its load of Roman deadness, but light and life greet us where the stream circles round the two hills, the spires, the winding streets and fascinating buildings assembled round Roger de

Montgomery's Norman castle and abbey foundation of Shrewsbury (156–157). Near at hand are the ruined abbeys at Haughmond and Lilleshall, and Battlefield church as well, still fine as it was when built for Henry IV to commemorate the victorious day in which Hotspur Percy fell and Falstaff saved his paunch. The broad plain extends from the Severn vale across north Shropshire. On Grinshill Hill at Clive (164), William Wycherley's birthplace, we can see at a glance this tranquil countryside. It is a land of wide pastures, many trees, secluded villages, sandstone Gothic churches and Georgian towers, quiet country towns like Wem and Whitchurch (170), and a little lake district owned by Ellesmere.

The bold, straight line of Watling Street takes us into Staffordshire. A Black Country to the south and the Potteries to the north of the Roman highway introduce our first sniffs of industrial England. But as these signs of the country's greatness do not suggest what Hitler called "strength through joy," we can ignore the scenic effects of smoke and arid earth, follow the Romans to their station at Wall (*Letocetum*), and then ruminate on uneconomic products of old England, here visible in the unique triple spires of Lichfield presiding with grace over Dr. Johnson's own city (182–183). Cannock Chase is in sight. This elevated tract, even now largely unspoiled by coal-loving man, shows diversified surfaces, woods and parks ringed round pretty Penkridge, Beaudesert, Rugeley, and Milford. Views from the uplands extend away over the western scene, a quiet, rural country notable for the churches at Gnosall and Eccleshall, and a battle-point of the Red and White Roses on the higher ground at Blore Heath. Up on the moors of the Staffordshire Highlands the River Trent begins a long course. It passes through Trentham Park, greets at Tixall the River Sow, fresh from Izaak Walton's birthplace and the shoemakers of Stafford. The stream glides between wooded banks past Cannock Chase, adds pleasantness to the village acres of the Ridwares and King's Bromley (189), meets the Roman road pointing to Derby, and sends the gypsum water along to the brewers at Burton-on-Trent. Landscapes across the vale denote the aged limbs and remnants of Needwood Forest, and limbs and features of gentry who owned the oaks we shall find wonderfully represented inside Hanbury church. At that high point, with Derbyshire in full view, the River Dove shows itself after coming down in lovely measures from the Fishing House of Cotton and Walton in Beresford Dale. Winding, ever winding, the stream leads us to Tutbury's Norman church and the castle, a smashed memorial of John of Gaunt.

Derbyshire promises the mountains, dales, and rivers for which it is famous. But first, if we cross from Staffordshire to south Derbyshire in the neighbourhood of Newton Solney, the landscapes there and beyond show in lowly key through the sandstone vale of the Trent. A pastoral stretch of England is this, true to the Midland type. Miniature hills break the level lines at such points as Findern, Ticknall, and at Chellaston Hill. Swarkeston's long and ancient bridge marked the limit of the Young Pretender's advance. The Church of All Saints, Derby, keeps the pride of Perpendicular towers for many a mile (195). At this point, where Prince Charles Edward came to a stop in 1745, the railway sheds and industrialism may not detain us, so we can advance in the tracks of the Pretender's hasty retreat, leave the sandstone, meet the mountain limestone and millstone grit, and enjoy a complete change of scenery. The hills grow higher and bigger. Upward from Belper and Ashbourne groupings become varied and bold. Darley, Monsal, and the dales and vales that everybody knows open out, fast streams and the Rivers Dove, Wye, and Derwent hasten from the moors, impressive panoramas fill the distances. Above the magnificence of crags, rocks, glens, and leaping waters the Peak rears its wild heights to more than 2,000 feet, the southern culmination of England's great backbone along which our northward quest will be through the Pennines to Cumberland. Buildings and field boundaries of stone rule again. Bulky walls, heavy roofs and low-pitched gables begin to show that we are meeting the northern expression in masonry. Stone greyly colours Stanton-in-the-Peak (207), Eyam, Bakewell, Tideswell; it tones scores of places settled round valley streams, on hilltops, and across the county to the vicinity of Chesterfield's crooked spire. Properly situated in nature's bounteous settings stand the great houses, relics of systems now worn out. Historic and renowned, they include Chatsworth, very splendid (201), and Haddon Hall, romantic and picturesque (202), two of England's great sights. The Norman ruin at Castleton, representing one of the old brigade, occupies a position dramatic enough either for William Peverel or *Peveril of the Peak*.

In Macclesfield Forest, at the *Cat and Fiddle* inn, or perhaps with a look back from Alderley Edge, we bid a temporary adieu to the mountains and dales, then descend to the plain of Cheshire. Wide flat landscapes broken by a few sandstone hills make the landscapes on our route to the River Dee and the Wirral peninsula. Level, rich farmlands stretch for miles. Gothic church towers, built pink and red from the native stone, give touches of colour to the villages and towns and locate the cathedral at Chester (221). Trees in Delamere Forest and elsewhere remind that dense woodlands once covered the county, and "magpie" buildings, plentifully in view, show how the earlier inhabitants used the timber. Their efforts promise exciting moments at Moreton and the group of noted halls, at Marton and Warburton churches, and inside and outside the unique rows of Chester (208–209). Malpas (215), and towns and villages in all directions, contain their particular specimens of oak used without stint, sixteenth- and seventeenth-century interiors, and massive low beams devised for bumping people's heads; perhaps the old timbers of Knutsford prompted unrecorded comments from Mrs. Gaskell and the taller ladies of *Cranford!*

On Merseyside and north of the High Peak we gird our loins to meet and leave the drab concentrations of industry in Lancashire and Yorkshire. Hemmed in stand reminders of times gone—cathedrals at Manchester and Bradford, Perpendicular churches, old halls well cared for by new owners and municipal authorities. Forests of chimneys, smoke, vapours, and twinkling lights by night yield characteristic effects, peculiar yet fascinating for those who appreciate them; and at least these areas of cottons and woollens demonstrate how far we have travelled since Adam and Eve first set the fashion with pristine leaves. Moors, valleys, and farms on hillsides (241) surround and neighbour the masses of stone, bricks, and mortar. The sandstone, extended from Cheshire, ends on the coastal belt at Morecambe Bay. Speke, near Liverpool, and Hall i' th' Wood at Bolton are among the last of the timbered houses before the reign of the northern stone buildings.

Clear of the signs and portents of manufacturing towns we meet pure air, prepare for mountains, rocks, passes, moors, torrents, and the tumbled stone that makes nature's own grand architecture throughout the Pennines and the Lake country (258). Great Whernside, Ingleborough, Helvellyn, Skiddaw, the fells and the highest peaks in England will point directions and serve for milestones. Villages, towns, lonely farms, and cottages crouched on the slopes and all built of gray stone present man's handiwork dwarfed by the bigness of natural shapes. Boldly constructed with massive walls and low roofs, the buildings seem to stand defiant to wind and storm. The dales run down into Yorkshire (247), to Grinton, to Wensley, and to the memorable scene at Bolton Abbey on the Wharfe (242). Rivers of fame and beauty, including the Ribble, Turner's Lune, the Eden, and Wordsworth's Duddon, leave wild birthplaces for luxurient vales. In this land of poets, song, and story the castles, peel towers (262), and fortified homes may stir thoughts on moss-troopers, raids, and strife. At scores of points between John of Gaunt's Lancaster (234–235), Appleby, and Carlisle (260–261) we can meditate in safety on times that were dangerous. More pleasantly perhaps if the Lakeland wet does not descend, the roofless halls of Brougham Castle will suggest a few lines from Wordsworth on the Shepherd Lord Clifford (263).

Legends of a Roman Wall now gone can lead our imaginations past the red city of Carlisle (260–261) and through the pleasant green vale to Gilsland, the village in which Walter Scott met and won his bride in 1797. The River Irthing leaps the rocks, shoots the bridge, then curves fast below the bluff of Birdoswald. On the height are stones and broken masonry, all that remains of *Ambloganna*, once the largest Roman station on the Wall (264). We stand on the ruins, look towards Bewcastle Fells and Scotland, see where the Ninth Legion advanced for conquest in the second century—and never came back. Strife not recorded in history or ballad brings this sketch of our itinerary to a full stop.

2. WESTWARD FROM THE CHILTERN HILLS

OXFORDSHIRE, GLOUCESTERSHIRE, MONMOUTHSHIRE

Good honest ground, real English, makes this area for exploration indicated on the map below. It spreads beyond the River Severn and is washed by the tides of the Bristol Channel; the Thames and Oxfordshire form boundaries in the south and east. Chiltern chalk, Cotswold oolite and lias, sandstone beds from the Severn vale to the River Usk and the mountains tumble geological time down the ages. Landscape shapes and patterns are richly varied by these formations. Combinations of nature's handiwork and the labours of man account for a wealth of attractive scenes. Many of the great sights, such as Tintern and the Cotswold towns, have worldwide repute. Early dwellers and Romans found the high points and big panoramas; they travelled along the Fosse Way and other routes now in use. Fine architecture developed through the local products of stone, chalk, flint, and plentiful woodlands. It is shown by splendid churches, towns, villages, and country houses built of stone, flint walls and timbered dwellings. Spoliation by modern industry is not generally well represented, but a number of objects, including the crop of aerodromes in operation, temporarily defunct, or captured by squatters, signify a district abreast of the times.

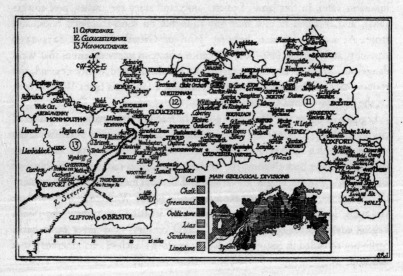

SOUTHERN CHILTERNS AND THE OXFORDSHIRE VALE

OXFORDSHIRE VALE from the Chilterns at Beacon Hill

Nowhere do the Chiltern Hills show better than on the 20-mile stretch in Oxfordshire. Landscapes are both widespread and intimate. The line of escarpments from Swyncombe to Chinnor Hill can give one the idea of being on the top of the world to view kingdoms; the seclusion in such parts as Bix Bottom (25) and Maidensgrove Scrubs may rouse a suggestion of being the only inhabitant on earth. All the best characteristics of chalk country are here—heights and distances, rises and falls blended in subtle curves, close valleys enclosed in steep banks, heaths, commons and airy spaces, hollow ways, hanging woods, and some of the quietest places under the sun. Mother Earth pervades the colour-schemes. Spangled tints on turned ploughlands, the opalescent shine of field greens, and bright accents of exposed chalk offer the thought of a divine artist at work and using white freely with the pigments on the palette. Brilliant effects are amplified by the stately depths of woodlands, the undergrowth of thorns and bushes; yews and hollies make their own deep notes, and juniper-trees, darkly clad, are regimented like soldiers on slopes of whitened green.

The south Chiltern woods are glorious. Where could be found more gracious massed patterns of trunk, limb, and foliage than in the sequence which extends from Crowell Hill and Aston Woods to Stonor Park, Nettlebed Woods, College Wood near Hardwick House, and the hill of St. Birinus at Berins? Oak and ash, sycamore, cherry, and a mixture of trees thrive. The beeches of course hold pride of place. Their branches and new greenery shoot up over the haze of oceans of bluebells in spring; summer warms the luscious tints; autumn decks the beech foliage with gold beyond price. November tunes its symphonies to golden showers, and all through the winter pearly smooth bark gleams like silver above carpets of rich brown leaves that rustle and prance in the wind.

Alas! many of these noble trees prematurely die. The woodman spares not the axe. Men wearing official hats walk round and pronounce doom far and wide. Dreadful slaughter happened during the war years; now the high price of nationalized coal has brought further degradation by reducing the beauty of branches to mere blocks of wood for fuel, scurvily sold at one penny each.

Old-fashioned craftsmen also do their bit, a very little bit nowadays, for their race is becoming extinct. Though they turn the growth of nature's patient years into legs for chairs to accommodate human beings in the passage from the cradle to the grave, these acts may be excused by realizing that they represent last skirmishes in a lost cause pitted against the conquering monarch called machinery.

Samuel Rockall, the old friend of H. J. Massingham, has been fighting this losing battle all his life. For this reason I set out to find him just beyond Stonor Park and discovered his flint cottage and wooden workshop on the edge of a heath fringed with beech trees, the ammunition for chair-leg bodgers. A knock at the door and an enquiry brought the reply, "You'll find him down the garden"; which to me seemed just as it should be when seeking a true child of environment who drew the essence of life from the earth, its gifts, and skill of human hands. Among spring cabbages and sprouting onions I met a hale, shortish man whose merry eyes, characterful features, and air of sturdy independence evidently were not born of a safety-first and penny-in-the-slot decade. He talked of plants and weather, trees and wood. We went to the workshop. Outside on the heath grew beeches. Trunks, felled by the bodger, lay piled on the near grass. The door of the workshop led to a cave fit for Arcady, Pan's very own, conglomerated with blocks for chopping, horses for sawing and shaving, the lathe for turning, tools suspended from beams and hung on walls. When the lathe spun round for my particular benefit the prime moments had come. The pliant wood yielded. Curly shavings scattered. Deft hand movements made the shapes. A chair-leg, properly finished off, finally was mine. I received more than that, held in my fingers a last link in the chain of traditional workmanship that brought pride and pleasure to both makers and users, and thus garnished life through past centuries in England. Here was exemplified the ageless economy of divine provision: growing trees outside, felled trunks, the wooden workshop, right tools, finished products, joy in work, seasonable beauty visible always, sweet air around, little money for labour, and—happiness. Natural supply, place, and pride in doing accounted for the man standing before me. He represented the end of a line that made the national folk art and from which sprang a Hugh Herland, a John Abel. His accomplishment, simple though skilled, offered one of those little episodes in ordinary workaday life such as Chaucer knew and an artist vignetted on the parchments of the *Luttrell Psalter*.

Whether Samuel Rockall still works in beech I do not know. The memory of my visit lives, a reminiscence formed in the mind like a faded cameo set in a Chiltern scene of springtime. Many winters have come since then. Sad to relate, chair-leg bodgers do not fit into new times. Machinery has conquered them one by one. If any survive, they might be thought just archaic and out-of-date jetsam by the human flotsam buoyed pleasantly or otherwise on progressive currents agitated by electric drills, prefabrication, and other diabolical inventions. Tears

BIX BOTTOM, *a secluded section of the southern Chilterns with a ruined church below Maidensgrove Scrubs. The woods of Stoner Park show in the distance.*

WATLINGTON. *The lines of the Chiltern escarpment seen from above the site of the old castle.*

HORLEY, *a stone village in north Oxfordshire near to the famous quarries for Hornton stone*

for the passing of an old brigade are therefore superfluous, nor is it heartening to sentimentalize on ancient and hand-made Windsor and rush-seat chairs, once eagerly sought by young folks and grandfa's with whiskers. Yet if any of my readers fancy an antidote to things as they are, or would like whiffs of old life and freedom before they are as extinct as the dodo, I recommend a journey to Summer Heath, beyond Stonor Park and just in Buckinghamshire, to see if the chair-leg bodger is still on view. If he is not, the Chiltern views will repay all the petrol expended.

Little of historical consequence belongs to this section of the hills. Grim's Dyke, fringed with beeches, holds its antique line from Nuffield to Mongewell, keeps secrets and tells nothing. The Icknield Way, senior in service, cuts the Dyke, skirts Ipsden and Ewelme; rising in elevation and beauty, it strides the greensand belt where the chalk promontories push out at Swyncombe Downs and Watlington, Beacon and Chinnor Hills. Lovely and silent in green and white stretches, the route invites no olden confidences among the solitudes. Gone are the signs and footprints of the unknown figures that went up and down from Salisbury Plain, the Berkshire Downs, and Norfolk in the forgotten centuries of B.C. Conscious of age and purpose, the primeval track still asserts authority, fixes parish boundaries, demands respect for original uses, laughs as it were at modern times. More than once it has done this to me while bringing discomfort for not using the Way as first planned. In wet weather the putty-like surface has clogged my bicycle wheels to a standstill, literally given the command to propel myself on Shanks's and carry the machine. In an age of human frailty it is sometimes salutary to be thus reminded of elemental origins and natural forces. White sticky mud in the Chiltern area is good for this purpose, having been puddled for about 100 million years if geologists speak the truth.

Neither villages nor population crowd the high lands. Settlements usually keep to the early arrangement of scattered hamlets grouped round greens and commons. The little collections of habitations, each decently small in the bigness of natural environment, make pretty pictures of houses, cottages, and barns properly featured in the native fashions, simple schemes of bright flint and brick walls, tiled roofs browned and mossy, bits of plasterwork, and timbering here and there to emphasize respectable lineage. The place-names, sampled by Hollandridge, Pishill, Maidensgrove, and Huntercombe End for a representative of the numerous "Ends," exactly fit Chiltern locations and qualities. Cosy pubs serve the district. At one of them recently, when the tough Argentine bulls were in short supply, I met a brave salmon in cut. I do not give the location of the fish because that announcement might cause an invasion; his presence is mentioned only to prove that a wayfarer may thrive quite well while exploring these sequestered haunts in which the finery of nature's work predominates. Architecture takes second place. It had little scope to develop strongly. In past times the district was remote, a camping-ground for robbers and odd sort of people, and the Chiltern Hundreds in the next county even now keep old memories green by accommodating extinct politicians. A sprinkling of lowly churches offer what might be expected in form and style—Norman arches at Checkendon; Early English windows at Ipsden; Swyncombe in a divine situation and interesting throughout from early walls to the fine modern rood-screen; and no more than a tangled ruin in Bix Bottom to recall Thomas de Belesham, the first rector in 1236. The idea of hearth and home, expressed in a bigger way than was usual in village and hamlet, brought the very good house at Turville Heath, a Georgian specimen open to the sky and the trees and in view for all to see.

And there is Stonor House in its park, a grand sight of lordly home and natural beauty blended to a high note of harmony. The footpath from the clap-gate in the village to Balham's Wood yields visions all the way, stately measures offered by the Restoration house and the chapel, gardens meeting grasslands, wide green slopes curving down, patches of shade from isolated trees, deer ambling in line, and the great semicircle swept majestically and toned with deep woods that mount to the rim marked out against the sky. Of all the combinations of homes and parks in England, few, if any, can excel this one for the artistry of leaving much alone and adding little. Tranquil and secluded, the scene remains an emblem of past spacious years. Yet in spite of the perfection and visual delight presented it seems ghostly to me now, a faded relic like a human beauty mellow in age but with course run and purpose served. Dead as a doornail are the inspirations and uses that caused and maintained the like of Stonor House and Park. My first visit of long ago suggested an ideal frontis-piece for *Burke's Peerage*. A school was in possession on my last visit. What next? I wonder! All who wish to see this rare sight intact should hasten there before the spoilers get to work.

Away to the west the Chiltern ramparts point their bosses and combes to the cornlands and the vale. Magnificent panoramas from every vantage point sweep over the great plain punctuated here and there by what Horace Walpole called "the dumpling hills." Eye and fancy travel over the valleys of the Thame stream and the River Cherwell, to the moated castle of Shirburn, Chalgrove battlefield, Oxford, Marlborough's and Vanbrugh's Blenheim, to Roman roads and coaching roads, towns, houses, and villages of long standing. Fine, too, are the looks back at the bold line of wooded heights when we say good-bye to the Chilterns and descend to the Lower Icknield Way running through Ewelme, Watlington, and Chinnor (25).

The mention of Ewelme reminds me that the showpiece of the neighbour-hood is handy, one justly famous and much visited by the knowing ones from English counties and foreign countries. Pretty cottages and houses, clear streams, little bridges, watercress beds, the site of a palace, a peerless group of fifteenth-century school, almshouses, and church (31), trees everywhere, downs around—what more could desire hope for on this earth, unless it be that the Benson aerodrome might retire instead of thrusting into the very borders of this demi-paradise. The story of Ewelme since its Domesday years already has been printed in dozens of books. It is therefore needless to slip back to the year 1428, when William de la Pole, Duke of Suffolk, married Alice Chaucer, the grand-daughter of the poet. Nor can anything new be said on their palace above the stream, the school and courtyard almshouses they caused to be made in lovely brickwork, the church they rebuilt in the Perpendicular style, and the treasures of craftsmanship it contains in monuments, hundreds of carved figures that include real masterpieces, sixteen brasses, old glass, the fifteenth-century font cover, the timber roof panelled and enriched. This village group gleams like a jewel, wonderfully wrought, finely set, toned by age; of all the places I know, marooned in the backwaters of an era distinguished for ugliness, few can awaken keener joy in past beauty. The palace of the Duke and Duchess, and later of Queen Elizabeth, gave up the ghost early in the seventeenth century. The only relics of it survive in the manor-house. It was from this palace that the Virgin Queen rode away on a pillion with her gallant Earl of Leicester to inspect the remarkable monuments of the de la Beches in Aldworth church, ten miles distant in Berkshire.

A ride in Kemp's bus from Ewelme will deposit those of us unfortunate enough to be without cars into Watlington. The end of the journey thus made can also provide some people with an anticlimax to the haunts of the late lamented Duke and Duchess of Suffolk. One-eyed, deadly, off the map—all sorts of laudatory expressions I have heard bestowed on this little town lying snug below the Upper Icknield Way and Chiltern slopes. Such tilts of language imply peace, charm, desirability. Watlington has these and other good qualities, even if it does not rank tawny and full-bodied in the choice vintage of small country towns. It centres round the market hall, arched below and built of 1664 brickwork, with the Georgian front of the *Hare and Hounds* conveniently placed opposite. Timbering, thatching, walls of flint, and plaster, and a sprinkling of good Georgian houses can be tracked in curious back ways and along the winding streets through which John Hampden made his last ride to Chalgrove battlefield in 1643. All in all, this one-eyed and deadly little town of much desirableness, near to the sources of bacon and eggs and far removed from tax inspectors, seems to me just the place that any harassed slave of the present dispensation might choose for ripening in age, comfort, and oblivion without even noticing explosions from Parliament Square, Russia, and other directions. The church, being largely rebuilt, need not make unusual demands for devotional exercises. Nicholas de la Beche and his castle, built in 1338, threaten no more, because both have completely gone (25); the site of their alarums is merely guarded by an artist of great distinction (Harold Speed), but he is quite inefficient in the arts of murder and only keeps watch when perched up a tree writing his books. In case of temporary ennui the little buses could show how the big world wags in the market on Fridays at Wallingford, or at Woolworth's near the Bodleian in Oxford. Now and then the funny railway train, after much labour, might promise connections for Fleet Street and a banquet at Guildhall. Not very often though, for I'm sure that any nice and wise person, once properly settled amongst old cronies in Watlington, would rarely dream of leaving them.

Shirburn Castle, really a fortified house of 1377, towered, moated, and built to replace a Norman stronghold of the mighty Robert D'Oilli, lies in aristocratic seclusion two miles along the Lower Icknield Way from Watlington. Next in order on King Cymbeline's road is Lewknor church, a beautiful reminder of the monks of Abingdon and very interesting, followed by the Lambert Arms. The inn, long famed as a port of call, marks a meeting of roads at the foot of Aston Hill, so we will follow the one that first leads past notable Tudor survivals of a Cistercian abbey in Thame Park, then enters the town settled near its namesake, the Thame river.

Thame is the jolliest place imaginable, whether in spring, summer, autumn, or winter, and the pubs will supply anything from tea to French wines of right vintages, at least one of them could when Landlord Fothergill reigned at the *Spread Eagle* and My Lord Asquith might be spotted making for the dining-room to tuck in. This bright collection of streets and houses meets the country and the country comes into the town, hinting a kind of marriage between corn-fields and shops, live beasts and roast beef, hay smells and petrol stinks. Hearty, browned, and healthy people walk up and down; scythes, bill-hooks, hoes, wheelbarrows, hedging-gloves, straps, buckles, and all sorts of marvels offered for sale spiritually belong to the world of soil and singing larks; signs up aloft embellished with painted symbols, such as black horse, nag's head, swan, eagle, and birdcage, keep up the nodding acquaintance with the beasts and birds of the field. Thomas Hardy's immortal Casterbridge always crops up in my mind when in the wide main street of Thame, a worthy rival of the one at Marlborough (32). Having settled down before the Conquest, the town of course is full of old things to show just what it should do for a marketing centre of mellow years. Inns, shops, and houses revive aspects of home life from the timbered and gabled period to the era of very good brickwork and eighteenth-century doorways. The reign of Queen Elizabeth brought the two school-houses; John Hampden attended one of them and, after the Chalgrove battle, returned to die in a timbered house near. A pretty picture riverwards through the trees includes the Prebendal House and Early English chapel, the work of Bishop Grossetête in the thirteenth century. Best of all and bordering the open

EWELME, *a gem of a village, has stood prettily at the foot of the Chiltern Hills since Domesday times. The church is a treasure-house of craftsmanship in stone, wood, carved tombs, and brasses. Adjoining are the quadrangle of almshouses and a school. All these buildings were schemed in the fifteenth century by the Duke of Suffolk and Alice Chaucer his wife, a grand-daughter of Geoffrey Chaucer the poet.*

STANTON HARCOURT. *Part of the church, Pope's tower, and remains of the Harcourt's early home. The church contains notable Harcourt monuments. In the tower Alexander Pope completed his translation of the fifth volume of Homer in 1718.*

THAME. *Tuesday market in the wide main street. The town is noted for its agricultural show, a noble church, prebendal chapel, abbey remains, Elizabethan grammar school, gabled and Georgian houses, and numerous inns including* The Spreadeagle *(right) and* The Bird Cage *(left).*

CHAPEL HOUSE NEAR CHIPPING NORTON. *Relics of the old coaching establishment at which, in 1776, Dr. Johnson delivered to Boswell his celebrated panegyric on the hospitality of inns and taverns.*

BANBURY. *Inn yard of the Reindeer showing the Globe Room before it was spoiled. The room had panelling of 1637 below an exceptional plaster ceiling, and served for a council of war at the time of the Battle of Edgehill. The entrance doors to the yard are dated 1570.*

OXFORD FROM ELSFIELD. *A distant impression of the city of towers and spires backed by the Cumnor Hills. One of the memorable views visible from the higher surroundings in the north-east.*

LOWER HEYFORD, *on the Cherwell stream. The parklands across the valley lead to Rousham House, a Jacobean home of the Dormer family with gardens laid out by William Kent.*

NORTH LEIGH, *near the Evenlode valley, Wychwood Forest, and the remains of a Roman villa. Stone houses and cottages neighbour the Saxon tower of the church, a building with medieval wall paintings, alabaster monuments, and beautiful fan-vaulting in the Wilcote chapel.*

ASTHALL (*above*) *and* BRIZE NORTON (*below*). *Two of the manor-houses that add distinction to many of the Oxfordshire villages. Next to Asthall the Windrush valley contains Minster Lovell and the ruined home of the Lovells.*

Sydney R. Jones.

BURFORD. *Cotswold towns offer some of the most wonderful streets in England. In and round this High Street are Elizabethan and later dwellings, the Tolsey with a clock (above), a remarkable church, the Priory house and chapel, the bridge over the River Windrush. Walls and roofs of local stone harmonize with the wold setting.*

green is the big church, a noble structure begun by the Bishop of Lincoln just mentioned. From the wealth it contains I can only indicate particular preferences—the central tower and lantern, Early English arcades, a rare south porch and parvise in the Decorated style, the Perpendicular rendering of the nave clerestory and roof, richness in the tracery of the south transept window, and the panelled tomb in the chancel with effigies of a lady and gentleman carved in alabaster. This monument, like a good many more, commemorates the art of getting on in the world, though more than alabaster perhaps may be needed for success in the hereafter. The gentleman in life secured the manor at the Dissolution, served Queen Mary only too well, assisted in burning martyrs at Oxford, became Lord Williams of Thame for services rendered, and finally retired into the gorgeous tomb at the opening of Queen Elizabeth's reign in 1559. His money built the almshouses, since defunct, and also the boys' school, now devoted to the book-learning of commercial Dr. and Cr. My Lord and My Lady continue intact. They are wonderfully presented, properly dressed, attended by greyhound and unicorn, railed in for privacy, and no suggestion of conducting bishops to martyrdom appears on the graven images. In a charming thatched house across the green lives Herbert Norris, the famous authority on English costume. Anybody lucky enough to meet him may learn all that can be known about the fur cloaks, armour, dress, and the trappings on the tomb of these great ones, once living figures in the lovely church.

Thame's present, however, is quite as thrilling as its past. In addition to Thame Show, an exciting and annual spectacle, every Tuesday market-day stages first-class shows all the year round, agog with cars, horses, traps, and waggons, country people shopping and bargaining, stalls in the street laden with gewgaws for every taste, pavements strewn with agricultural and household fancies. A general liveliness prevails, made all the merrier by the music of cattle, sheep, sows, and little porkers penned in wattles. And what is this? Myself wedged in a crowd of farmers round an auctioneer and a cow. The bidding starts: " 18, 10 —18, 15—19—19, 5" and so on to " 25—26—26, 10. Any more bids on 26 pounds 10 shillings?"—and in the excitement of the moment I nearly bid higher and might have secured a brown and white heifer, though what on earth to do with it would have sorely troubled my brain! A great place is Thame, both for past and present. Go there as soon as you can, dear reader, look well around, lunch with jolly farmers at the *Spread Eagle* or the *Black Horse*, and perhaps return with a pig or a cow to help out the rations!

South-west of the town true rural country stretches in peaceful and quiet acres to the Thames valley. Remote villages and hamlets continue from the Miltons, Wheatfield, Cuxham, Britwell Salome, Newington, and on to Warborough, prettily clustered round a stone and flint church tower and a big green, the local focus for cricket and August feasts of tremendous gusto. Buildings begin to show that we have reached the oolite stone. Many thatched roofs indicate an old craft still alive. Men can be met and talked to while they fix yelms and sprays and carry their burdens. The thatchers' "burden," it may be explained, is the wooden frame used for conveying heavy loads of straw up the steep angles of roofs. This implement resembles a large edition of a boy's catapult; it is rightly named when loaded, as I have discovered while lending a hand to one of these thatchers who is a friend of mine. Interesting sights and scenes are plentiful in this district, but my space only permits the bare mention of a few of them—Jacobean woodwork in Rycote chapel; the church of Henry VIII's brave topographer, John Leland, at Great Haseley; the wedding-house of John Hampden at Pyrton, good for Tudor chimneys and brickwork; an old barrel-organ for Sunday voluntaries in Brightwell Baldwin church; the big eighteenth-century house in full view at Newington; gatepiers, a pigeon-house, and a granary at Ascott, only survivors of the home of the Dormers, built in 1662 and immediately burned down. Those who prefer lunch before devotions can aid digestion by attending the only Sunday service inside Berrick Salome church at three o'clock; this permits meditations on the woodwork of the seventeenth-century gallery and roof. The name of Salome hereabout, be it noted, owns no connection with the wicked lady of the Bible. It survives from the Sallom family and the local pronunciation of "Saloom" is near the mark.

On the old London road over the Chilterns and near to the Thames stands Benson, though it might have stood no more when the Benson aerodrome expanded by pinching part of the historic highway and Beggarsbush Hill. Happily the village survived, just as Offa did in the year 777 after trouncing the West Saxons at the Battle of Bensington and thus pinching for the Mercian kingdom the district now called Oxfordshire. The battle is a forgotten thing; Benson's place on the great coach road is not. The bow of the *Castle* inn, the white front of the *White Hart*, timbering at the *Crown*, odd openings, long yards, and the nice architectural assortment in houses and inns clearly belong to a horsey past. While the new cars and red coaches swish past, stop, and go on, an air of departed days breathes balmily about this very good village street. Standing evidences trace back to the ages of roadside life agog with packhorses, heavy waggons, latten bells, chaises and sixes, flying-machines, and parsons jogging along with Mrs. parsons behind on pillions. And the following words told to me recently, and handed down from Landlord Costar who kept the *White Hart* in Georgian days, preserve what transpired when a large personage drove down from London.

"Good morning, landlord. Have you got any boiled bacon to-day?"

"Yes, at your service, your majesty," replied Costar, with a low bow.

"Let me have some, please. Don't forget the pickled cabbage. Never mind about the Majesty. I'm tired of that. Call me Farmer George down here."

OVERY MILL *on the Thame stream.*

After that dialogue King George III was known by his farming title whenever he called for the famous boiled bacon and cabbage of the *White Hart* at Benson.

Three miles distant towards Oxford, and near the end of the Thame stream's course, another faded relic survives in a backwater quiet as one could hope for in a noisy and hustling age. This is Overy Mill. It had a mention in Domesday Book, and William the Conqueror's scribe did not forget to put in a good word for the eels; natives who do not worry about Doomsday still say, "It's a good place for eels." Many a long year has passed since the monks of Dorchester Abbey went "over the rie (water)" to grind their corn at Overy. It is a long time, too, since Master William Turner, last of the line of millers of that name, passed in and out of the doorways, ground the corn, and, whitened from cap to boots, looked over the mill-dam and perhaps pondered on stewed eels. Nothing is doing now. A silent wheel in a gloomy chasm and bits and pieces tumbled down give suitable elements for the sentimental kind of picture favoured by Victorians and titled "Life's work ended" or something like that. Yet of all peaceful spots this is one of the rarest. You may sit for a whole day where I sat to sketch with never a human being in view, watch patterns of light and shade change on the weathered mill and the trees, hear water for ever singing into the pool. Hour by hour minnows turn and sparkle, tadpoles burrow, moorhens dart gracefully. Descendants of the Domesday eels of course do not show themselves, nor, fortunately, do the hasteners along the polished tarmac of the busy London–Oxford road only a quarter of a mile away.

Dorchester's splendid abbey and choice houses, and Oxford too, are beyond our present tracks; both these points properly belong to my previous book, *Thames Triumphant*. Divergent roads, or the Roman way from Dorchester, will lead us from the Thame valley to higher ground and on to Ot Moor, a fine solitary expanse in my youth, then marvellous for blackberries and quietude, and now marked on the map, "Bombing Range"! This way also goes perilously near the unlovely sprawl that demonstrates how an incomparable city is treasured by the English race. Nevertheless a number of distant prospects of Oxford seem to have escaped the notice of the spoilers. Round about Stanton St. John, Elsfield, and Beckley you see visions of towers and spires dreaming in the vale (34–35). Distance, lending enchantment to the views, softens the excrescences and surrender of beauty outward to Marston, the village with the manor-house in which Oxford surrendered the sword of war to Cromwell. Away to the west, and beyond the range of these views over Oxford, the upper Thames valley expands to meet the uplands. Here is announced the long course of stone building awaiting ahead. Stanton Harcourt (32), Bampton church, Brize Norton (37), Witney, North Leigh (36), and houses, cottages, and churches on every hand begin to show the delicate tints of oolite and the work of

NORTHLEACH. *A sermon in stone from the great days of Cotswold wool. The fifteenth-century reconstruction of the church seen from the south. The window traceries and porch are finely designed and executed and the interior contains famous memorial brasses to the woolstaplers.*

STANTON, *a village with charming homes and two manor-houses placed on a spur of the Cotswolds above the Vale of Evesham.*

old-time masons who shaped doorways, mullions, chimneys and carvings, graded slates from ridges to eaves, and cunningly laid boundary walls without mortar.

These pictures in stone continue up the pleasant valley of the River Cherwell. They sparkle in meadows, on wooded ridges, and feature brightly in villages and hamlets from the Heyfords (36) and the Astons to the gables of Fritwell manor-house. Rousham House, erected early in the seventeenth century and furbished in the eighteenth by William Kent, supplies a touch in the grand manner; complete with gardens designed by Kent, it moved Horace Walpole to prate of "Daphne in little" when he wandered among groves, fountains, and statues in 1760. Cool uplands over the stone lead to Bicester church, an interesting structure near to the meeting of Roman roads and within hail of meets of foxhounds. More than once the sporting Bicester pack has urged me to Cropredy Bridge, the exact point held by Waller after the fighting on June 29, 1644. The venerable church in the village keeps many good things, including a cannon-ball to recall the battle. This inspected, and without more thoughts of war, we advance to realms of peaceful stone, trouty streams, uplands of departed sheep flocks, with the Cotswold Hills calling in the distance.

COTSWOLD COUNTRY

The oolite stone land to the north of the Thames mounts up towards the west. It begins to rise in a rough curve marked by Cirencester and Fairford in the south, and continued through Witney, Woodstock, and Deddington to Banbury in the northern tip of Oxfordshire. After meditations on the cannon-ball, the genuine old eagle of the brass lectern, and other attractions at Cropredy, a few miles onward will lead us into Banbury. But first, bound as we are for delectable harmonies in Cotswold scenes and stone, glances through the villages spread round Banbury Cross will give foretastes of joys to follow. Great Bourton, Horley (26), Hornton, still famous for quarries, and place after place grouped on slopes and in valleys glow with the delicate colouring of the local product. They exactly fit their natural environments. The brilliance of the golden tints on the walls of Deddington is so arresting, one almost forgets to find the parsonage house in which King Charles slept after his short-lived victory at Cropredy. Much of the masoncraft in the district is remarkably good; it rewards a constant lookout for walling laid in trim coarses, arched doorways, gable adornments, and the artistry of stone slates laid in diminishing sizes from eaves to ridges of roofs. Little date panels give inklings of human lives, make one wonder who answered to the initials of W. M., G. B. H., or R. A. I. and caused their monograms to bloom on the homes they reared and evidently loved.

Among the village churches Bloxham and Adderbury are splendid. The local saying tells of three spires in a line,

> Bloxham for length,
> Adderbury for strength,
> King's Sutton for beauty.

The last one, perfect in grace, is in Northamptonshire and therefore outside my present borders, yet the other two churches lack nothing in beauty. John Harvey, scholarly champion of Gothic art, traces the fineness of Adderbury's chancel to Richard Winchcombe, a master craftsman working early in the fifteenth century. Homes schemed on the bigger scale for squires and notables add particular sights to these pleasant north Oxfordshire scenes. One of them, at Hanwell, is no more than a relic of the courtly Copes' Castle; seen from the churchyard, it makes a pretty picture of Tudor stone and brick. Another churchyard view includes Wroxton Abbey, fortunate in continuing much as it was when built in 1618 on the site of a priory. Jacobean gables rise and big windows glisten just as they did for earlier owners, Lord Keeper North and George III's Prime Minister, Lord North, director of the Boston tea-party. Broughton Castle is the prize of the neighbourhood, an early fourteenth-century foundation reconstructed by the Fiennes family in the sixteenth century and fully meriting all the expressions of admiration already aimed at it. Complete with moat, gatehouse, hall, oriel windows, and a hiding-hole up aloft, here are all the elements for "a haunt of ancient peace in the good old days!" Even so, peace did not always reign. One member of the family lost his head during Jack Cade's rebellion, another fell in the Battle of Barnet, and mysterious visitors used to mount a secret staircase to plot Civil War conspiracies. The household also provided a "Fiennes lady on a white horse," the one that made any precocious infant "Ride a cock-horse to Banbury Cross." Doubtless due to the rise of democracy and the consequent eclipse of nobility, the "Fiennes" lady slipped in the social scale to become merely "fine," just like any June Smith with a flaxen perm riding in Hollywood. This loss of caste is a pity because it has flattened an elevated point in the nursery rhyme.

Banbury, ancient in fame for cakes, ale, and cheese, thrives to-day at the centre of old coach roads and new motor highways. In certain particulars it is a town of has-beens, a cemetery of late lamenteds without gravestones or epitaphs. The castle, erected in 1125 by a bishop of Lincoln and heroically defended without hope for the King in 1646, merely survives as somebody's doorstep. A mid-Victorian erection, often called bad names, serves as best it can for "the goodly cross with many degrees (steps) about it," seen by Leland and later knocked down by local vandals. The big church rears its masonry over the ashes of a splendid medieval predecessor, one hardly excelled in all Oxfordshire and therefore blown up by the Banburyites in 1790. All the town gates have disappeared and the stone town hall obviously dates from the modern sham Gothic period. The Globe Room no longer adorns the *Reindeer* inn with panelling of 1637 and a plaster ceiling that was good enough to be copied for the South Kensington Museum; this room sailed away to America within my recollection. Nor do the above complete the town's losses. In past years of fruits and fats my visits to Parsons Street were schemed for gormandizing the same kind of Banbury cakes that Ben Jonson and George III relished. My appearance at the same spot for the same purpose in 1947 ended in disappointment. The welcoming fragrance had departed from the threshold of Lamb late Beesley. Brutal printed words barred the way. They read, "No Banbury Cakes for Sale." I turned from this emblem of those who arrange our bodies and souls, and consigned modern times to the devil for these particular reasons. Cakes eaten in Banbury were scrumptious and unique; made from a secret and traditional recipe, they proved how well people filled their insides in the happy ages of Unsocial Insecurity; while consuming and gloating you could ponder on the old wool trade by recalling that the peculiar shape of the Banbury cake derives from the weaver's shuttle.

Enough of Banbury's losses. The town retains plenty to mark its continuance and gains. Even the ponderous church, spacious and theatrical inside as planned by the Cockerell architects, attracts admirers to-day, probably because we have gone from bad to worse. Fashion is fickle, has changed since 1810 when a writer to the *Gentleman's Magazine* thought the church "more like a gaol than a Christian temple." Below the heavy tower the vicarage stands meekly, a charming survivor from the blow-up of 1790 and preserving gables and windows characteristic of the mid seventeenth century. Church and parson's home face a capital stretch of historic highway joining North Bar to the Cross; generous in width, good for the red buses and motor cars, it yet looks just the thing for shades of phantom horses and coaches between the wide verges, and ruby coachmen, too, who of course used to wink at pretty maidens fresh from matins in the departed Gothic shrine. Streets, Church Lane, Butcher Row, and curious ways keep tight to the medieval town plan and consequently offer antiquity nicely blended with modernism. For instance, pointed gables, curved windows, and external plasterwork look very well above the bright colours of agricultural implements arranged by Messrs. Neale and Perkins. Those who require them can swallow Mr. Goodman's pills behind the same square window-panes that attracted gouty and dyspeptic Georgians. Best of all is the Market Place. It upholds ancient custom, continues true in deed as well as name. Grouped around are reminders of past marketing days, the gabled and Georgian frontages, Jacobean timbers, pierced wooden pendants, the panelled and carved doors of the *Unicorn* inn perpetually guarded by heraldic animals under the date of 1648. When the stalls are set up in the open, the hubbub of chattering, jokes, laughter and shouting echoes round the mature background, just as it must have done for centuries. A great sight is this market, jolly, crowded, and assorted with bloaters, ice-cream, the Women's Institute, flowers, fruit, gospellers, suspenders, and every known commodity for mankind's pleasure, profit, and discomfort. A power for starting movements in cash is irresistible. As sure as eggs are eggs and sometimes bad, few human beings could conquer parting with money for things needed or never likely to be wanted. One day while there my publishing friend acquired two fly-catchers for useful service in sultry London; at the same time I gained two religious tracts (for nothing).

In spite of the above acquisitions a suggestion of the town's losses persisted on that occasion until my departure from Banbury. For accuracy of facts in this book, I went to the *Reindeer* to ascertain if the historic fame for ale had disappeared like the actual Banbury cakes. Though shorn of its treasure, the Globe Room, the inn yard had not been completely spoiled (33). The doors to the yard remained intact, fine solid doors generously made of oak. There was the date, ANNO · DIN · 1570, and the carved names as well, IHON KNIGHT · IHONE KNIGHT · DAVID HORN, each separated by a little carved heart. A pretty fancy, I thought; but while wondering who the owners of these names might have been an aged man fresh from the bar said to me, "Make a fine lot of firewood!" Perhaps he felt impelled to uphold the town's reputation for destruction? Certainly he mentioned the coal shortage and quite confirmed my intuition that Banbury ale had not vanished.

The uplands spread southward from Banbury. Landscapes shape in gentle slopes. Streams water green valleys. The Evenlode river makes lovely windings. Big and little woods mount to particular richness at Great and Little Tew, Blenheim Park, and Wychwood Forest. The local stone colours the villages, mutely tells the annals of rural centuries. It amplifies stories of country squires, as at Chastleton and Shipton-under-Wychwood, locates the home of Lucius Cary, Lord Falkland, at Great Tew, and stone walls round Blenheim Park, extending for furlongs beyond Woodstock and laid in the best dry stone walling I have ever seen, enclose Vanburgh's immense palace reared for the great Duke and Sarah.

All the villages in this region repay exploration, either for beauty in stone, history, and sometimes for surprises. Idbury, for example, one of the high places facing the Wychwoods and the Evenlode, has the customary curiosities—a clerestoried church partly Norman, stone cottages, and a manor-house. Yet this manor-house, though correct in traditional masonry, once helped to give me quite a surprise. Enquiring at this home of *The Countryman* for the founder and then editor of the quarterly, the reply was, "He is in the orchard pruning fruit-trees." Very strange that seemed! The words shattered my belief that editors of works on every known subject drew inspiration from Fleet Street and similar

CHIPPING CAMPDEN, *the old wool town prime with the fineness and pattern of stonework.*
Its distinctive features include the church rebuilt by the wool merchants, a fourteenth-century
woolstaplers' hall, William Grevel's medieval home, the market hall (above), lovely seventeenth-
century almshouses, and remnants of Viscount Campden's mansion, burnt down in the Civil War.

WINCHCOMBE lies in a hollow on the fringe of the Cotswolds. Once it was an important Mercian town and the place of a Benedictine monastery with a shrine to St. Kenelm. The great abbey has gone but a wonderful fifteenth-century church remains unspoiled. Picturesque houses line the streets. The inns show a stone frontage of The Old Corner Cupboard and the courtyard gallery of The George, a reminder of the pilgrims.

conglomerations of bricks and mortar. How and why *The Countryman* evidently "comes from the country" needed no further explanation.

Another cause for surprise, not to my knowledge previously illustrated, exists at Chapel House, a draughty hamlet on the old coach road directing past the Rollright Stones to Birmingham. This object, being an archway the worse for wear (33), keeps so many memories inside its worn stones that I specially followed in the tracks of the coaches on the good motor road through Woodstock and Enstone to Chapel House. When centuries oozed with big joints of roast beef and pork, port wine in cobwebby bottles, etc., etc., for the delight of man's internal apparatus, and until after a princess, later Queen Victoria, honoured the spot, this archway and adjacent buildings, once components of a very celebrated inn, welcomed alike travellers of great, famous, notorious, and inconsequent stature who arrived variously sun-burnt or blue-nosed, according to the behaviour of Sol or Boreas on the bleak Oxfordshire uplands. And lo! on one memorable day, March 21, 1776, to be exact, the bulky Doctor dined excellently, so Boswell related, soared to the heights of inspiration on wings developed by a satisfied tummy, and uttered his immortal panegyric:

"There is no private house (said he) in which people can enjoy themselves so well, as at a capital tavern. . . . You are sure you are welcome: and the more noise you make, the more trouble you give, the more good things you call for, the welcomer you are. No servants will attend you with the alacrity which waiters do, who are incited by the prospect of an immediate reward in proportion as they please. No, Sir; there is nothing which has yet been contrived by man, by which so much happiness is produced as by a good tavern or inn." He then repeated, with great emotion, Shenstone's lines:

"Whoe'er has travelled life's dull round,
Where'er his stages may have been,
May sigh to think he still has found
The warmest welcome at an inn."

Every true explorer of England knows these words by heart; yet they are so wedded to my soul through benefits enjoyed and in expectation, pardon is asked for quoting them again. Johnson, Boswell, coaches, horses, chaises, callers, landlords—all semblances of their ghostly selves and dinners have faded from Chapel House. Now the chapel of the priory of Cold Norton merely marks a ground-plan under a lawn. The archway with a leaky roof looks likely to tumble down. A solitary pull-up at the cross-roads alone struggles to keep alive the spirit of hospitality. Therefore, on the December day of my sketching, when the wind blew chill from the north-east, I went down the hill to Chipping Norton and fed in the modern fashion behind a good old frontage of the *White Hart*.

The airy and spacious centre of Chipping Norton, a combined High Street and Market Place lined with stone buildings sprinkled with seventeenth- and eighteenth-century features, is so contrived on a slope that masculine dwellers downstairs on the high side could study their feminine neighbours in bedrooms opposite; this may be possible, but of course does not happen in a town so respectable. The new Post Office, built of stone in the Georgian Style, is nearly good enough to be an old one. Things more hoary include dull earthen relics of a castle erected during the reign of Stephen, a guildhall with mullioned windows, Middle Row obviously in the middle, a pretty lot of dormers and chimneys on the seventeenth-century almshouses, a fine big church entered through a notable two-storied porch and wonderfully lit in the nave from a fifteenth-century clerestory daringly constructed of more glass than stone. In addition to sculptured monuments the church contains a collection of memorial brasses. One of them, to John Yonge, with woolpacks at his feet, has particular interest for us at this stage of our progression. The gentleman's footstools imply that we are reaching the true stone land of Cotswold sheep and wool, a land in which you now can wander from morn until eve without seeing a flock of sheep or a shepherd, more's the pity.

Everybody knows that onward from the fourteenth century this wool trade rose to be a prop and mainstay of the country's prosperity, and the immigration of foreign weavers, first encouraged by the Edwardian kings, developed the great cloth industry. The peculiar constitution of Continental towns, each jealous of independence and continually at war with each other, made keeping sheep flocks in western Europe a hazardous enterprise. Thus England gained the advantage of being the chief supplier of wool to the weaving countries beyond the Straits of Dover. The woolpack on the brass in Chipping Norton church, similar tokens elsewhere, and emblems throughout the wold country related to this story of wool can summon speculations on a multitude of things. One can think of the Cotswolds, once a vast sheep walk; the port of Bristol, an early staple for wool; the staple established at Calais in 1363 for the European market; merchants and nobles trafficking in wool and kings doing likewise (before the battle of Crécy Philip of France sneered at Edward III, "the royal wool merchant"); the rise and expansion of the home cloth industry; the decree for everybody to wear woollen caps and be "buried in woollen" to keep trade thriving; Queen Elizabeth, ever sagacious, planting her Lord Chancellor on the Woolsack in the House of Lords, ever to remind him of the white source of golden prosperity in case his mind went woolgathering elsewhere. Standing evidences in these Oxfordshire and Gloucestershire lands, now awaiting our exploration, emphasize the tremendous importance of this olden industry. Reminders abound to vitalize anew the centuries when "Cottys" fleeces were in high favour, great demand, and called buyers from the Continent and home centres, sent strings of pack-horses laden with precious burdens over the wolds to the ships at the ports, and fed weavers in Cotswold valleys and more distant

Cottages at BIBURY

parts of England. So much is on view for delight, suggestion, and contemplation, it is rather nice to be reminded of sheep, shepherds, and tinkling bells on the open wolds under the broad sky, billowy wool on pack-horses, merchants mixing bargaining with attending mass, and other aspects of man's work and enterprise in the process of making money and buying immortality. This way of life, indicated by the weathered properties of its stages, even gains in romance when spied from this era of clattering machinery, assembly lines, murky industrial towns, dull suburbs, and times of advantages now enjoyed while all bodies and souls are manœuvred as economic robots for equation on the national balance sheet. Even the words current in those past days of trading vibrate cosily. Woolly brains like mine can sometimes weave fantasies from the very sounds of "fells" (skins with wool on them), "in pile" (wool heaped up), "tod" (28 pounds weight, usually made of three or four fleeces, valued in 1481 at 13s. 4d.), "woolpack" (about 250 pounds of fleeces), "poke" (a small sack, nowadays usually associated with buying a pig), "sarpler" (a large sack containing 80 tods); and the word "woolstapler" itself always rings a tuneful note.

Sheep farming, trading in wool, and the consequent flow of prosperity influenced the development of architecture as a matter of course, for religious worship and artistry belonged to the accepted scheme of daily life and work. Nature not only provided the sheep walks; it also gave good stone which was turned to advantage through the wealth, devotion, labours, and talents of men. The buildings that constitute the unique charm of the Cotswold scene therefore did not happen from tricks of luck, accident, or sentiment. They were the logical result of divine provision, fortunate circumstance, enterprise, skilled work spiced with genius. Masonry served for a true expression of a people who made the towns, villages, and manor-houses while they chiefly depended and thrived on wool, or were connected with the commodity in one way or another. Their story is told by villages high among walled fields and lying in wooded valleys watered by clear streams—at Snowshill and Stanton (44), Bibury on the Coln, Chalford in the Stroud valley (55), and everywhere throughout this area bright with walls and steep roofs of stone. Streets of the incomparable towns, ringed by Chipping Campden (49), Burford (38), Cirencester, Tetbury (9), Wootton-under-Edge, Painswick, and Winchcombe (50), send their messages from halls of woolstaplers and marketing, from gable, archway, and pediment. Churches, responsive one to another with arch and tracery, embattled parapet and crocketed pinnacle born of riches accumulated by the woolmen, join in harmonies of grey and golden beauty over hill and dale. Frequent manor-houses and the larger dwellings in the towns bespeak a spacious and cultivated life. They localize families and names, show home quarters such as those of William Greville of Chipping Campden, "the flower of the wool

CHALFORD, *stone built and steep, in Gloucestershire's Golden Valley.*
The cloth industry, introduced by the Flemings and Huguenots,
brought centuries of prosperity to this bright vale of the River Frome.

OWLPEN MANOR-HOUSE *near Dursley. Secluded on a slope below high woods, it was built in the sixteenth century and occupied by the Daunt family for generations. The clipped yew-trees in the gardens are ancient and noted.*

merchants of all England," Daunts of Owlpen (56), Fettiplaces of Asthall (37), who owned "all the parks and all the places," and the gables and towers at Chastleton remain as built and occupied by Walter Jones, the Witney woollen merchant, before he retired to a heavenly woolsack in 1633.

The building style that developed, marked strongly with local characteristics, was a true child of the English tradition. It matured late in the fourteenth century, rose in the full flower of grace and majesty during the fifteenth, and the native manner of work continued through Elizabeth's reign until the Restoration. Old in years when Queen Anne and the Georges ruled, the style then gained new delicacies with pilasters and angle quoins, classic doorways and eaves cornices, now often to be viewed standing beyond formal paths and pillared gateways. Obsequies these might be called, wreaths for the final page of the great English epic that came to a full stop in the wars waged by economics, competition, and the coal, smoke, and mechanical industrialism of England's northern towns.

To paint the lily is wasteful and ridiculous, wrote Shakespeare. It would be equally foolish for me to attempt additions to the words already available on the jewelled stonework set in the Cotswold scenes. Since Guy Dawber produced the volume on Cotswold architecture nearly fifty years ago and Arthur Gibbs penned *A Cotswold Village* in the manor-house at Ablington bearing this inscription carved over the entrance, PLEAD · THOV · MY · CAVSE · O · LORD · 1590, writers have issued acres of pages on the delights, and also the defects, presented by these wolds and valleys. Some of them, clear of vision, have told all that can be known on the lie of the land, craftsmanship in stonework, and fertility of design in masonry. Others, looking through mental eye-pieces coloured rose-pink, perceived much ammunition for sentimentality in mossy walls and roofs overgrown with roses. A writer here and there merely found the wolds bleak and draughty, and certain silly individuals, armed with smoky spectacles and minds insensible to colour and beauty beautifully rendered, discovered no more than an absence of damp-courses and articles dependent on drainpipes. The poets, perhaps, have most nearly revealed the Cotswolds' heart and spirit of place—John Drinkwater in *Cottage Song*,

> When down the silver tides
> The moon on Cotswold rides.

Odell Shepard on Bibury in *The Harvest of a Quiet Eye*,

> I shall remember cottages
> Carved out of silver and gold,
> And how the great beech-darkened hills
> Tenderly enfold
> That little human island
> Washed round by meadow and wold.

And surely John Masefield must have had his own Cotswolds in mind when he conceived,

> For they'd the skill to draw their plan,
> And skill's a joy to any man;
> And they'd the strength, not skill alone,
> To build it beautiful in stone;
> And strength and skill together thus . .
> O, they were happier men than us.

Better than any word or drawn pictures, best of all it is to explore the Cotswolds, the real thing. You can put up at the *Lygon Arms* in Broadway (if it is not full up), at the *Lamb* in Burford, dating from the fifteenth century, the *Bull* in Fairford (oh! my trout for breakfast there!), at any of the inns and anchorages of ancient peace for ancients not in a hurry. What is seen then can be enjoyed and admired. Mind and memory are enriched with impressions gained from churches, manor-houses, towns, and villages left by earlier dwellers, the standing memorials of themselves, their lives and thoughts, evidences clearly and strongly made in stone and incapable of telling fibs or proving that white was black or black was white, a trick so easily done nowadays by manipulators of modernism. Amongst all the loveliness it may be difficult to ward off sermons in stone and that sort of preaching. Such temptations nearly captured me at the moment of gathering these words while sitting on a wall of stone. Swinbrook, Asthall, and the ruins of Minster Lovell manor-house glinted in the sunlight down below in the Windrush valley. The hill behind me hid Coln Rogers, Winson, and Bibury. Uplands spread in curve after curve to meet the Rissingtons and Bourton-on-the-Water. Very quickly all chance of attack from sentimental moodiness retired before the onslaught of a string of lorries snorting past my stone wall and bearing sections of the prefabricated houses! Yet these emblems of house and home did preach a jolly good sermon on ugliness allied to convenience in this epoch of England's progress. They reminded me that the Cotswold tradition of building is as dead as anything can be. Attempts to revive it were made by Sir E. Guy Dawber at Coldicote and elsewhere, C. R. Ashbee at Campden, Ernest Gimson and Ernest Barnsley of Sapperton, Charles Bateman (who owned a delightful house at Bourton-on-the-Hill), and other architectural friends of mine. They did splendid work, brought new life to a building style evolved in past generations and exactly suited to the local scene. But their efforts represented no more than individual specks in the ocean of a lost cause. Modern thought and conditions have no affinity with the way of life that adorned the Cotswolds with golden glory.

The main routes for Cotswold exploration are good, and very obliging for our purpose of finding and seeing the landscapes, the villages and towns built of stone. The Fosse Way bisects the area from north to south. It mounts from the

Vale of the Red Horse to Moreton-in-the-Marsh, then points up and down in an immemorial line to the end of Gloucestershire near Tetbury. The Way sends out arms right and left to Bourton-on-the-Hill, Upper and Lower Slaughter, Bourton-on-the-Water (prettily grouped round the stream crossed by little bridges and once likened to Venice by somebody who had not seen the Grand Canal), Chedworth noted for the Roman villa, Coln St. Denis and Coln Rogers, North Cerney, Ampney Crucis, and many more villages of attraction and memories. Stow-on-the-Wold, perched high, stands like the hub of a wheel with spokes radiating in every direction. These promise yet more notable villages, among which are Wick and Little Rissington; Naunton and Sevenhampton; Temple Guiting, screened in woods once owned by Knights Templars; Stanway; Broadway, still a charmer in spite of popularity; and Stanton (44), Weston-sub-Edge, and the villages grouped round Chipping Campden in a locality which I think exhibits the stone architecture in its very best mood. Witney lies at the fringe of the hills. A stone town throughout, it possesses a good church under the high spire, the seventeenth-century butter cross neighboured by a quaint town hall carried on pillared archways, and most unusual, a new and convenient housing scheme built to tone and harmonize with the work of the ancients. Here old fame is kept alive by manufacturing the "Earlyworms," in which we awake somewhat later than the birds; and my mind went wandering down centuries when in Bridge Street I read a notice, "Weavers wanted." The highway at the butter cross, finger-posted for Cheltenham, is a capital leader to Cotswold moods and graces. It mounts above the Windrush valley, shows village after village from Minster Lovell to Barrington and Windrush, rises higher and higher, skirts the vale of the Coln bound for Fosse Bridge, Bibury, and Quennington. Turnings on each side will take you over the wolds and into a quiet world of soft green pastures, warm-coloured earth, lucious shades of spinneys and woods, and dry stone walls follow the curves of the land to collections of cottages grouped round churches. More to the south the route from Cirencester to Birdlip Hill and Gloucester cuts a straight and bold Roman line through finely wooded hill and dale scenery; attractions to the left and right include Daglingworth, the Duntisbournes, Norman sculpture at the highest wold church of Elkstone, and the halt in King Charles's wandering at Coberley rectory. The Golden Valley holds treasures at Chalford (55) and up the Frome stream to Sapperton; and for the romantic scenery of the southern Cotswolds a fine round I can recommend shows the beech woods down to Owlpen and Uley, North Nibley, the tower of Ozleworth, Boxwell, a hiding-place of King Charles after the battle of Worcester, and a view of the historic keep and gatehouse at Beverston before reaching Tetbury.

Here, there, and everywhere are the famous manor-houses, one and sometimes two in most of the villages, and exhibiting all the variations of local style in gables, kneelers and finials, windows divided by mullions, entrances made by old squires for their ladies (and themselves), the matchless stone roofs, and squared chimneys finished with moulded caps. Those who know the owners of these houses can see stone fireplaces, panelling, and all sorts of wonderful things inside; less fortunate wanderers, not on visiting terms, usually may squint at these lovely homes from roadsides or neighbouring churchyards. The number is so large and my stock of paper so small, I can only mention this short selection from my choices to send my readers in search of more: Snows-hill, high at 850 feet; Stanton Court, built in the sixteenth century to serve prisoners of war and their hutments in the twentieth century, and Warren House, of 1577, round the corner; Stanway, with a gatehouse, a notable group erected by a land-owning Tracey early in the seventeenth century; Upper Swell, Upper and Lower Slaughter, three prizes close together; Whittington Court, mainly early sixteenth century with a later wing added, poetically con-nected with the names of Denham and Dobell; two specimens previously mentioned and illustrated, at Asthall and Owlpen; Bibury Court of 1623, and Ablington, dated 1590, a mile distant; Moor Hall, in a very bad way at my first introduction, but now happily thriving after being re-christened More Hall; Little Sodbury, a fifteenth- and sixteenth-century house in which Tyndale began translations of the Bible. The later style of building to balanced and classic designs brought charming results. One of the best is at Lower Lypiatt, near Stroud, erected in 1717 behind a sweep of stone piers and a gateway made by Warren, the celebrated smith. Medford House, Mickleton, re-fronted in 1699, also shows a very pretty face within a walled forecourt; it so attracted me at first sight in years long ago that I explored beyond, slept under the stone roof, sketched the doorway and the urns, and of an evening walked in the manor park up and down the fine avenue of elms planted by Shenstone, the poet, to get a kind of feeling of being Morgan Graves, the eighteenth-century squire. That did not come off. Times had changed. Evidently the defunct squires of these manor-houses never would do for modern days, based on the sacredness of one vote for every one man and woman and the omnipotence of political fry. Members of an extinct race, their years and deeds are remembered by the homes they made and memorials in the near churches where they worshipped, and sometimes slept, in big family pews while the sands of the hour-glass trickled down. Their courses run, they retired to the places of worship to sleep for good. Now we can gaze on graven images and records of the Trinders of Westwell, Fettiplaces of Swinbrook, and their like, who passed quiet country lives on ancestral acres, built in faith with durable stone for themselves and their progeny, reared sons and daughters to follow on, set examples both good and indifferent for neighbours, tenants, and the nation, farmed and planted, tickled

CLIFTON. *The Georgian and Regency terraces high on the bank of the River Avon near the Gorge and Suspension Bridge.*

61

BRISTOL. *The cathedral from the south-east and ruins of the bishop's palace wrecked by Reform rioters in 1831. The cathedral has the remarkable late Norman chapter house and medieval choir aisles of unique design. It remained without a nave from the dissolution until 1868.*

BRISTOL. *St. Mary Redcliffe, the famous parish church of rich Perpendicular architecture which commemorates the piety and munificence of the merchants. Notable memorials include the Amerycke brass. Here Coleridge and Southey were married.*

The Gloucestershire vale, the Severn bend, and the Forest of Dean viewed from the Haresfield escarpment of the Cotswolds near Stroud. Abergavenny Sugar Loaf and the Black Mountains show in the far distance.

the trout, shot the birds, and then departed to spheres of silence, commemorated with little more than monograms and dates figured on gables and porches, and inscribed slabs and carved effigies in churches, to inform posterity that they had breathed, lived, and died.

From villages and manor-houses we reach the towns, grey towns, golden towns, shining out from sunlit landscapes in exquisite harmonies of tone and colour. Evening light amplifies their mellowness; on moonlight nights I have seen pearly shades and slanting shadows blended mysteriously; and even in dull or wet weather there is a good deal to be said for a fine stock of masonry as an outlook. Children of time, these aged towns speak volumes. Their weathered stones in churches, dwellings, inns, and halls of trading offer solid stuff to illuminate the annals of communities that prospered during centuries of summers and winters while Tames of Fairford, Sylvesters of Burford, the Grevilles, Torteys, Midwinters, Smalwoodes, Biddles, and hosts of notable and workaday natives spread their family trees and built for comfort and beauty. It is no cause for wonder that Cotswold towns have charmed writers, artists, and lookers from all corners of the earth, choice specimens as they are in the collection of smallish and little towns so remarkably matured in England's past years. No towns in the country quite equal this Cotswold group and their contiguous neighbours in Wiltshire and Somerset. Built with stone throughout, the most expressive material used in building, they rose to the highest point of excellence in what may be termed democratic architecture; that is to say, a regular method of building devised and encouraged for the uses of the common life. These towns still accurately reflect the guiding motives that made them. Particularly do they show the influences of local product, climate, environment, and the degree of material prosperity and spiritual enlightenment attained by a people naturally bright in temperament and invention.

Lack of space again forbids me even to mention all the Cotswold towns that have given me hours and days of pleasure; but they have wide fame and no doubt a map and the joy of finding will direct my readers to them. One is tempted to say that the main street of Chipping Campden cannot be bettered in England (49); pardonably the town may claim to be the most perfect small one on earth, with its combination of seventeenth-century market hall, Greville's fourteenth-century house, Woolstaplers' Hall (where I gossiped with C. R. Ashbee in distant days), inns, house fronts gabled and square (behind one of which F. L. Griggs used to hide), gardens and vistas at the backs of the said houses, and for a climax the almshouses and church, acme of magnificence, facing all that is left of Sir Baptist Hicks's mansion, burnt down by Royalists in the Civil War to cheat Roundheads of a prize. Then you light on Burford High Street (38), and Sheep Street too, waver, do not know where to award the palm, and retire inside the *Lamb*, the brick-fronted *Bull*, the *Cotswold Gate*, the *George* (King Charles's pub), or the *Bear* to think it over. Here, again, is the delicious cohesion of stonework grouped down the slope to the Windrush stream crossed by the old bridge; and lots of sights, too, with one of the largest and most interesting of the Cotswold churches, the Warwick almshouses founded in 1457, Symeon Wysdom's Elizabethan grammar-school, the Tolsey, houses for beauty and stories, and the Priory and seventeenth-century chapel combined, tumbling to pieces when I first found it, but now intact to recall the Elizabethan mansion of Lord Falkland and the safe retreat for Speaker Lenthall after the Restoration. Tetbury is another charmer, not widely known to the outer world and therefore deficient in "luncheons and teas provided." It crowns the hillock surrounded by valleys; thus elevated and topped by the church spire, the groupings from the Bath and Malmesbury roads and other directions compose remarkably well. Spire and tower developed from a rebuilding to the old pattern in the 1890's. The body of the church is an amusing curiosity. Designed and built by Francis Hiorn, of Warwick, it has spaciousness and a certain dignity, in spite of the spindly piers made of wood and iron and the spiritless window traceries in the wiry "Gothick" style fashionable during the ascendency of Horace Walpole and the "Committee of Taste" who cultivated romantic sentiments as an anchorage from classicalism. The present building followed a medieval predecessor, so large and handsome that it was knocked down in 1777 to enable Tetbury to change a real monument into a sham one. Genuine articles are offered in the picturesque, hilly streets and byways round about. Gables, Georgian façades, shell door-hoods, and a mixture of features seem to tell of an easy-going past while the town clock bell pips out the hours in high, squeaky notes or you look out on placid scenes from under the arches of the seventeenth-century market hall (9); placid scenes, that is to say, if the outlooker is not perpetually spied on, as I was, by a bright youth with a bicycle, a local scion of the ubiquitous tribe specially created to terrorize artists with such expressions as, "Mister, what are yer drawin'," "My! Rosey, isn't it lovely!" or more politely, "Pardon me, may I look?"

Other sights, scenes, and interests are unending in the complete group of Cotswold towns. Certainly the collection is remarkable when one remembers Stow-on-the-Wold, "where the wind blows cold" in winter, dreaming away summer days on the height mellowed by the houses round the Market Square and the church, used in 1646 as a cage for Royalist prisoners after the last battle fought in the Civil War; Moreton-in-the-Marsh, by no means marshy, but situated over 400 feet high on the march or Cotswold boundary; Winchcombe (50), the old Mercian town, pilgrim point for St. Kenelm's shrine, a name-place for Jack of Newbury, the town with the perfect fifteenth-century church, stone houses, inns, and the *George*, the pilgrims' rest, where you can sleep above timber inscribed with the initials of Richard Kyderminster, past landlord and

SHIPTON
OLIFFE
13c. bell turret

WINCHCOMBE
Arms panel
Chandos
Almshouses

NORTHLEACH
15c. porch
Upper figure Blessed Trinity
Lower Virgin & Child
Bell turret above
Left pinnacle pierced for chimney to pervise

PAINSWICK
18c. House near church

COTSWOLD NOTES

STOW on the WOLD
Renaissance house
Market Sq.

67

wealthy Tudor abbot of the departed monastery; Painswick, very arty, and particularly good for eighteenth-century houses; Stroud, more remarkable for its situation between the hills than for the contents centred round the Elizabethan town hall; Minchinhampton with a good seventeenth-century cloth hall standing on columns and arches; Nailsworth, surrounded by fine heights, and perhaps most curious for a street which natives say is like a penny because they can have a pint at the *King's Head* at one end and another pint at the *Britannia* at the other end; Dursley, thriving afresh with engineering in place of wool, yet still sedate with its town hall and market house presided over by Queen Anne; Fairford, known throughout the world for the glass windows in John Tame's "wool" church, a late-fifteenth-century shrine most handily placed for reaching the ancient *George* and the *Bull*, cherished in my memory for pre-war comfort, chicken and trout; and Cirencester, the villagers' Ciren, the Cicester of the nobs, entrancing always, and briefly noted in my earlier book, *Thames Triumphant*.

Northleach, situated right in the middle of the wolds, demands more than two words. This large village-cum-small town has kept a warm place in my heart since I first found it in the 1890's, then a Rip Van Winkle kind of spot lost and forgotten in a pushing age. Grass actually did grow in the streets. Apparently strangers were rarely seen, for the welcome given to me by the natives mounted almost to a point of embarrassment. The landlord at the *Wheatsheaf*—I can picture his cheerful, hale, and bearded features now—treated his only guest with the devotion of a loving parent; the huge sirloin of roast beef presented for my solo performance is yet tender in memory, and companions in the smoke-room assured me of ample provision for whatever might happen because the town was noted for a workhouse at one end and a prison at the other. Northleach has a different look now. If the workhouse exists no doubt it is otherwise and beautifully named, perhaps a St. Christopher's home schemed to serve democratic travellers. Judging by the meal consumed before writing these words, roast-beefy savour is not even on smell. Below the stone walls the main road is principally tarmac. Coaches, lorries, and cars buzz along for Cheltenham, Oxford, and London. The coaching days of petrol have livened up the town that was left high and dry when the coaching days of the horses faded. Go-ahead fogies must be pleased with the town's progress, even though Northleach may be less fascinating than in my earlier years, when it advanced backwards.

A number of years ago, say four or five hundred, this town probably flowed with milk, honey, beef, mutton, sack, and malmsey. Without doubt it was then right on the top of the times; in fact, it appreciably assisted in making those times what they were. The church most distinctly proclaims this fact. It is a glorious work of art, a pride of Cotswold; it illuminates more clearly than

MONMOUTH. *The defensive tower on the medieval bridge over the River Monnow in the birthplace of King Henry V.*

The valley of the River Usk and the Sugar Loaf (1955 feet) near Abergavenny.

LLANTHONY PRIORY, *romantically situated in the Honddu valley of the Black Mountains. Built about 1115, it was largely*

words can tell a tale of men's worldly striving and prosperity, religious devotion, and trust in things beyond this earth (43).

In common with other Cotswold town churches, this one represents great dignity of thought expressed in local stone by exuberant craftsmanship. Brief particulars of the edifice are these. Little remains of the twelfth-century building. At a later date a great reconstruction happened. The present tower, nave, and clerestories, the south choir aisle dated 1489, and the south porch, mounted up in new splendour between the approximate dates of 1400 and 1500. That means about one hundred years to create a joy for ever, if mankind ever should think it worth while to keep such things of beauty for so long. The nave interior is lofty and spacious, wonderfully lit by the clerestory windows. Arcades of singular pillars and arches plainly denote the late Perpendicular style; they closely resemble those at that other grand Cotswold church of Chipping Campden. The timbered aisle roofs adorned with carved bosses may cause the eyes of shrewd worshippers to wander upward from prayer-books. One boss, quite noticeable, flaunts the bear and ragged staff; this symbol of the house of Warwick, with others at Cricklade, Chipping Campden, and elsewhere, recall the past mightiness of the Beauchamps and the Grevels in this land of wool and denote how useful sheep were for brightening earl's coronets. Window traceries, particularly in the nave aisles and east chancel, are good enough to be called remarkable. Two choice works appear in the chancel sedilia crowned with canopies and the original fifteenth-century pulpit. The font, very gracefully supported and probably of early-fifteenth-century date, is peculiar for the series of heads carved all round it. These curious faces may represent benefactors to the church. It is very thrilling to trace the masons' marks scratched on many stones and so unite the building with the makers of it, almost say "How d'you do" to William Nutto, Simon White, and the skilled company whose brains and hands created this emblem of faith and work. Amidst all the finery they left for posterity it is difficult to stop even making a catalogue of things to be seen. The most marvellous one of all, however, must be mentioned. This is the south porch, the late-Gothic masterpiece. To find its equal in inspired masoncraft would mean searching through all England. So much for a story in stone of past times. At present a notice in the porch reads: "This is a large church and costly to maintain. This is a small and poor parish." Any charitable soul who now scans this page of mine and straightway tips up to the Vicar a fiver, or more or less, for the preservation of this noble structure will thereby do high service for God, England, home, and beauty.

A sermon in stone is not the only one here. A complementary story is told in brass. The numerous and famed memorials of Northleach preach from the floor all about the building. As a good structure must always depend on its foundations, so these brasses represent the foundations on which this rare church was built. They commemorate the power of wool, the prosperity, benevolence, and piety of those who traded in it. Looking down, or crawling about the floor, you can actually meet the woolstaplers, see depicted the men who thrived, grew rich, and with profits made paid for a worthy monument to the source of all goodness, or in the idiom of their own age of faith and religious fervour, "To the glory of God." There they lie, set out here, there, and everywhere, engraved at full length in brass as if awaiting their final earthly call and meanwhile offering themselves for inspection. Notable among them is John Fortey at the east end of the same nave that he directed to be made "lightsome and splendid" with the contents of his purse before he departed this life in 1458. Himself, Thomas Bushe, with a bush, William Midwinter, and others in this crowd of forty portraits repose with feet on sheep and woolpacks, their emblems of comfort on earth and perhaps of joy in heaven. Very fascinating are the particulars displayed, the details of costume and the merchants' marks.

The good folk of Northleach fully realized the importance of wool, the source of their own and the country's wealth, and the brasses in the church show that they took care to depart this life with representations of their feet still firmly planted on the sheep and the woolpacks which had served so well in the passage on earth. The situation of the town gave it particular importance. Burford, Chipping Campden, Winchcombe, Cirencester, in fact most of the old wool towns stand at the fringes of the hills. Northleach alone is right in the middle of the Cotswolds. It therefore developed into a famous collecting point. Wool poured in from every direction. Merchants flocked there to secure the prizes stored by the local woolstaplers in great stone warehouses. Bustling must have been the scenes when the inns were crowded and woolstaplers offered hospitality in their stone houses as buying, selling, and packing progressed and pack-horses set out on their journeys. The published letters of the Cely family, London merchants of the staple with business in Calais and Bruges, afford interesting sidelights on a busy Northleach in the 1480's. They introduce the actual person of William Midwinter, with whom the Celys principally dealt, and for a pretty garnish they illuminate a flirting interlude between young Richard Cely and Miss Lemryke during matins and mass inside the church of my illustration. These figures and the wool trade vanished years ago. The great warehouses went to pieces; only the relics of one did I discover and record. Northleach dwindled into a phantom of its former self. No longer the merchants passed into the church under the Blessed Trinity and Our Lady carved on the lovely porch. Those of my readers who travel that way I trust may follow in their footsteps, stop, admire, and put a big or little something into the box to help preserve this beautiful monument erected through the piety and generosity of the woolstaplers in spacious times when grace and devotion had a real place in day-to-day life.

Away to the west the Cotswold escarpments sweep in bold succession across Gloucestershire, growing richer with trees and verdure in the southward march. Camps crown point after point, tumuli are in good supply, archæologists crawl into the long borrow near Uley to inspect funeral arrangements made in the year goodness knows when, and the stone implements and iron currency bars which I handled evidently had been made and left on Meon Hill by Neolithic and Iron Age ancestors. The Romans provided more recent proof of occupation. They found and adapted what they wanted in the way of ancient earthworks and sites, reconstructed, planned afresh, and so left their unmistakable signs all along this impressive line of defence which directs through Meon Hill, Shunbarrow Hill above Stanton, Hailes, Haresfield Beacon, Uley Bury, and Little Sodbury. Within reach, and handy for military leave and week-ends, lay the cities of Gloucester and Cirencester, and the villas known to-day by remains at Chedworth, Elkstone, Charlton Abbots, Woodchester, Witcombe, and elsewhere. Very big snails now living at Coberley, thought to be descendants of those first introduced from Italy in early years of A.D., indicate how Roman epicures tickled their palates. Apart from antiquated associations, these camps repay finding because the ancients had such good eyes for country. Uley Bury, for instance, occupies one of the grandest of fortified sites. To climb up into it means enjoying the present in finest mood, breathing pure air high above the vale, and meanwhile treading fresh green turf that rooted in man's centuries years before Romans used the great camp of about half a mile long from earthwork to earthwork. In addition the Bury served for a kind of Aldershot to the chain of forts extending between Meon Hill and Clifton Down.

While bits and relics left over from early days may be very entertaining to those who like them, more important for ordinary mortals are the panoramas in view from the Cotswold escarpments. Heights and the places of forgotten wars emphasize in breath-taking fashion that there are visible, and always have been, the miles and miles of vales, hills, and woods fading away to blue distances and grey horizons, the work of powers greater than those possessed by insignificant humanity. Romans and their predecessors looked far to the west over these expanses. We do the same to-day, see what they saw, and newer patterns added with centuries of patient labour to glorious wide stretches of peaceful and smiling landscapes. I illustrate one only (64), a scene from the Haresfield Beacon enclosure embracing the River Severn and its famous bend at Newnham, the Forest of Dean, the River Wye country in Herefordshire and Monmouthshire, with the Abergavenny Sugar Loaf and the Black Mountains in the distance, both plainly obvious on clear days. Similar view-points over these coloured miles can be found by the score in following the escarpments of the Cotswolds that guard the river vales of the Avon and the Severn from Meon and Broadway Hills to the high lands leading to Clifton and Bristol.

LOWER RIVER SEVERN, ITS TRIBUTARIES AND BORDERLANDS

A watery line for the Severn, hills and woods beyond, distant mountain shapes on the Welsh border, and the pattern and colour seen in the panoramas visible from the Cotswold escarpments call us to rare scenery further west. Passing the near stretch of country for the present, extending from Bristol to Gloucester and Tewkesbury, we will in reality or fancy find ourselves on the far side of the River Severn where it bisects Gloucestershire and bounds Monmouthshire.

We see a proper vale, real English in character and of the kind that Tom Hughes loved—wide, flat, fertile, and bounded by hills. You can sample its true quality all the way along the high road bordered by orchards and pastures from Gloucester to Westbury, Newnham, Blakeney, and Chepstow. The road also offers ways down to the tidal river. Here the stream and sandbanks are a good mile in width at The Noose, Oldbury Sands, and other points; level lands on our right bank lead to the heights of the Forest of Dean and the ridges between the Wye and Usk rivers; eastward the green miles of the Berkeley Vale meet the wooded slopes of the Cotswolds. These elements yield landscape effects of peculiar quality, rarely spectacular, but charming always. Horizontal scenic lines combine with passages of water and sand. Big skies form overhead. Sunlight and shadows from clouds variegate the widespread subtilty of colouring. The pictorial motives suggest subjects by a Dutch painter of the seventeenth century or from our own school of great water-colourists; in fact, Turner, Peter de Wint, and Patrick Nasmyth painted in this neighbourhood. These expansive and pastoral lower Severn scenes, the Cotswold escarpments we have just travelled, and nature's demonstrations of the grand manner awaiting to be seen in the near Wye valley, each emphasize England's trick of ringing the changes and presenting much variety in little space.

The annual exploits of the Severn bore foaming past the golden sands of the Noose, salmon fishing at Beachley and Awre, eels at Epney, and other distinctions and peculiarities of the lower River Severn are too well known for me to dwell on. Of less widespread renown, yet of unique interest to students and painters of birds, is the long stretch of low land called the New Grounds, facing the river below the very pretty village and big green of Frampton-on-Severn. The Grounds are "new" because they were reclaimed from the water in the fifteenth and seventeenth centuries. For hundreds of years they have been a sanctuary for birds, protected and cared for by the Berkeley family. Here in winter gather the greatest collections of wild geese in England, wildfowl, and migratory birds from near and distant countries. Most wonderful sights can be observed. Whether you know all, as Peter Scott does, or nothing whatever about pink-feet and white-fronts, the birds feeding, flapping their wings, flying,

RAGLAN. *Ruins of the stately pile erected in the last years of great castle building. It developed in the fifteenth century, an elaborate construction of lofty walls, machicolations, courts, the moated keep and fine gatehouse.*

TINTERN. *The ferry arch near the ruined abbey.*

MATHERN. *Moynes Court, a stone home with a gatehouse built in 1603 by a bishop.*

and circling round thrill beholders with their expressions of grace, strength, and beauty. Gratefully remembered is my own experience on a December day when a pale, wintry sun glinted through wisps of mist and on to the white wings of the moving life gathered on this quiet and secluded lowland. The Severn bend begins here, a very notable scenic composition and one of England's best. Its course has been noted in the Introduction (pp. 13–14) and already we have traced the distant curve from the Cotswold camp above Randwick (64). A closer and best point of view is from Pleasant Stile on the upward road from Newnham. The majestic sweep of the stream winds round the peninsula; rich passages of woodland and trees, vivid green of pastures, and the accent of roofs clustered at Newnham combine in a memorable prospect, one that would fire any enthusiast who performs on big canvases and large areas of drawing paper. Such performers might feel happy settled at Newnham inside the old inn adorned with a stone pediment, vases, and an eagle over a porch roomy enough to shelter a mayor and corporation. These functionaries, alas, and the ceremonial sword they liked to think was presented by King John, disappeared when the town lost its ancient status. The spacious main street remains none the less pleasant in spite of the loss of a mayor and the kingly days, too, of Henry II, who sailed away in 1171 to annex Ireland after Dermot MacMorrogh ran off with O'Rourke's wife and O'Connor went to the rescue.

Pointers of our arrival in the Forest of Dean are given by the names of Little Dean near Pleasant Stile, once a Roman station, the quiet old town of Mitcheldean lying between the groves and the tump, and Ruardean heights, in command of wide landscapes patchworked with fields and woods to the foothills of the Black Mountains. Stretching for about 20 miles in length and 10 in width, the Forest is big, a worthy rival to the New Forest. Large enough for the flight of arrows from the bows of strong kings, at an early date it acquired royal standing as a hunting ground. No arrow here deposed a Rufus by disposing of him, but a like fate befell the Earl of Hereford while hunting on Christmas Eve in 1143; the remains of the Cistercian abbey at Flaxley, founded by his son, commemorate this mishap. For centuries verderers and miners assembled to guard their traditional rights and privileges. Where the verderers eventually met in the reign of Charles II, and still do so, can be inspected under the timber roof of their Court Room at the Speech House, an interesting survival of old English custom. Harking back towards the beginning of A.D., the most exciting archæological curiosity to my way of thinking is at Blackpool Bridge, about 3 miles from Blakeney. Here you can walk up and down a section of road trodden by the Romans, paved as they left it, and well preserved for a hale old article aged more than 1,500 years. Farther on, between Bream and Lydney, a spooky hollow shrouds dark holes dug by Romans who searched for iron ore with oak spades. The coal-mining district of Cinderford, useful though it is just now, may not be ideal for holidays or honeymoons, and parts of the Forest are popular with human beings and much frequented by them. But many ways, far from madding crowds, remain unspoiled. They lead to the Forest's heart, where silences are broken only by rustling leaves and songs of birds, and the majesty of nature's own work rises supreme in tree forms, leafage and flowers. Above the glades and the ponds the ridges are prolific for near and distant views. Eastward is the Severn and its vale bounded by the Cotswolds. In the west the River Wye sweeps from Welsh Bicknor and Symonds Yat to the great vista visible from Staunton, and cliffs and woods massed in peculiar grandeur indicate the river's southern course past Offa's Dyke and the height crowned with the castle and Norman church of St. Briavels.

The narrow streets at Monmouth, reckoned to be on a Roman site, are just outside the Forest at the junction of the Monnow with the Wye. Needless to state, the present natives do not wear the Monmouth caps trimmed with leeks that Fluellen told Henry V were so becoming, but the town retains other past adornments for observation. Castle ruins, mouldy for a birthplace of the gallant Henry V, show best from the opposite side of the river, and a representation of the hero of Agincourt decorates the early eighteenth-century town hall supported on an open colonnade. Geoffrey's window, an enriched Perpendicular oriel of five lights, presents historical complications; it would be nice to think that Geoffrey of Monmouth worked hard on King Arthur behind the mullions and produced one of the earliest best-sellers, but this attractive piece of masonry obviously dates from years and years after the daring fabulist's own twelfth century. The River Wye accounted for the seventeenth-century bridge, since widened. River Monnow did better, caused the town to get its best present showpiece. This bridge, guarded by a medieval gateway, is picturesque when seen from the waterside. Thus it has been presented by thousands of artists of varied abilities and sexes in many periods. For the sake of variety I tackled the subject from the King's highway while in a motor car (69). Turner's fine drawing of the arches and gateway grouped from the usual angle afterwards convinced me that in affairs of art, as with things in general, it is better to be conventional and good than unconventional and shaky.

Whatever of fable may have hitched on to the Monmouth oriel, the name attached to it, Geoffrey of Monmouth, hints with truth that we are at the gateway to a home of old romance. Geoffrey, with Walter Map, born in the neighbourhood, and Layamon, who lived on Severn bank, make a valiant trio among writers of twelfth-century truth and fiction. Celtic vivacity, continually exploded in the racial wars of the Marches, gave moving incidents and names to history. The face of the land hereabout tells its romantic stories without aid of words from romancers. Offa's Dyke bordering the Wye is visible upward from Chepstow. Dozens of earthworks and camps show on vantage points. Castles on the Wye, the Monnow, and the Usk bristle up over rippling waters, and castles on hillocks and with moats in peaceful rural landscapes look quieter now than they used to do. All of them exactly fit the type of scene, here mounted romantically in natural effects of hills, woods, and winding rivers (69, 81). Ruined, picturesque in decay with towers and walls fallen, the castled pictures are just the subjects for ruminations on Normans and Lords Marchers who continually harassed the natives, and in return were harassed by visitors from the Black and other mountains looming dark in the west. It is quite understandable that George Borrow, when he groped round Chepstow Castle, fell to repeating for nearly one hour *The Norman Horse-shoe*, remembered from Scott:

> From Chepstow's towers, ere dawn of morn,
> Was heard afar the bugle-horn;
> And forth, in banded pomp and pride,
> Stout Clare and fiery Neville ride.

Stories and views of FitzOsborn's and de Clare's castle at Chepstow are famed, and the superb combination of ruins and setting at Raglan (75), fitting last scenes for the last act of medieval military architecture, quite rightly attract the gaze of multitudes doomed to inhabit a mundane age deficient in knightly and heraldic trappings. Upward from the castle of Prince Hal's birth in 1388 at Monmouth the windings of the Monnow, and of Time, offer further warlike embellishments. They present a round Norman keep at Skenfrith, the keep with adjacent thirteenth-century ruins at Grosmont, and a moated White Castle remarkably preserved 6 miles inland from the river. Each lovely and away from beaten tracks, these units in a triangular system of Border defence give little hint of past hurryings and scurryings. Only in fancy can be pictured Henry III personally in charge at Grosmont, the surprise attack launched on him by Llewelyn ap Iorwerth at night, warriors minus clothes stampeding into the darkness, and a probable quick exit of Queen Eleanor covered only with the medieval equivalent of a Burberry, for of course early-English ladies, even if French, did not favour nightdresses or pyjamas.

Castles again are framed in the River Usk's settings. Running fresh from the mountains, the stream sweeps and curls grandly through its vale, brightens Llanover, Llanbaddock bridge, and other joyous spots, passes the Went Wood ridges and reaches Roman *Isca* at Caerleon. Abergavenny's ruined walls and towers and the pretty town of Usk with its keep and gateway figuring in the ruins, each offer old stonework suitable for pictures or for souls with a romantic tilt. William de Braose, a most horrible knight, furnished at least one appropriate episode at Abergavenny when he invited seventy Welsh warriors to dinner and had all of them murdered after the coffee and liquors. No such misfortune is likely to occur in Usk to-day. Historic and charming, the town amply compensates for any stains on hospitality in the past by affording comfort without murder and much more than safety in food at the *Three Salmons* hotel. More castles and signs of perils and surprises appear towards the Severn estuary in the neighbourhood of Roman conquest at Caerleon and Caerwent. Penhow Castle occupies a hilltop; the early walls, round tower, and fourteenth-century gatehouse at Caldicot make a memorable group; and houses near and far, as at the Bishop's Palace, Mathern, and Moynes Court (76), show that the old inhabitants felt most comfortable when behind gatehouses and fortifications. Even Llanthony Priory, wonderfully situated in the Honddu valley of the Black Mountains, is more piquant with the romance of strife than of holiness (70). Built by Augustinians in the first half of the twelfth century with the powerful de Lacy's money, and at a site thrice blessed with traditions of St. David of Wales, a hermit's cell, and a church of 1113, "savages, thieves, vagabonds," weather and wolves soon made things either too hot or too cold for prayer, meditation, or praise. Rather than be doomed to purgatory before it was due, the monks flitted from the Honddu (black water) to Gloucester, left their temple to go to ruin. Early in the nineteenth century it became an unfortunate plaything for Walter Savage Landor, who in due season flitted also. Now you can settle inside upstanding leavings of the monks and perhaps feel quite as romantic as Geoffrey of Monmouth in surroundings that surely are unequalled by any other hotel in the land. You live in the prior's own quarters, go out to fish, scale Hay Bluff and the mountains, wander away to find de Lacy's castle at Longtown just in Herefordshire and the fifteenth-century rood loft at Partrishow church. At night, without being modernized by thoughts of bathrooms, you wind up the circular stone stairway, stepping in correct transitional Norman–Early English style. And so to bed, to wing afar from these dull times into dreamlands, chivalry's own, romantic with Queens of Love and Beauty, fields or, plumes waving argent and gules, and proper charges of fierce warriors, villains, dragons, wolves, and heavily armoured knights tumbling off hefty horses. Whatever Augustinians and W. S. Landor may have thought of Llanthony Priory, I call it a charmer.

My space, like Time, flies. Reluctantly I must leave the mountains, the rivers, the rural scenes and the grand scenes of these Monmouthshire lands, telling of much more than pillage by Lords Marchers and onslaughts by Welshmen. The Wye, guiding to Gloucestershire again, cannot be praised afresh; it is Richard Wilson's "River Wye," Turner's "River Wye," Wordsworth's "Sylvan Wye," the river of countless pictures and innumerable books, the famous valley for the charabancs and motor cars, yet still continuing sublime and perfect. Hastening on I pass Tintern (76), the Wyndcliff (here the wind cost me one hat while drawing for p. 81), Chepstow, and reach the camp at Sudbrook where the conquering Roman general, Julius Frontinus, is supposed to

RIVER WYE FROM WYNDCLIFF *and overlooking Chepstow,
the Wye and Severn confluence, and distant Cotswold Hills.*

New Inn
Teatime
Three China Festival
Sept 1947

Sydney R.
Jones

Timbering in
SOUTHGATE ST.
House of Robert Raikes

15th century
Angle Post
NEW INN

GLOUCESTER

have sat after crossing the New Passage nearly 2,000 years before I sat there myself, to construct a picture of a new Severn Bridge which threatens to desecrate the watery landscape. A dive through the Severn Tunnel and my arrival under the trees on College Green permits me to introduce—Bristol.

Contrasts Bristol certainly offers after the country pictures, broken-down castles and deserted monks' quarters of Monmouthshire. Here is the romance, if any, of modern times in exchange for our recent encounters with ruins. Situated close to the River Severn, the estuary, the Cotswolds, and glorious Somerset, it is well placed for living in or getting out of. Being very big, this is the first centre of commerce and industry that we have met as yet in our wanderings through western England. It savours of both the land and the sea; you can stand on pavements or look out of factory windows and see ships. Streets are busy, packed, full of hair-breadth escapes from motors; and commotion, noise, a fine high tower of a new university, a cathedral half modern, factories in view, and a hundred sights give lively impressions of a city right on the mark and up to date, the embodiment of that peculiar, illusive, and often very unsatisfactory quality called progress. Bristol kept in the vanguard of progress for centuries. Merchants, explorers, sieges, riots, wars, politics, and a constant lookout from presents into futures helped movement forward. Thus Bristol rose to be the second city in England during the seventeenth and eighteenth centuries. When steamships were born Bristol founded a new era with the first regular service to America. Railways developed, so Bristol produced the biggest goods shed in the world. Much earlier, before William the Conqueror arrived or Britons had learned to sing *Rule, Britannia*, Bristol held foremost fame for being the principal slave market in England. Much later, even in the 1940's, Bristol East sent a Chancellor of the Exchequer to Westminster to improve on the pre-Conquest idea by manufacturing Britons into slaves out of the azure main while singing *Rule, Britannia*. Such happenings and notable records during a very long time certainly entitle Bristol to its pride for progress.

Bristol does not suggest, as many old towns do, an ancient dependence on royal, feudal, or ecclesiastical privilege. Two rivers, the sea, and trading made the city. Its character was developed by people of commerce and enterprise who knew how to act, get things done, to adventure and prosper, and who found time and means for piety, charity, and culture. Before the German raids this city and port, with buildings old and new ringed by a group of fine churches, reminded me most of the City of London, itself a growth of trade and settled by the river leading to the oceans of promise.

Though merchants and trade ruled in Bristol, footholds of aristocratic overlords and the monks accounted for a castle and a monastery. The castle ended with Cromwell's order for demolition after the memorable Civil War siege. Relics exposed by German bombs and the name of Castle Street are the inglorious reminders of the Conquest stronghold that was rebuilt in the twelfth century by Queen Matilda's half-brother, Robert, Earl of Gloucester, and used by the queen for keeping King Stephen quiet while chained round the feet in a dungeon. Books on the brave old days explain how Robert also got himself into a similar uncomfortable position and thus enabled the king to regain the use of his legs and walk on to his throne again.

Works built by the monks fared somewhat better than those made by the feudal lords. Although another destroyer, Henry VIII, finished off the monastery when he turned the abbey church into a cathedral in June 1542, ancient beauty has survived from the great Augustinian foundation of Robert Fitzhardinge, first Lord of Berkeley, which began to shape in 1140 on the border of College Green at the traditional place of St. Augustine's preaching in *circa* 602 (62). Before the Tudor plunderers appeared the Norman great gateway had been rebuilt in 1515 and a demolished nave awaited reconstruction. Thereafter time and circumstance dealt hard knocks to the cathedral and precincts. From the Dissolution until the nineteenth century the church remained without a nave. Reform rioters, Bristol's harbingers of progress, wrecked the bishop's palace in 1831, but failed to reduce the cathedral. Gothic revivalists duly arrived. G. E. Street designed the nave and western front for completion in 1868 and J. L. Pearson reconstructed the bulky central tower in 1892. These and other alarums completed, memorials of monkish years and the prime time of English art survived in the choir, chapels, transepts and chapter house. Beauties now displayed particularly include the Elder Lady Chapel of about 1200, the fourteenth-century Berkeley and Newton Chapels, fifteenth-century transept roofs rich in carved bosses, canopied tombs, with the one to Abbot Newland, very splendid. The chapter house, with vaulting, arcades, and surface patterning, is one of the most impressive late-Norman interiors in the land. Very ingenious, and not to be seen elsewhere in England, are the arrangements of stone arches, beams, and spandrels in the choir aisles. Here is evident the bold originality of the progressive school of Bristol masons. Though these features may be more notable for novelty than beauty, they do show the birth of an idea, one that is found fully developed in the choir of Gloucester Cathedral.

Through the ups and downs of early castled and monastic years the townsfolk reigned top dogs. Neither wars and rebellions, very severe devastations from the Black Death, nor whiffles of other sorts quelled the people's progressive spirit and independence. When necessary, as in 1312, they ran a siege on their own account. Their ships sailed the seas, carried the English wool, fought in the wars of Plantagenet kings, and for services rendered to Edward III Bristol was created a self-contained county in 1373. A hundred years later legends and rumours stirred these dwellers by the Avon Gorge. They dreamed of a golden West. John Jay's two ships set out in 1480. John Cabot followed in 1497. They led the way for adventurers and explorers to scour uncharted oceans. The Armada threatened, so Bristol ships fought for Queen Elizabeth as they had done for Plantagenets and were destined to do for the hero of Trafalgar. While merchants and seamen, their foresight, commerce, and hard work continuously brightened national glory and local fame from century to century, Bristol developed into a place of close-packed streets on the peninsula formed by the River Avon and a new channel cut for the River Frome in the early days. A bridge led over the water to Redcliffe. Tall masts at the quays meant prosperity and enterprise, and ships safely in port savoured the native air with a fragrance of distant lands. Many churches enriched by merchants graced the scenes below the downs. Merchant venturers, coopers, cutlers, and the good companions of various guilds met in their halls; no doubt they mixed business with jolly times and Bristol milk, then a convivial kind of punch inspired by the West Indies trade. The fruits of individual effort and adventure in active life prompted kind thoughts and deeds. Hospitals, almshouses, and other quarters were created and endowed for the sweet advancement of charity, education, the arts, and citizenship. Thus the people advanced the place and purpose of their home town, made it of importance second only to London. Events, like years, pointed forward. Bristol marched with times on the move. The *Great Western* forged new links with America in 1838 by starting the first steamship service across the Atlantic. Docks expanded, the railways came, the Suspension Bridge begun by Brunel was completed. The *Greyhound* and numerous coaching inns changed tactics, and the *Royal Western* hotel on College Green boldly informed all and sundry, "Omnibus to and from every train. R. P. Ham, Proprietor, Turtle and Wine Merchant." Modern Bristol developed and spread in size if not in beauty. Industries grew and multiplied. The name of the ancient and ever-new city went round the world on chocolate boxes, cigarette cards, motor vehicles, aircraft, and a hundred and one big and little products carried to the ends of the earth from the docks on the Avon. The year 1940 brought a new kind of interlude. During thirty raids Hitler's bombs churned up signs of past and present. Much remained steadfast. Representatives of the early lights, the lords spiritual and lords temporal, retained position, and the real makers of the city, trade and worldly enterprise, carried on. The monastery-cum-cathedral therefore stands. Castle relics are on view again. A progressive municipality forges ahead with all latest developments in welfare; and a civic restaurant, in which I observed fish and chips in great favour for tea, daily operates a parable of loaves and fishes. But the busy scenes, the general alertness, and gaunt gaps made by the German raids hardly imply the glamour of those far-off years that made Bristol.

Sitting under the trees on College Green, an oasis in the middle of noise and hurrying, it may be pleasant now and then to get back a bit; to fancy, for instance, the year 1756 transported from the first chapter of *The Virginians* and alive again with Mr. Trail, merchant, large and grave, Harry Warrington in mourning, their talk on negro slaves, and all the vividness of Thackeray's picture of Bristol on that summer morning when the *Young Rachael*, Virginian ship, came up the Avon on her return from the Potomac with Edward Franks captain, in charge, who invented the wonderful advertisement for W. D. and H. O. Wills when he said, "There's no sweeter tobacco comes from Virginia, and no better brand than the Three Castles." Mr. Pepys may help a more distant mental flight and with facts rather than fancies garnered onward from 2 p.m. on June 13, 1668, after being "parboiled," dried, and sweated in Bath at four o'clock in the morning. Thus fortified, he decided that Bristol was "in every respect another London." He saw where the merchants met in Corn Street "and a fine cross yet standing, like Cheapside" (since counterfeited on College Green). He walked through Marsh Street (now drab with garages and a waterworks department), visited the "most large and noble quay," inspected "the new ship building by Bally" (a naval architect of the time). "No carts, only dog-carts" in the streets recalls the fact that horse-drawn vehicles were prohibited for about three centuries because their iron tires damaged the street paving. Deb's uncle, "very good company," pleased him mightily, and the merchant's "good entertainment of strawberries, a whole venison-pasty cold, and plenty of brave wine, and above all Bristol milk" evidentally cheered the cockles of the Pepysian heart.

Charming times! Still they dimly echo in streets, byways, and quiet corners on the flats and up the slopes. You can dodge about in the traffic, at the same time see quays, water and ships, and easily twist a thought back to wooden bulwarks, spreading mainyards, "argosies of magic sails." Broad Quay expands wide in centuries of fame, peopled with visions of John and Sebastian Cabot looking to the promised west, Martin Pring bent on discovering a landing-place for Pilgrim Fathers, Admiral Penn's son finally destined for Pennsylvania. Stones, bricks, mortar, and dirt are telltales for stages in long development. Courts (Dusty Foot and Pie Poudre are good names for two of them) and narrow streets that have survived efforts for destruction by municipal authorities and Hitler preserve the lines of the packed and close planning mentioned in medieval records. Christmas Steps—a quaint bit—show the "steppering" done in 1669. Development beyond the city walls produced King Street at the restoration of King Charles, the spacious quadrangle of Queen Square fixes a building line for the reign of Queen Anne, terraces above the Avon at Clifton mark the outward stride for Bristolians and fashionable spa visitors in Georgian and Regency years.

Progress and the recent raids have not helped to preserve original works

THE CHELTENHAM VALE *and distant line
of the Malvern Hills from Upper Dowdeswell.*

GLOUCESTER. *The fifteenth-century tower, finished with pierced masonry of*
splendour in choir and Lady Chapel, Norman piers in the nave, the shrine of Edwar
the city preserve the Roman plan and old buildings show a

Gloucester coronet," predominates in the vale below Cotswold Hills. Perpendicular
and the finest cloisters in England are among the riches of the cathedral. Street lines in
of medieval stonework, timbering, gables and Georgian fronts.

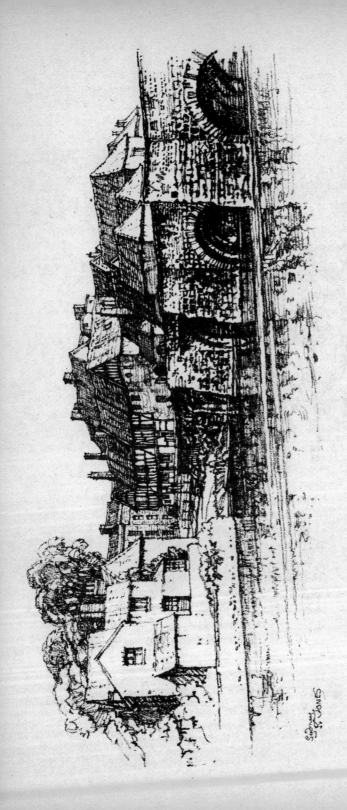

TEWKESBURY

A group at King John's Bridge. Many old houses line picturesque streets leading to the abbey church, celebrated for the Norman tower and west front, tombs and chantry chapels. The battle here in 1471 ended the Wars of the Roses.

created after the fashion usual in old English towns. Survivors include the eighteenth-century façade of Coopers' Hall; an open timbered roof of the Cutler's Hall in Rosemary Street; the Exchange well designed by John Wood of Bath and amplified on the pavement outside by curious posts dated 1594, 1625, 1631, known as "nails" and used by merchants for settling bargains "on the nail." Oldest institutions of their kind in England are the Library, patronized by Wordsworth, Coleridge, and Southey and built in the local classic style pre-eminent in Bath, and the Theatre Royal of 1766. The home and domestic front has its reminders of fashion and period. There are the notable Regency and Georgian terraces and crescents at Clifton (61), sedate white walls with cornices in Berkeley Square, Queen Anne houses in Queen Square. No. 6 King Street leads the fine series of doorways with shell hoods. Excellent Georgian rooms and fittings are open for all to see at No. 7 Great George Street, the house in which Wordsworth first met Coleridge. The homebred earlier manner of beam, oriel and gable has a showpiece in the timbering of 1664, which includes *Llandoger Trow*, the inn with the strange name derived from Llandoger, in Monmouthshire, and trow, a type of boat sailed long ago by a nautical landlord. Older still are the remarkable pavings of tiles removed from the Canynges house and now in the British Museum, proofs that the homes of great merchants did not lack beauty and luxuriance in the fifteenth century.

Churches: they have held their places well enough to suggest the towered scenes that were the city's pride when nineteen of them stood within the walls and ringed the space with high masonry and joyful chimes. Loveliest of all rises the great collegiate Church of St. Mary Redcliffe, spired over the city and the docks, an emblem of faith for both (63). Choir, transepts, nave, and porches extend in a noble design; arcades, clerestories, and vaults soar to lofty heights, and traceries, pierced parapets, flying-buttresses, and pinnacles unite in the resplendent harmony born of the late Gothic time. It is a true expression of the merchants, a memorial to the Canynges family and their fellow citizens, who determined to have and to pay for the best that money could buy. The spire collapsed in a storm soon after completion and awaited the nineteenth century for renewal, but the splendour seen and praised by Queen Elizabeth remained and has continued in this "fayrest and most famous parish church." Memorials inside, puppets and properties of old tales, commemorate priests, knights, sailors, soldiers; the Medes, the Jays, and the prolific offspring they could afford to have in the fifteenth century join with the company of merchants that added lustre to their own years and church. Thoughtful, blest by angels, lies William Canynges, the merchant prince of his day, patron of this architecture at St. Mary's and with enough spare cash to entertain a luxurious Edward IV, himself a fellow merchant in wool. The brass face of Joan Brook looks outward, raises but never solves the enigma on the origin of America's name; for of

Joan
dau. of Richard Amerycke
Sheriff of Bristol

from
the Amerycke brass
St. Mary Redcliffe

course a few old Englanders and all New Englanders know that the living Joan was daughter of Richard Amerycke, Sheriff of Bristol and John Cabot's friend. Memorials such as these, screened from outside noise and visible in the dim religious light of church after church, perhaps best of all afford the liveliest commentary on the years and the spirit of Bristol's great past. They represent the actual people who traded, adventured, brightened the fame of their city, added passages to England's far-flung story; men who did very well for themselves (and others) and went inside churches pretty often to offer prayer, praise, and thanksgiving for benefits received (and expected). Among this crowd of silent figures are Martin Pring, most admirable and impudent of navigators, and George Snygoe at full length in a furred robe, both at St. Stephen's; Edward Colston, grand old benefactor fresh from the hand of Rysbrack at All Saints; Henry Gibbes in the skull-and-hourglass fashion at St. James's; John Whitson at St. Nicholas's, famed for naming Whitson Bay, Massachusetts, in 1603; John Aldworth, clad in scarlet at the Lord Mayor's chapel of St. Mark's. Knights, mayors, aldermen, merchants, seamen, even the Canynges's cook, all are there cut in stone and brass. You can go close up to them, look into their characterful faces, see how they dressed, study the arms they bore, and feel all the fresher for a breath of valiant times that neither knew nor desired safety first from the cradle to the grave.

Away from sepulchral gloom and facing the four winds of heaven the Cabot Tower stands high in elevation and fame on Brandon Hill. It commands a range of towers, spires, chimney-pots, factories, miles of green England, silvery streaks of water. The structure is not particularly beautiful nor older than the year 1898. Even so, a very noble tower is this. Placed high for all to see, it symbolizes dreams, memories, the spirit of a city whose pioneers began to make the English tongue a language of the world. A penny-in-the-slot fitting and a lift will raise sightseers up to the top. There, if the earth were not round and human eyes could see better than they do, the United States and Canada might be discerned far away in the west.

Neither tower, tablet, nor flourish commemorate Bristol's first brave attempt in 1480 to conquer the West. John Jay's two little ships, the *George* and the *Trinity*, piloted by Thomas Lloyd, then "the most scientific mariner of all England," sailed the uncharted Atlantic and failed to reach their goal, a legendary "Isle of Brasile." They gathered little glory and no medals. But they went not in vain. The spirit of hazardous exploration, already astir, was quickened. What happened seventeen years later every schoolboy knows; and some oldsters remember that John Cabot, the Venetian, settled in Bristol, made a friend of Richard Amerycke, the Sheriff, obtained letters patent from the King for himself and "his sonneys" to sail for the discovery of islands and countries then unknown "to all christians," left Broad Quay in the *Matthew*, manned by an English crew, discovered new-found lands in North America, and on St. John's Day, June 24, 1497, a year before Christopher Columbus discovered the South American mainland, John Cabot unfurled the Royal banner on Cape Breton Island and "took possession in the name of King Henry VII." This feat of tremendous promise brought Cabot a reward of £10 from the King and a pension of £20. The second voyage, more discoveries, a safe return in the autumn of 1498, then death removed the brave adventurer from the stage of worldly history. Better than the cash reward and pension is John Cabot's credit in perpetuity, brightly kept on Brandon Hill and at Cabot Straits leading to the Gulf of St. Lawrence.

On a September day after the close of this last world war I walked to the base of the Cabot Tower and there met two strangers, a pretty girl dressed in blue, evidently English, and an officer from overseas. We talked together, admired the views. Then I said, "You can see even more from the top of the tower and the lift will take you up."

"Fine," answered the man. "We'll go."

He looked through his cash without finding coppers for the penny-in-the-slot, asked me to change a shilling; I couldn't, so gave my only pennies, for which he offered the shilling.

"No thank you," I said. "This is my privilege. If we happen to meet in New York we'll make up the change there!"

"Do you think I come from Noo York?" he asked laughingly.

The enormity of my military crime at once was obvious on noticing that he wore the uniform of a Canadian officer. "Well," I added apologetically, "in Toronto, Montreal, or wherever it may be."

He laughed again, the girl smiled roguishly, click went the pennies into the slot. With a mutual, "Until the next time," they disappeared upwards. I went downward to find the relics of the fort, defences of Bristol during the sieges of 1643 and 1645. "Halloo! halloo!" and words shouted down made me look up. The words were lost on the wind, but two figures on the tower, clear against the sky, waved again and again. I hallooed and waved in return, then finally descended the hill. With a last look back I saw the pair up aloft, lit by the western sun and faced towards the Atlantic. "A very pretty picture and an emblem," I thought. "Charming young England and brave young Canada, just suited for an Atlantis up-to-date and not according to Plato or Bacon. Perhaps they are engaged, maybe just married, and bound for a united adventure. Wouldn't old John Cabot have loved to see them, 450 years after his own adventure!"

Northward from Bristol level and wide landscapes border the Severn leading to Gloucester below the southern and best wooded scarps of the Cotswolds. Villages look snug with thatching, timbering, warm-coloured brickwork, and tiled roofs. Grouped round church towers and manor-houses, they give the local type of rustic pictures that continue through Gloucestershire to Shakespeare's land and Worcestershire. Black and white and the thatching at Frampton-upon-Severn are wonderfully set off by the long and wide green— Rosamond's Green by name, one of England's biggest. Slimbridge, a traditional birthplace for William Tyndale, has the old cider mills, tools of time-honoured industry which remind of being in the apple and orchard country. Thornbury and Berkeley, each picturesque with a splendid church and a castle, and both creepy through murderous associations, keep the flame of history lurid. Tudor battlements, bays, oriels, and moulded brick chimneys at Thornbury, begun in 1511 by Edward Stafford, third Duke of Buckingham, localize a noble work never finished because the duke provided the farewell speech for Act II in *King Henry VIII* and expired on the block at the Tower in 1521. The embattled and buttressed pile pierced with squint-holes seen from the meadows at Berkeley is proper material to shake up notions on chivalry or bloodthirsty crimes of a long time ago; quite enough to send shudders down anybody's back is the knowledge that these fourteenth-century walls screen Fitzhardinge's Norman tower and the place of Edward II's murder in 1327, where shrieks broke the stillness of a September night and Bristol citizens came on the morrow to view the distorted face of a King of England who had refused to be bullied, starved, or tortured to death.

Travelling in the footsteps of Abbot Thokey we next reach Gloucester and see one result of this murder at Berkeley. John Thokey ruled in Gloucester's Benedictine abbey church of St. Peter, a rebuilding begun in 1089 and now partly visible in the strong Norman design of the nave. The abbot was loyal and apparently cute. More than once he entertained Edward II at the abbey. One day, when the king mentioned the absence of his own painted portrait in

MAXSTOKE CASTLE, *a moated fortified home begun by William de Clinton in 1345 and still inhabited. Two Kings of England slept here; Richard III on his way to Bosworth Field and Henry VII on the night after the battle.*

GRIMSHAW HALL, *probably the finest timbered hall of the sixteenth century in the Forest of Arden country.*

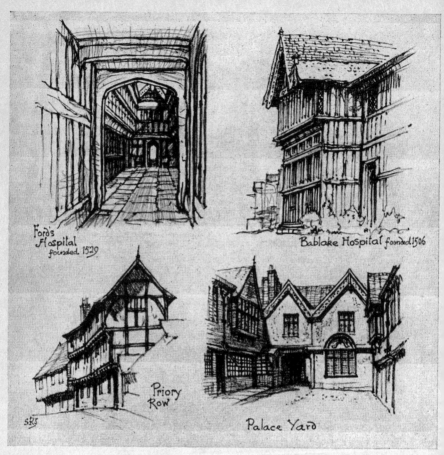

Ford's
Hospital
founded 1529

Bablake Hospital founded 1506

Priory
Row

SRS

Palace Yard

COVENTRY. *Notes made before the war raids.*

STONELEIGH ABBEY. *The classic frontage of 1704–20 adjoins remains of the Cistercian abbey*
King Charles stayed in the older rooms with the loyal Leighs at the opening of the Civil War in 1642

the hall where they dined, the abbot replied that his royal master's features should adorn a more distinguished position—as in fact they did, though for reasons then never dreamed of by the speakers. The murder at Berkeley accomplished, followed by refusal from the monks of Bristol and Malmesbury to bury the remains of an unpopular and deposed king in their abbeys, loyal Thokey himself fetched the body "from Berkeley Castle in his own chariot" and with procession and solemnity buried it "in the north aisle, hard by the high altar." During 1329–34 the abbot's earlier wish came true. Edward II, in the alabaster effigy of death, occupied a place of honour by the high altar; sublime in repose the figure still sheds royal dignity with features finely tooled and enclosed in a canopy of pinnacles richly carved in Caen stone. Time and popular feeling quickly elevated the murdered king to martyr and saint. The relics were thought to work miracles. Pilgrims flocked to the shrine. Wealth thus accumulated enabled the great reconstruction to proceed on the eastern Norman fabric. The Severn masons advanced their experiments made at Bristol. They developed the transepts, achieved the choir lit by the immense and superb east window, memorial to Edward III's victory at Crécy. Thought and execution brought the spaciousness, the brilliant lighting; high vertical lines to piers and mullions, windows of many lights cut by transoms, surface panelling lightly worked in stone, urged fine architecture forward into the revolution of the Perpendicular style. Fan-vaulting and pierced screens in the cloisters, unsurpassed in the world, led the way for similar triumphs elsewhere. Onward from 1450 the central tower rose predominant over the composition, elevated 225 feet high and crowned with the pierced parapets and pinnacles of the famous "Gloucester coronet." Late to arrive, the detached lady chapel and the gallery-bridge set the seal of delicate grace on this grand scheme in 1500. Glory accumulated in chapels, screens, tombs, stalls, misericords, and the marvels of stone, wood, metal, and glass, carving and imagery that have been described again and again since Henry VIII turned the Benedictine abbey into a cathedral of the new foundation on January 4, 1540.

Stone gateways and curious exits lead from the spiritual calm of the close to the twentieth-century air and crowded pavements of the secular capital of Gloucestershire. Here are pleasant and lively mixtures of the old and the new. Northgate, Southgate, Eastgate, and Westgate Streets follow the exact lines planned by the Romans for *Glevum*. At their crossing the curfew bell in the old tower of St. Nicholas still tolls the knell of parting day. A lot of church towers, medieval masonry, timber framing and Georgian brickwork keep their places shoulder to shoulder with modern erections, areas of plate glass, and an outer fringe of those skimpy little houses in which happy people now enjoy life. The charming local burr is heard spoken in the streets, though not by the nobs who patronize the collection of good shops and county doings; and of the city's good days, which are many, those of the Three Choirs Festivals cannot be bettered for music, grand effects, and human sights. Things of the old order include remnants left by the Black Friars, the Grey Friars, and the monks who removed from Llanthony. The Robert Raikes house (82) faces the Crypt Grammar School of 1539. Timbers and good wooden windows over-hang at the house in which Bishop Hooper lodged on the night before his martyrdom in 1555. More interesting buildings of various shapes and periods reward the seeker in this ancient place that accommodated William the Con-queror when he issued orders for compiling Domesday Book. The *Fleece*, with a courtyard and vaulted cellars, the *Bull, King's Head, Leather Bottle*, and *Grey-hound* are samples from the nice collection of names for hospitable institutions. As for the *New Inn*, this is one of the oldest and finest survivors of the ancient type and one of the jolliest providers for modern days in all England. It has a gorgeous fifteenth-century angle post outside, an inside courtyard introduced by the archway (82); there are snug rooms to eat in, the courtyard gallery for going to bed and perhaps finding a wrong bedroom in Pickwickian style, and the general mellow atmosphere can make one feel either Johnsonian or Eliza-bethan, or just as cobwebby and medieval as John Twynning, the monk, to whom the foundation is traditionally ascribed. The city is difficult to see whole because it lies in the flat vale. The top of a tower or something high, such as I found, can be handy for spying down to discover wonderful and unexpected groupings (88-89). More distant compositions seen from the Severn meadows show the cathedral's tower, clerestory and broken roofline soaring above clusters of domestic roofs, calling to mind Peter de Wint's picture painted in 1840.

The end of this chapter brings me to the river and valley country from Gloucester up to Tewkesbury, the beginning of the noble vale that sweeps away between the Malvern and Bredon Hills into the heart of the south Midlands. A fertile and well-tilled countryside, and the buildings on it, give the quality of more to follow in our course northward. Pretty villages have pretty names—Stoke Orchard and Woolstone are two samples. Cottages and houses show the black-and-white and the red brick constructed and grouped in the homely Midland manner. Upleadon introduces one of the church towers built of half-timber, and at Hartpury begins the series of tithe barns conspicuous for great length. Pauntley old court, dovecote, and church are London-ish with fourteenth-century associations of Sir William Whittington and his son, the real but not fabulous Dick. A spirit of longer ago still haunts the Saxon church and chapel in quiet meadows by the stream at Deerhurst; it is no ordinary experience to see the walls undoubtedly used by St. Alphaege for worship, to be in this place of pre-Conquest times, to recall an abbey's thousand years of romantic vicissitudes which came to an end when George Throgmorton obtained the buildings and the tithes at the Dissolution. Two towns hereabout represent a small and a large one. Newent, little, historic, and surrounded with bloom in spring, marshals itself round the spired old church and timbered market hall. Cheltenham, big, clothes its own piece of the vale below the Cotswolds and in sight of the Malverns (87). Those who like the stucco and verandah grace overflowed from the age of elegance will find the correct doses in this early example of a garden town; the delicate combination of Promenade, Regency terraces, Papworth's villas architected for Lord Sherborne, tree-lined avenues and gardens, now gracious in maturity, may stir a thought for old tunes and gaieties, Byron and celebrities, "Indian" settlers conscious of livers, and the fashion that flocked to the spa after George III drank the waters in 1788, benefited his inside, and caused the town to rival Bath.

Lastly Tewkesbury, rare old Tewkesbury, where Severn and Avon meet and dozens of artists could fill dozens of sketch-books. Everything is here—beauty, history, memories, river and waterside, King John's Bridge (90), picturesque inns, streets of timbered houses and tall brick fronts. For thoughts and emotions beyond the scope of words there is the abbey church, its Norman tower, western arch, vaults miraculously poised, the flowering of architectural styles as at Gloucester, the marvellous chantries, perfect carving in miniature, old glass in the Despencer windows. But I must tear myself away from my beloved, as we are overdue for Warwickshire. Merely can be mentioned the *Black Bear* under the sign of the house of Warwick, the *Berkeley Arms*, *Wheatsheaf*, Clarence House and Cross House in the specimens of timber and plaster of the sixteenth century and pre-Cromwellian period; the half-timbered *Bell* for "Abel Fletcher's home" in *John Halifax, Gentleman*, the *Hop Pole* for Mr. Pickwick's dinner, "Thick as Tewkesbury mustard" from Shakespeare; and my inadequate words on a treasured English town end with a homily for my readers, painted in medieval lettering on plaster behind a High Street frontage,

> Three thinges pleseth booeth God and Man.   Concorde Be twene
> bretheren Amytie betwene nayghbowers : And A man and his wyfe
> that agreeth well to gether.

3. THE MIDDLE OF ENGLAND

WARWICKSHIRE, WORCESTERSHIRE, HEREFORDSHIRE, SHROPSHIRE

Mapped below, this is an ideal land for oaks and glades, leafy lanes, elms and orchard trees. Footpath ways to jog on, and the intimate scenes characteristic of the Midlands, we like to think bred and helped to make Shakespeare. The Midland Plain meets the noble vales expanded round the Avon and Severn rivers. Clee Hills and Wenlock Edge, leading to the rugged heights of the Marches, divide the vales of Hereford and north Shropshire. From Warwick to Worcester, Hereford and Shrewsbury buildings show this area to be chiefly on sandstone. It is also a great district for seeing past timber construction; names of Arden, Wyre Forest, and the general woodiness explain why. Henley-in-Arden, Evesham, Ledbury, and Ludlow are samples of the lovely old towns, and scores of villages are so pretty that explorers may wish to stay in them for ever. One reminder of early days is the straight line of the Fosse Way across Warwickshire. Watling Street and Wroxeter stand notably for Roman years. Offchurch, and Offa's Dyke suggest being in ancient Mercia. The crop of castles, war sites from Edge Hill to Battlefield, monastic relics, two cathedrals, moated houses, mansions in parks, and expressive architecture typify the human motions and ideas that constantly stirred at this heart of England.

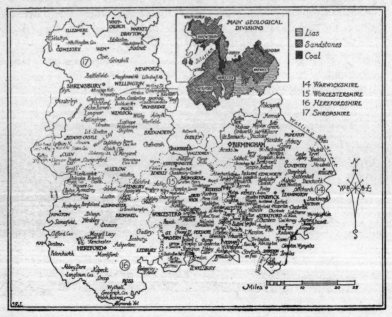

ASHOW. A scene in the Stoneleigh Abbey domain near to Leamington.

LEEK WOOTTON (page opposite). "The Skylark," a study in the upper Avon country.

WARWICK CASTLE. *Cæsar's tower built by the first Thomas Beauchamp about 1360. The castle, developed round a Norman mound above the River Avon, was successively held by the Beauchamps, the Nevilles, and the Grevilles. It is one of the great monuments of chivalrous splendour that remains habitable to this day.*

WARWICK. *The Leycester Hospital, an ancient foundation re-established by Queen Elizabeth's favourite, Robert Dudley, Earl of Leicester. It then became what it is now, a home for pensioners under the badge of the Bear and Ragged Staff.*

STRATFORD-ON-AVON. *The Birthplace in Henley Street associated with the birth of William Shakespeare on 23rd April, 1564. With its museum and garden, one of the most famous goals for pilgrims in the world.*

STRATFORD-ON-AVON. *Holy Trinity Church on the riverside, Shake-speare's last home in 1616. This celebrated building is distinguished for thirteenth-, fourteenth-, and fifteenth-century architecture, chapels, tombs, and the modern screen. The graceful spire, erected in the eighteenth century, replaced a timber steeple.*

WORCESTER. *The cathedral, much restored throughout, st*
window between turrets distinguishes the west front design, and
dicular features. "The Faithful City," true to the Royal cc

Sydney R Jones
Worcester.

...utifully on the bank of the River Severn. A vast Geometrical
...rious tower of circa 1365–74 is the earliest of these great Perpen-
... to Cromwell in his "crowning mercy" on September 3rd, 1651.

STRATFORD-ON-AVON. *Harvard House of Shakespeare's time adjoins the Garrick Inn. The elaborate timberwork was built in 1596 for Rogers, the Stratford alderman. His daughter Katherine married Robert Harvard, and Harvard University in America is a perpetual memorial to their son John.*

SHOTTERY. *Anne Hathaway's Cottage, the most visited cottage in England and once the home of the bride who married Shakespeare by licence when he was eighteen. This characteristic specimen of Warwickshire rural building, its contents and garden are perfectly maintained by the Shakespeare Trustees.*

KENILWORTH CASTLE. The keep (centre), the beautiful fourteenth-century hall (left), Leicester's Elizabethan buildings (right), and site of the great lake in foreground. Cromwellians ruined the castle. No ruins in England are richer in associations with the great names of English history. These extensive remains stir memories of kings, queens, de Clinton, de Monfort, John of Gaunt, Robert Dudley, and the Wizard of the North, Sir Walter Scott.

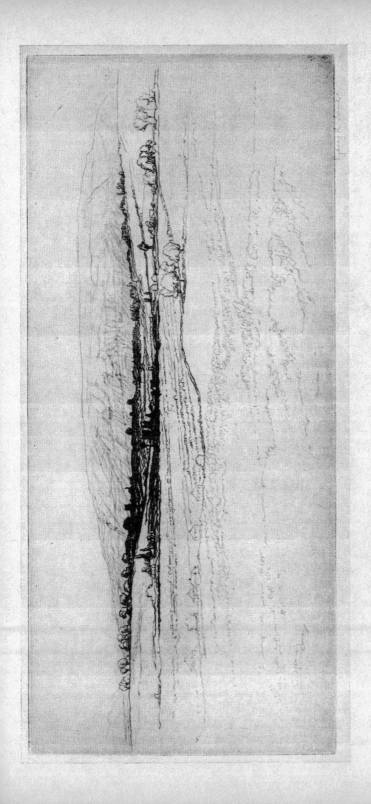

THE VALE OF EVESHAM, *a land of rich cultivation, old fame and beauty. A view over Offenham, Evesham, and extended to Bredon Hill.*

EVESHAM. *The most conspicuous reminder of one of the mightiest medieval abbeys, founded on Avon bank about 702 and once the shrine of Simon de Montfort. The Bell Tower belongs to the brilliant years of tower design in the Perpendicular period and was still incomplete at the Dissolution in 1539.*

COMPTON WYNYATES. *The moated home of the Comptons and the Spencers, one of the finest Tudor examples in England, has remained practically unaltered since the reign of Henry VIII. The name is derived from the vineyard that once existed there.*

ABBOT'S SALFORD, *an Elizabethan Roman Catholic home that came to the Eyston family, descendants of Sir Thomas More. It is full of surprises in panelled rooms, a long gallery, odd staircases, a hiding-hole, and additions of different periods.*

CLEEVE PRIOR. *One of the many picturesque villages in the River Avon borders below Stratford. Cleeve has a good church, farms and cottages of timbering and stone, the old King's Arms, and a manor-house framed in clipped yews.*

Long Marston

Hillborough *Pigeon-house*

Pebworth Church *with dormer windows*

Bidford Bridge

S.R.J.

IN THE SHAKESPEARE VILLAGES

Piping Pebworth, Dancing Marston,   *Dodging Exhall, Papist Wixford,*
Haunted Hillborough, Hungry Grafton,   *Beggarly Broom, and Drunken Bidford.*

WICKHAMFORD, *one in the series of pretty villages near Bredon Hill.*
Penelope Washington lived in this manor-house and her memorial in the
neighbouring church shows the stars and stripes of the Washington Coat of arms.

OFFENHAM, *traditionally associated with King Offa,*
and now in the centre of market-gardening and orchards.

SHAKESPEARE'S COUNTY

Warwickshire has been so prettily made by God and man and so often written of, it is difficult for me to decide on a point for opening this page or to think of anything that has not been stated before on the county which is sometimes presented as the private property of William Shakespeare with an entail on his name for ever. Yet my beginning must be made somewhere; so I will imagine myself where I have often sat, under the Shakespeare Oak, gnarled and bent over the River Avon in Stoneleigh Deer Park. Nobody can say with certainty that Shakespeare ever saw it. Only foolish people own this truth. For wiser folk the truth about the oak is just as you like it. It even may be the very tree used by Orlando when billposter of rhyme to Rosalind,

> Hang there, my verse, in witness of my love.

Shakespearean or not, the tree serves very well for a starting-point into one of the most wooded of English shires. It stands at the heart of England. A few miles away are the Lillington Oak and the archery turf of the Woodmen of Arden at Meriden, each claiming to be the centre of our island, whose irregular shape could not possibly have a fixed middle. Approximately central, and appropriately so, the Forest of Arden extended. Not very definite in boundaries, it seems to have spread over most of Warwickshire north of the River Avon, but not quite so far distant as Michael Drayton poetically fancied,

> Her one hand touching Trent, the other, Severn's side.

In other ways the Forest had no limits. It set no bounds of space or time for romance, love-making, deeds aboveboard and below, and the frolics and mysteries of life adapted to shades under the greenwood trees. We know that a banished duke, "his co-mates and brothers in exile," Touchstone the clown and Phebe the shepherdess did very well here and found the uses of adversity sweet. When required the Forest could produce ragged staffs for bears to maul; a particular one was embellished for the Black Dog of Arden when he proved to be one too many for Piers Gaveston at Blacklow Hill in 1312. Another aspect of the Forest's usefulness, dated just over a century ago, is given by a letter now before me.   The writer was my ancestral relative, then on a visit from Shropshire to Malvern Hall, Solihull, to attend the Musical Festival at Birmingham. Travelling through the Forest near Solihull, a village even at that time almost lost in the woodlands, highwaymen attacked the coach. The lady arrived intact at Malvern Hall, but alas, she sadly wrote,

> I have lost all my smart clothes, five best gowns & my two fine Bonnets & the handsome silk lace veil. I cannot go to any of the concerts not having an evening gown left! All my nice new Canezous are stolen and all my blonde trimmings!

To-day there is still no doubt of being in Arden when in Warwickshire. The old tract, which in fact was well wooded but not an impenetrable area of dense forest growth, is suggested on moving from place to place, from Morton Bagot, Beausale, Forshaw Heath, Temple Balsall, Berkswell or Wishaw, for example. Scenes are close, intimate, friendly, near at hand, rarely expanded in great widths and distances; they would have suited Birket Foster, or David Cox when in his home county. Trees in abundance, and especially oaks, border the lanes and group in the fields. Landscapes show leafiness everywhere, sturdy grace of boughs and trunks, all the harmonies of greens and browns, patches of grassy heath. Villages, hamlets, cottages, farmsteads, and moated houses with walls timbered in oak look just right in their woody settings. Oaks in the glades of Stoneleigh, grand aged monarchs at Packington, a deer park at Combe Abbey, Lady Luxborough's retreat and immense double oak at Barrels, ancient acres of the Archer family at Umberslade, wooded slopes of the Dugdales at Merevale, the old grounds of "Syr Thomas Malory, Knight" at Newbold Revel, and more of the parks for which the county is remarkable preserve the true Warwickshire glory of fine trees. Many of the place-names have a woodland ring in this district stretching east and north from Aston Cantlow, Henley-in-Arden, Tanworth-in-Arden, Packwood, Hampton-in-Arden, and Acock's Green, Birmingham, marked on old maps for a boundary of the Forest.

Apart from the Arden Forest, typified at my starting-point under the Shakespeare Oak standing over bracken on the Stoneleigh bank, this Warwickshire ground is well stored with more vernacular features of locality. One of these is the celebrated river, the Avon. Others are the villages and towns of distinct native flavour, and picturesquely made. They show harmoniously in wooded field and hedgerow surroundings, the characteristic scenery of the Midland Plain; they continue at about 200 feet lower level across the Leamington and Red Horse vales to their boundaries at Edge Hill, Burton Hills, and the hills of Shuckburgh. Standing on these hills, or at such points as Liveridge Hill above Henley-in-Arden, the eye travels far over the rich and patterned lands of Shakespeare's country. Throughout this district of vale, plain, and forest are the sites, mansions, houses, and buildings of sundry patterns, altogether a notable lot, which accommodated the human resources of the neighbourhood and also served the splendid people, likewise a notable lot, who helped to make these Midland shires a cockpit for the action, enlightenment, and success that illuminated medieval, Tudor, and Civil War times and the later years of intellectual polish, invention, and commercial prosperity. But observers topographically minded sometimes have said, and perhaps a few of my readers may think, that the splendour of persons never can equal the splendour of oaks, elms, hedgerow flowers, rivers, or sermons in stone, timbering, and brickwork. Whether this idea be true or not we will at this page-point of progress look around for objects other than people, spy along rivers, rushy banks and meadows, meet villages and towns of old standing, and here and there notice houses with low beams, classic heights, hiding-holes, and various inconveniences once enjoyed by the defunct splendid persons.

The Warwickshire Avon, weighty with fame, in spate from beautiful expressions of Garrick and other poetical admirers, and the recipient of very bad words from dwellers in the houses it regularly floods in rainy seasons, has managed to keep fair and lovely along most of its winding course. Though it has been useful in attracting dollars from American tourists, the river is not considered an ideal economic proposition by the modern type of iconoclast because it is not especially fitted to make man work harder and harder or influence international rates of exchange. Hence factories, gasworks, and such monuments of progress are not well presented. It is true that the lords of Nationalized Electricity lately conceived a notion for erecting monstrosities to blear miles of placid beauty round Hill Wootton, Leek Wootton (103), and Guy's Cliff (rightly called by Leland "a place meet for the Muses"); an historic region thus might have gained things most horrible and sufficiently terrifying to send jerks through the ghosts of Piers Gaveston and Guy the Hermit while prowling about the riverside at midnight. Through the valiant acts of the Mayors of Leamington and Warwick these arrangements have not yet come to pass. The river at present generally keeps out of date, flows and curves placidly, delights with quiet scenes, charms from the source to the end. Graceful in motions and decked with rushes and arrowheads in the stream, it passes wide stretches of pasture, ploughland, and orchard, snug villages, old church towers. Willows, hundreds of them, stand in lines and avenues, joined one to another to show green arches like Gothic arcades. The stream meets the bridges of ancient towns and reflects on its surface the tapering spire of the national poet's shrine (107).

Coming into Warwickshire the Avon makes one Roman point at the bridge on Watling Street near to Rugby, Charles Dickens's "Mugby," in the "dullness of the scenery" disliked by Arnold; the river passes a second Roman point on its last stage out of the county from Bidford's fifteenth-century bridge (117) and the ford, which mark the line of the straight road leading through Alcester and Beoley to the stretch of original track preserved in Sutton Park close to Staffordshire. The stream's infant prances, begun in Leicestershire, continue round Dunsmore Heath, a bleakish region and bleak indeed on the 5th of November, 1605, for Sir Everard Digby and the one hundred conspirators who assembled there, only to learn that the gunpowder arrangements entrusted to Guy Fawkes had not blown up the King and the Parliament. Past these spaces of gloomy remembrance the Avon shows off its own true qualities. At Bubbenhall it has grown in width. The real vale begins to open out. The stream ambles down to Ashow (102), bound for Warwick and Stratford, Wasperton, Luddington, Binton bridges, Cleeve Mill, and more shy haunts fit to love and retire in for ever. Scenes have that delicate beauty that is so very English, exactly right for this heart of England. The waters move placidly between low banks, chatter over little weirs and mill-races. Bushes and branches screen the holes of fishes, and eels and tench hide in the mud. Willows and alders wave silvery leafage in the breeze. Hedgerows, oaks, and bosky shapes of elm and ash mark out broad meadows painted with the colours and wild flowers of the seasons. Quiet places abound in which to forget and remember. Lazing in one of them under a willow near Charlecote (Shakespearean name!) I saw a sleeping fox in the next tree wake up, stretch himself, jump down, give me a sidelong glance, then trot leisurely across the grass, turning his head now and again with as much as to say, "Catch me if you can!" Such a meeting with Reynard may not happen twice in a lifetime.

Otters live at Bubbenhall. I've seen them under the river bank just below the place where Alfred Parsons sat to picture the church tower and cottages amongst trees beyond the greensward. This mention, not of otters but of a Royal Academician and a village, reminds me of scores and scores of pictures offered by these villages on or near the Avon, and of hundreds of artists who have had a go at them. Early sketching-grounds of mine, these villages and their border-lands embrace Stoneleigh and Ashow, the winding stream from Barford to Wasperton, Weston and Welford below Stratford, Salford Priors and Abbot's Salford, and

> Piping Pebworth, Dancing Marston,
> Haunted Hillborough, Hungry Grafton,
> Dodging Exhall, Papist Wixford,
> Beggarly Broom, and Drunken Bidford,

the Shakespeare villages popularly but doubtfully associated with the poet's pub-crawling and his meditations on the morning after the night before under a crab-tree by the roadside between Bidford and Stratford (117). Full of pictorial motives, and also furnished with ancestral antiques and antiquated human descendants of ancestors before antique dealers and weekenders dissipated both, this attractive area has been well spied on by artistic professionals and amateurs. It rose to much favour in the days when Edwin Abbey and Alfred Parsons penetrated over from Broadway, and Yeend King might be noticed under an umbrella; artists then strewed the earth round the mill, the medieval lych-gate and the timbered cottages at Welford, while now and again white ponies pranced gaily along with Marie Corelli, out for a talk to the old sea-captain by the maypole or bound for Dorsington in search of copy for *God's Good Man*. Natives, properly featured and dressed without need of make-up, were ready at hand for painters of the subject pictures liked and bought by the public before the advent of world wars and atomic bombs; pictures of the popular kind titled in the style of "Gleaners returning," "At

GORCOT HALL. *Built of brick and timber, and full of oak inside, this old home of the Chambers family stands on Gorcot Hill near Redditch. One window of 365 panes shows the arms of Queen Elizabeth. A spider dial painted on another window tells the time when the sun shines into the room.*

HUDDINGTON COURT *prior to restoration. The moated and timbered house with an elaborate Tudor chimney, once the home of Catesby's cousin, Robert Wyntour, a conspirator in the Gunpowder Plot. After the capture of Guy Fawkes, thirty fugitive plotters sheltered here on November 6, 1605, attended Mass, and prepared for death.*

milking time," "By candlelight," "When all the world was gay." In these figured the glove-makers, whose work done at cottage doorways went to Worcester; William, heavily whiskered, and voluble with "O blame, O day!" "Odds rat me!" and explosions in speech apparently derived from Elizabethans; the rosy-cheeked dame who expanded marvellously after sundown on the laying of ghosts with parsons and bottles; and a range of local types, young or ancient and suitable for all sorts of artistic occasions and pigments. Now it is nice to remember them, the last of a generation and a race extinguished by progress; soothing it is to recall their features, whiskers, stories of their day-to-day life, "the short and simple annals of the poor," which in narration sometimes were very long indeed and full of truths stranger than fiction.

Since these good folk went to quiet acres where rude forefathers sleep many of their haunts and habitations have continued whole. Though perilously near progressive districts full of people that specialize on spoliation of landscapes and weekends, symptoms of auld lang syne still persist in villages of the Avon vale and throughout the Warwickshire countryside. Local conditions and old-fashioned influences are clearly defined. They are well suggested north and south in the county and particularly mark such regions as Curdworth, Berkswell and Tanworth, Newbold-on-Avon, Lighthorne and Preston-on-Stour. In all directions stand the typical timber-framed cottages, houses, and farms with panels of plaster or brickwork, the thatched roofs, the coloured tiling. Big chimneys tapered upward to the stacks denote open fireplaces inside, the vast apertures that provided natives with warmth, smoked bacon, downdraught, smoky atmosphere, and gave Shakespeare a reason to write,

> Though little fire grows great with little wind,
> Yet extreme gusts will blow out fire and all.

Sightseers who quiz Anne Hathaway's Cottage (111) and Mary Arden's Wilmcote cottage, at least cannot fail to notice two good specimens from the local hundreds of these framed and thatched providers of home, sweet home. This mode of construction in oak and panel, elaborated to gables, bargeboards, brackets, porches, and windows divided by wood mullions, served for the larger village homes and small manor-houses. Often moated for security in Arden, now frequently used as farmhouses or freshened in age by new and enthusiastic owners, they are to be seen at Bott's Green, Grimshaw Hall (95), Berry Hall, Gorcot Hall (123), Clifford Chambers, in parish after parish and always worth finding for the pictures they yield, the stories and names they recall. Southward, where the lias of the hills meets the vale, stone chiefly rules for building. It colours adorable villages, named to include Shuckburgh, Burton Dassett, the Tysoes, and Tredington. Yet the prevalent Warwickshire timbering is not absent; the fifteenth-century and haunted manor-house of the Ingrams at Little Wolford is but one instance of the effective combination made with stone and oak. When timber for fuel absorbed by the near centres of manufacture made oak scarcer and bricks and tiles became generally used, the later Midland style for house and home spread through the towns and the villages. It developed the characteristic red-brick walling, string courses, tiled roofs with dormers, little bay-windows for cottages. Bigger bays and taller windows lighted the larger houses. Moulded hoods protected Georgian and Regency doorways. A few entrances had shell hoods, like the one you can see by the roadside at Wootton Wawen, prettily adorned with modelled fruit and flowers for pretty brocades and wigs to pass under when dishes of tea went round and gossip expanded Mr. Knight's South Sea Bubble money spent at Barrels or glorified young Mr. Jago's Beaudesert poems.

It comes easily in Warwickshire to make a transition from small to large, to pass to bigger things from the circumscribed signs of even and long-settled life in hamlet and village. The country invites this. Central, old in use, rarely has it been out of touch with national expansion and temper. Much fought over, the land long knew the alarms of war and political intrigue. In years of peace and plenty alarms no less exciting sprang from industry, invention, discovery, and intellectual ardour urged forward by a shrewd people disposed for action, enlightenment, and material advantages. The local spirit of time and circumstance reacted far beyond the local fat pastures and borders. Joseph Priestley and James Watt perched statuesque at Birmingham, a birthplace of trade unionism at Joseph Arch's Barford cottage, the Jennens family home of great iron-masters at Nether Whitacre, Sanderson Miller's centre of polite intellectualism and Gothic Revival sproutings at Radway Grange—such outward forms with big meanings are expected constituents of the scenes, belong to them no less naturally than a birthplace for Shakespeare fits Stratford, Warwick Castle stands for Richard Neville the King-maker, Kenilworth recalls Simon de Montfort, pillar of English freedom.

The bold stretch of the Fosse Way from south to north gives to the county a sure mark of immemorial importance. Speculators handy with cars, or, better still, good on their feet, can spend happy and full hours tracing this straight life-line. It runs off the Cotswold stone at Stretton-on-Fosse, enters the Vale of the Red Horse, continues past Compton Verney house and park, Chesterton Roman camp, the site of a forgotten battle at Offchurch, the fortified mound of Brinklow, and at High Cross meets a hoary comrade, Watling Street.

Far and wide passages of national history can be read without books. Pages of it open at Warwick Castle (104). A modest 2s. 6d. per head delivered at a turnstile of romance will assault and carry the barbican and fourteenth-century gatehouse to the stronghold of the Beauchamps, the Nevilles and the Grevilles. Early walls and towers joined to later additions and rebuilding stand firm and erect high over the River Avon and the original medieval bridge, now broken down. As plainly as can be, the battlements, machicolations, and masonry carry the flow of centuries through the years of the Black Dog of Arden (slew Piers Gaveston, 1312), the King-maker (slain at the battle of Barnet, 1471), Queen Elizabeth entertained with fireworks, peaceful penetrations by later royal guests; re-created are seasons of "grim-visaged war" and many a "piping time of peace" to elucidate the words of a Shakespearean Richard III, himself Richard Neville's son-in-law and a visitor to this castle. At Kenilworth walls of the castle are ruined and baileys overgrown. Cromwellians drained the great lake and destroyed the park (112). Unlike Warwick, the placing of Kenilworth Castle in a hole is not spectacular, nor have the relics the advantages of charges at 2s. 6d. per head to stem assaults in close formation by crowds that may or may not know of a book by Scott called *Kenilworth* and what Simon de Montfort did for all of us. When I lived within two miles of these ruins, and therefore was liable to brood over them at all hours of days and seasons, it was remarkable to discover the peculiar feelings aroused inside the human apparatus by these pink and grey stones and grassy mounds, particularly when the sun was low or the moon was high. These effects may have proceeded partly from the state of vision, liver, and mind, but no doubt very much more from the unseen yet potent spirit of the still air, the stuff of remembrance born of past years and deeds that helped to fill chapters of England's story. Few acres in the land are richer in meaning, great names, and memories than these at Kenilworth. Outer towers, the tilt yard, inner and outer courts, wreckage of de Clinton's Norman keep, John of Gaunt's beautiful hall (*c.* 1390), and Leicester's Elizabethan buildings abide like a fabric of dreams. Robert Dudley's gatehouse continues intact and fitted with finely sculptured alabaster and oak chimney-pieces, prime from the grand days of Queen Elizabeth's visits in 1566, 1568, 1572, and in 1575, when 320 hogsheads of beer celebrated that great occasion, and very likely young Shakespeare, aged eleven, yelled with delight while the wonderful fireworks exploded into "birds flying and cats and dogs fighting, serpents of fire, a dragon as big as an ox." No fireworks illuminated the historic occasions of Maxstoke, a dozen miles distant, when dynasties fell and rose and the first Tudor succeeded the last Plantagenet. One night in 1485 Richard III slept in the castle on his way to Bosworth Field. Immediately afterwards Henry VII did likewise —on his way from Bosworth Field. Begun by William de Clinton in the middle of the fourteenth century, wonderfully preserved, and still a home, Maxstoke Castle is a perfect survivor of a moated Edwardian quadrangle with embattled walls, angle towers, a gatehouse and living quarters made more for days of peace than of fighting, a fortified house but weak for war's hurly-burly. It is the most lovely and quiet retreat imaginable. You can encircle the walls on the path by the wide moat, look out for dragonfly blue, peer down at the fishes, the only signs of armies that I or Henry VIII's commissioners discovered (95).

Differences of opinion between Royalist and Roundhead impressed later stamps of history on these lands. Few parts of Warwickshire escaped the hammerings and turmoil of the Civil War. Not everywhere is one conscious of the ghosts of kings; yet when I used to work in the panelled room at Stoneleigh Abbey near to the Norman stonework of the Cistercians, it was sometimes enervating to fancy time set back to the fateful year of 1642 and to wonder if Charles I's silk nightshirt rustled inside the four-poster just behind me. To this mansion grown from an abbey (96) Sir Thomas Leigh welcomed the King when on his way to set up his standard at Nottingham after the citizens of Coventry had shut their gates against the King. At Radway Tower, built by Sanderson Miller on Edge Hill in 1750 (a wonderful viewpoint for Warwickshire's patterned miles), you can stand where King Charles stood on the day of the first Civil War battle. The near beacon on Burton Hills signalled news of the conflict; soldiers sleep in Warmington churchyard. About the Fosse Way beyond the county boundary near Stow-on-the-Wold the last local fight of the conflict ended in 1646, when Astley, the silver-haired veteran and captive of Morgan the Cromwellian, sat on a drum and said, "Gentlemen, yee may now sit down and play, for you have done all your worke, if you fall not out among yourselves." Open war on Warwickshire soil thus temporarily closed until recent displays from the air spread ruin in Coventry and Birmingham, and the windy batteries of politics and economics opened up on the mansions and the landscapes.

Messages of the Warwickshire churches seem to be mostly of peace, though fighting knights lie inside them, grooves on outer stonework show where archers of Arden sharpened their arrows, and Civil War bullets and bullet-marks are in Tredington church door. Gothic forms, solid and workmanlike, group well among the timbered and brick homesteads of the villages and country towns. Far and wide stand the embattled towers, locally very characteristic, fine at Kineton and splendid at Brailes. Here and there a spire is seen far off or near, and well shown at Southam and Tanworth. Out of the ordinary are some of these churches. One at Wootton Wawen developed remarkably from Saxon and Norman times. Knights Templars achieved dignified expanse and the series of wheel windows in the thirteenth century at Temple Balsall. Lapworth gained the beauty of a detached tower and spire, the high Perpendicular clerestory, the chantry chapel over a western porch. Snitterfield (the church of Shakespeare's uncle Henry) acquired carved wood figures, panels, and heraldic shields when Renaissance design mingled with the Gothic. Masterpieces arose in the great Perpendicular style. One was the Beauchamp Chapel, Warwick (101); another, the tower and spire of St. Michael (1394–1433), subtle and superb, and still erect at Coventry. Later on the alert people in this district of progress and expanding industry naturally followed the fashions of

BROUGHTON HACKETT, *one of the secluded villages between Alcester and Worcester. Hundreds of nesting-places are inside the pigeon-house illustrated. The district preserves several of these survivals of manorial privilege.*

KYRE WYARD *near Tenbury. The pigeon-house and great barn of the older buildings. The main front of the house dates from the eighteenth century. Capability Brown laid out the grounds, and the park is notable for grand trees, including fourteenth-century oaks.*

HEREFORD. *The fifteenth-century bridge over the River Wye leads in*
the fourteenth-century cathedral tower is remarkable for ball-flower decoratio

e pleasant capital city of the orchard and hop country. Broad and sturdy,
rises over the largest collection of chained books in the world.

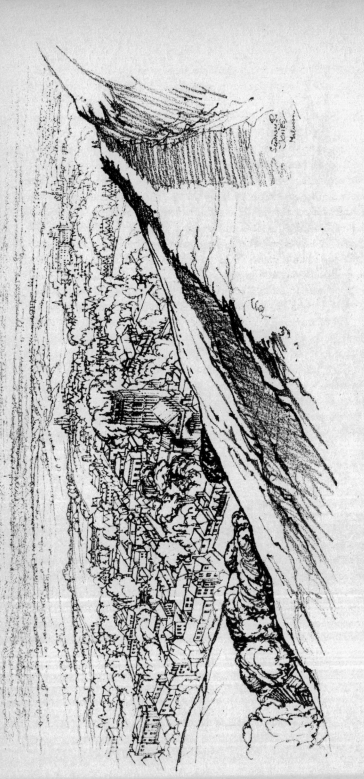

GREAT MALVERN, *from the Worcestershire Beacon. The view includes the priory and Perpendicular tower of the mid-fifteenth century, the Worcestershire plain, and the Severn Vale.*

Stuart and Georgian times. Good crops of eighteenth-century churches matured. They ripened in fair or strange growths, harvested a kind of Christianized paganism. The English soil bore Corinthian pilasters at Honily in 1723, a classical temple of 1731 at Castle Bromwich; Bonomi, the Italian, devised Doric columns at Great Packington in 1790 for the Earl of Aylesford; and a masterpiece was completed after 1725 when Thomas Archer's tower rose over the west end of St. Philip's, Birmingham (195). From early to late centuries simple folk, gentry, and splendid persons made last visits to these churches in the way common to humanity. Little stones on churchyard grass, memorials on sacred walls and floors, tombs in suitable and superior positions alike record inevitable fate. Carved effigies, lifelike or from stock patterns, heraldic ordinaries and charges, brasses, and inscriptions present opportunities without formal introductions for making silent acquaintance with once live beings who kept their little worlds moving and bright while they answered to such names and places as Boughton (Newbold-on-Avon), Fulke Greville (Alcester), Lucy (Charlecote), Compton (Compton Wynyates), Verney (Compton Verney), Throckmorton (Coughton), Ferrars (Baddesley Clinton), Shuckburgh (Shuck-burgh), Holte (Aston), Adderley (Lea Marston), the incomparable Dugdale (Shustoke), and of course Shakespeare himself at Stratford. Worth a day's march or a ride is a call on the Peyto family in the perfect seclusion of Chesterton, a remarkable crowd with two members made by Nicholas Stone. A visit to Richard Beauchamp's brass portrait in St. Mary's, Warwick, superbly rendered by John Massingham in 1450, and a study of every figure and detail on this marvellous tomb, means a revelation of how things were done in England's golden age of craftsmanship.

A good showing is made by houses of families commended in the churches, homes nice in size, but never so gigantic that inmates felt little in stature and puny of mind, as for instance anyone might do under the four acres of roof at Blenheim. Compton Wynyates (115), Stoneleigh Abbey (96), and other mansions in the vicinity certainly are quite big enough. But nobles owning such large titles as Compton, Leigh, Hertford, Willoughby de Broke and Craven, their relatives and friends no doubt were not overpowered by mere extent and shape in abbey remains, courtyards, long galleries and rows of gables; quite easily would they breathe and live while living up to Cipriani's ornate Labours of Hercules in the white saloon of Stoneleigh, Palladian impressiveness and Homeric decorations of Ragley, mixed Vanbrugh and Adam effects at Compton Verney, brilliance of gilt, rococo, and Captain Wynne's front at Combe Abbey, Grinling Gibbon's carvings at Arbury.

If Compton Wynyates is the prime showpiece of this district, well worth finding and rightly found by the many who appreciate a jewel of Tudor loveliness beautifully set, ordinary mortals perhaps may derive most satisfaction in seeking the less pretentious establishments, the expressions of home that so admirably fit the leafy scenes and symbolize past day-to-day life and sentiments of substantial families comfortably placed or settled in squirely fashion on ancestral lands. Masters and mistresses then did not do all their own housework and washing-up. Servants were plentiful in that lost age of willingness when everybody either had to be willing to work or was quite willing to be worked for. Even passing glances at the large areas that evidently were dusted and polished, or the very size of the kitchens can act as sedatives to minds fashioned by the present era of domestic terror governed by the non-appearance of "chars and dailies." The manorial and secluded homesteads have a fragrance of old years about them, suggest calm and manageable days and quiet, sleepful nights. Few parishes have not one of these homes representing the local architectural currency and the changes of schemes in living. Biggish or medium in size, some are timbered, some are moated; many have the brickwork and stone of the sixteenth, seventeenth, and eighteenth centuries. Grimshaw Hall (95), Gorcot Hall (123), and a few more specimens have been indicated on earlier pages. Another one is the Catholic family home of the Eystons at Abbots Salford, captivating both outside and within, and offering the chance of getting lost in a hiding-hole (115). Among the large number that have kept status, lost it, or continue in useful ways for farmers, you may light on the fashions of domestic years in all directions and range through generations and periods. The farmer's home at Wormleighton, for instance, has Tudor brickwork and stone erected by the Spencers, and through the arched gateway, dated 1613, Prince Rupert rode when he arrived to spend the night before the Edge Hill battle. Arlescote, on the roadside below Edge Hill, evidently fits the late seventeenth century with nicely balanced hipped roofs, dormers, projecting wings and walls of stone, and a similar effect in brickwork and tiles, though somewhat larger, appears beyond iron gates at Clifford Chambers. With quoins at the angles, eaves cornices, chimneys prim and uniform, Honington by Shipston-on-Stour is fully developed; busts of Roman emperors on outer walls and lavish decorations inside evidence the Italian tint of mind once so fashionable with the English. Foxcote, in the same neighbourhood, points the eighteenth century onward with the pilasters, pediments, and stone urns of the Cannings, a family descended from the famous merchants we traced at St. Mary Redcliffe, Bristol. Pinley Priory in Rowington parish tumbles time back to the close timbering period, while Coughton Court of the Throckmortons offers an impressive choice of style in Tudor, Jacobean, and the "Gothick" locally popularized by Sanderson Miller. The Lucy's Charlecote (noted for the Shakespearean deer-stealing fable charmingly resurrected by Washington Irving) clearly indicates the first year of Queen Elizabeth's reign and offers one hallmark of that period in the gatehouse elaborated with ornamental parapets and octagonal corner towers. It is joyous to thread the Arden lanes and suddenly discover the groupings of gables, Restoration brickwork, gates and piers, and the topiary garden of seventeenth-century yew at Packwood House, reminders of the Featherstone squires who were followed by the Ash family. Old centuries belong to the battlements and brick walls of Pooley Hall, Polesworth, a place of the Cockaynes in the reign of Henry IV and rebuilt by them in 1509; here Michael Drayton served as page to Sir Thomas Cockayne, and theorists also like to fit in young William Shakespeare and thus account for the poet's evident personal knowledge of north-east Warwickshire.

Of the ancient houses Baddesley Clinton, rarest of the rare, diffuses a spice of late medievalism. It lies secluded. Walls rise steeply from a broad moat. A Queen Anne bridge, in place of the old drawbridge, leads to the massive fifteenth-century oak door of the gate tower. Beyond is the courtyard built round three sides of a square in a mixture of sandstone, timber, and brick. The hall with a carved and dated fireplace and room interiors have all the elements for anything you like to think of or fancy from past Catholic days when bearers of the name of Ferrers had good uses for the secret staircase and the priests' hiding-holes. One still evening while I was there and a low sun mellowed colouring, a lady dressed in black velvet looked down into the courtyard, smiled from an upper casement, and made one of those pictures that stick in memory. To me the scene appeared just such a one that Edwin Abbey might have penned for an illustration to Shakespeare, with perhaps a title inscribed "O mistress mine" or something like that. An opposite point in the swing of architectural time is marked by Malvern Hall, Solihull, classic with wings right and left, the eighteenth-century home of the Greswoldes, proud in one of those broad and wooded parks typical of Warwickshire when I knew it a long time ago. Afterwards a secondary school took possession, a housing estate developed. Fortunately, before the years of myself, school, or housing, John Constable finely painted a characteristic and rich canvas of the hall, park, lake, and superior sky, thereby preserving the aristocratic bearing that a system of living once could impart to English landscape. The National Gallery is the place to see how Malvern Hall looked before it actually and figuratively lost an upper storey and came down in the world.

Church bells merry at midnight to welcome Christmas morning in Southam; Shipston-on-Stour good for Georgian stone houses; brickwork and black-and-white round about a seventeenth-century town hall in Alcester; Henley-in-Arden's long and picturesque highway below de Montfort's castle mound of Beaudesert; a medieval bridge over the river, the Georgian houses, a lovely church spire, fifteenth-century windows and Digby tombs on the hill at Coleshill; and much more I remember and might write, if my short space did not forbid, would be in praise of Warwickshire's little towns, examples of those special products of England that are nice to find, pleasant to look at, comforting to stay in, perhaps for ever and ever.

The larger towns of Rugby, Leamington, Warwick, and Stratford line across the county on or near the River Avon. Leamington continues in popularity, thrives, keeps a spa look even in these degenerate days. The gardens and groves are fresh and bright. The Old Well House and the Royal Pump Rooms stand firm and imply that the beneficent waters have not yet evaporated under the stress of national economy. When in the town I never fail to sip the unpalatable liquid, though not for the good it has showered on so many human insides or might do on my own, nor because it enabled John Ruskin to write, "I have gone back to brown potatoes and cherry pie!" Rather does the magic water, just one taste of it, set my mind thinking of the sprouting spring discovered by the shoemaker, Benjamin Satchwell, and those other springs that sprouted in unison to shower not only water but honour, fame, and success. Royal honour flowed in with the Prince Regent in 1819, followed by more from princes and princesses, and fame and popularity streamed along, while the nobility, notables, and all sorts and conditions of gay, sober, and liverish water-drinkers and abstainers came and stayed in the procession of nineteenth-century years, filled the Assembly Rooms built in Bath Street in 1821, promenaded up and down the Parade, found the Metropolis repeated at their own doorsteps in such quarters as Oxford Street, Regent Street, Euston Place, and even a miniature Covent Garden Market. At the appointed times the throngs departed, left their ghosts behind to haunt the Regency and Victorian villas that stand elegant, shapely, and creamy-faced with stucco make-up in Clarendon Terrace, Waterloo Place, Newbold Terrace, Willes Road, and other well-planned groupings embowered in greenery. In their own particular years Charles Lamb, truly great essayist, made a first acquaintance with Elliston, truly great comedian, "over a counter in the Leamington Spa Library"; Nathaniel Hawthorne settled at No. 10, Lansdowne Circus, in "one of the cosiest nooks in England or in the world"; Charles Dickens fitted Mr. Dombey and Major Bagstock inside the "Royal Hotel," found for Edith Granger and Carker "a deep shade of leafy trees" (locally fancied to be in Holly Walk). Yes, it is quite amazing what a mere glass of water can do when taken in this trim and attractive town. While benefiting the digestive apparatus, it also may act as a tonic for travelling a long way from to-day through the avenues and terraces of white and green, or to the Regency days of the little square window-panes and covered walks in Covent Garden Market behind Warwick Street; anybody who likes to do so can slip out of the present and enjoy re-creating yesterdays at the first hotel, the *Bath*, erected by William Abbotts after the discovery of the waters in Bath Street, at the very good frontage of the *Clarendon*, at the *Regent*, so named by command of George IV—and where, in good old days

ROSS-ON-WYE. *Market day at the pillared market hall, a building dating from the reign of Charles II.*

CRADLEY *near Bosbury, two picturesque villages below the Malvern Hills in Herefordshire.*

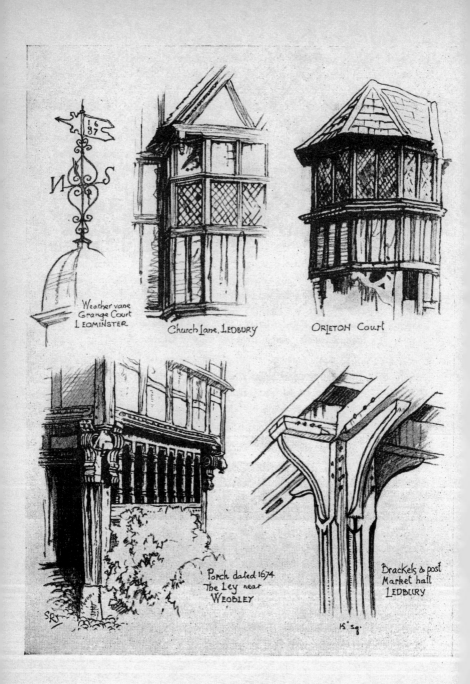

Weather vane
Grange Court
LEOMINSTER

Church Lane, LEDBURY

ORLETON Court

Porch dated 1674
The Ley near
WEOBLEY

Brackets & post
Market hall
LEDBURY

HEREFORDSHIRE DETAILS

before the advent of world wars, I used to consume grilled salmon steaks without need of the chalybeate spring for a sedative. They (the steaks) have since retreated to my ventricle of memory. If one of my readers now happens to find more of them at the *Regent*, and can generously spare and forward a slice of the browned pink delicacy for my consumption in this epoch of collapsed currency and short rations, I shall feel deeply grateful and acknowledge an act of remembrance for happy days spent, long ago, with the pretty white features and green leafage of Leamington Spa.

At Warwick, adjoining Leamington, we hitch on to the touring circuit of the Shakespeare Country proper, an event signalized by the ceaseless clatter of every known kind of thing on wheels up and down High Street. This proof of much coming and going—it has robbed me of sleep on more nights than one—relieves me considerably at this page on the county town, suggests getting away with it lightly because dozens of written guides and critical surveys already exist for the benefit of sightseers and seekers after knowledge who are delivered on wheels or otherwise. Humbly, therefore, I merely present my pictures (15, 101, 104, 105). Robbed of ammunition by previous explorers, I am left with nothing new to disclose on the castle, St. Mary's real Gothic and its peculiar Gothic finished in 1704, the Earl of Leicester's Leycester Hospital, two town gates existing and two missing, Sanderson Miller's fine Shire Hall completed in 1753, the dignified eighteenth-century birthplace of Walter Savage Landor in which he now could have said, "Put me amongst the girls," the antiquated appearance of Mill Street, the view from the Georgian bridge on the Banbury Road. These and more sights and associations make Warwick adorable when touring crowds have gone; then Leicester's pensioners in blue gowns saunter on shady sides of pretty streets, and the van Dycks and the Canalettos radiate glory undisturbed inside the castle. The bits of less common information, summarized below, are all that I can safely offer without endangering my life through knocks on my head from ragged staffs directed by captious bears and highly informed experts. 1. The great fire of 1694, which destroyed about 250 houses and caused St. Mary's to lose a medieval nave and tower, cleared spaces for the later frontages, doorways and fanlights that look so well in Church Street, High Street, Jury Street, and a perfect Northgate Street. Behind are dainty, well-proportioned rooms, and even an early Quaker meeting-house of 1695, so secluded, private and silent amongst clipt yews and hollyhocks that I will not disclose its whereabouts. 2. Can any town in England show a better interior than Sanderson Miller's masterpiece at the Shire Hall? It's a tremendous sight at night with dancers, music, and soft lighting. 3. Quaintness at the eighteenth-century law courts is so arresting, any law-abiding citizen might be pardoned for doing a murder or other crime for the chance of appearing inside the criminal or civil department. 4. Whatever may be said for or against Sir William Wilson's architecture of the spacious and high nave of St. Mary's, it makes a wonderful setting for ceremonial occasions of the Mayor and Corporation, soldiers, sailors, crowded congregations, the organ pealing, and parade hymns. 5. The *Warwick Arms* has been done up very nicely since the lords of war departed.

And so to Stratford-on-Avon, as Mr. Pepys might have said, though apparently the busy traveller was one of the few illustrious persons who left no mention of Shakespeare's town. Dr. Johnson, who did, because it lay on his posting route to Lichfield, I think told somebody that to marry once is brave, twice, heroic, or words to that effect. Yet of greater courage would be the man or woman bold enough to think of presenting any facts or fictions not already offered once, twice, or a thousand times on what has been called the play town of the world. Much more than that is this ancient place. Known by evidence from Saxon and Domesday years, rich in a long and prosperous medieval history, standing in the heart of a true countryside, and settled on the tree-lined banks of the Avon between Sir Hugh Clopton's bridge and Lucy's mill, if bombs or other destructive inventions by man remove all else but Stratford, still will remain an epitome of England. No doubt the powers of destiny acted on that assumption when locating a birthplace for Shakespeare.

It is often said that popularity has spoiled Stratford. I do not think so. I have known the town at all times and seasons, in the quieter past years, in the later phases of invasions by crowds, ice cream, chars-à-bancs, restorers, antique shops, and a commercial vitality that has driven me to Keith Prowse in London for the only hope of securing a theatre seat at Stratford. Yet to me the town ever seems impervious to spoliation. In the face of popularity and other adversities it has kept a heart and spirit pure, fresh and permanent as its poet's works. To seekers and lovers it speaks like Rosalind, "Can one desire too much of a good thing?" Would-be spoilers it can reproach and lightly drop a hint from *Henry IV*, "I know a trick worth two of that."

Forestalled by distinguished producers of facts and fictions that have made Stratford the matter for square miles of printed and drawing paper, my task at Shakespeare's town already has been done for me. Apologetically, therefore, I offer my handiwork of scenes known the world over, coupled with a spice of Shakespearean advice for my reader to follow,

> I'll view the manners of the town,
> Peruse the traders, gaze upon the buildings,
> And then return and sleep within mine inn.

Tales twice told again and again then will be remembered and located in their famous places—Holy Trinity Church, one of the most beautiful in Warwickshire (107); a group to fascinate at the fifteenth-century Guild Chapel, Guildhall and Shakespeare's school; nothing to see of New Place, the house built by

Sir Hugh Clopton, purchased by Shakespeare in 1597, knocked down by Parson Gastrell in 1759; Shakespeare's birthplace in Henley Street (106); the Hathaway Cottage outside the town at Shottery (111); Hall's Croft in Old Town, finest of the Tudor houses, probably lived in by Shakespeare's daughter Susanna; Harvard House built by Alderman Rogers in 1596 (110); pictures unending in streets of timberwork, brick, and stone; the gabled *Shakespeare*, a timbered *Falcon* (supposed to have been Shakespeare's pub), the *Red Horse* (with Washington Irving's "little parlour"), and more inns galore of all ages and patterns with provision inside them for all sorts of tastes. There is also a Memorial Theatre, a recent product of "this iron age." This intruder in the gracious scene of river, bridge, trees and meadows incorporates bits left over from the burning of an earlier erection, its predecessor. The bits are liable to remind old fogeys of the glamorous days and nights of the Bensons, George Weir, Oscar Asche, Frank Rodney, H. O. Nicholson and attendant hosts, when all and sundry, including myself, made annual and joyous family parties of players and audiences in the odd and spiky old theatre, one equally inglorious with its successor for a worthy tribute to the creative genius and immortal memory of the great Elizabethan Englishman.

Without presuming to offer one word on the ancestry and life of Shakespeare, why he married Anne Hathaway, deer-stealing, pike called luce, who wrote the plays, and other subjects reserved for minds of the very learned, I now say with Gloster, "Enough, enough," repeat Hamlet's last words, "The rest is silence," bid a temporary farewell to my lifelong friend, Stratford-on-Avon. In so doing I gratefully remember that many people are quite satisfied to have the plays whether written by one Shakespeare or not, that Stratford exists and is lovely, and that a railway porter named Shakespeare used to direct pilgrims from Warwick station platform to the shrine of a man for all time who was bred on Warwickshire Bacon.

A suspicion of smokiness must dim the end of these notes on Shakespeare's county. Geographers know of the existence of Nuneaton, Bedworth, Coventry, Birmingham, and their environs; geologists tell of a Warwickshire coalfield; and political economists have expended much wind, ink, and paper on a number of things since Adam Smith, a Scot, and the Industrial Revolution began to tackle the green lands of England. Places and views in north Warwickshire illustrate various aspects of the matters above-mentioned. Invasions of industrialism on nature's landscapes nevertheless are not quite my subjects for these pages, though the Nuneaton district might have offered an excuse for expanding my memories of South Farm, the birthplace of Mary Ann Evans, "Cheverel Manor" at Arbury, the "Hall Farm" at Corley, and Chilvers Coton for "Shepperton" in the George Eliot books. Coventry, the ancient city of religious, civic, and domestic treasures related to spires, friars, royal visits, guilds, pageants, mystery plays, charities, wool, cloth, watches, and ribbons, by good fortune could have remained one of the most wonderful town sights in all the land. It didn't. Destroyers obliterated city walls, ten of the twelve gates, the cathedral of St. Mary, built with three spires like Lichfield, Butcher Row and other things; factories that revolutionized the uses of human legs surrounded the city's heart, and German raiders did their dreadful work. The spires, St. Mary's Hall, and Bablake are among the standing reminders of old glory, and casualties such as Ford's Hospital and Priory Row I am told yet may be kept from falling (96). But my own constant reminder of intimate Coventry years is an old patchwork quilt that covers me up at night with silken bits of the true "Coyntrie Blewe" praised by Michael Drayton and Ben Jonson, a very cheering sight to see when waking up in the morning in these days of the blues.

Lastly, it would be foolish to deny the existence of smoke for a halo to Birmingham, great and beneficent city though it is, one certainly never seen by Shakespeare but now possessing the best library of Shakespearean books in the world. To penetrate within this halo is not quite the thing for these pages of mine, most unsuitable sheets for papering large industrial cities. Nor are the following words interposed for the reason that first impressions of the Midland metropolis when gained from railway trains romping in from Euston, Paddington, or Wolverhampton sometimes offer satisfactory suggestions for a Dante's *Inferno*, just as first sights also can do at Manchester, Leeds, Sheffield, and other monuments of England's greatness and commercial prosperity. Rather does Birmingham now figure here because it will be my one sample, my representative of more of the kind to be seen in our progress northward, and at places where it is not my purpose to tarry long. And further. This city ranked second in the kingdom, with a University, and a famous School of Art guided years ago by Edward Taylor, first directed me along the thorny ways of drawing, architecture, and the crafts. Gratefully I salute thee within thy smoky nimbus; and also recall that my illustrious namesake with a hyphen, Edward Burne-Jones, here had his natal habitation, discovered the *Morte d'Arthur* of Malory at Cornish's in New Street, began to devour it free gratis in that bookshop until William Morris appeared and bought the copy. Thereafter the magnificent Burne-Jones windows appeared in the church of St. Philip, and the artist endures perpetually bright in the unique collection of Pre-Raphaelite works kept at the city's Art Gallery—or rather, in parts of the fine gallery left intact after the German raids.

The strength of Britain depended on coal, said George Stephenson, when he suggested that the Lord Chancellor ought to sit on a bag of coals instead of on the Woolsack. And if England's early source of wealth and good fortune,

KILPECK. *The Norman sculptor's genius for decoration and surface pattern.*

ROCHFORD *church on the bank of the River Teme. Norman pattern in the tympanum, one of the twenty-seven English representations of "The Tree of Spiritual Life and Knowledge," a mystic device deep rooted in antiquity.*

MANSELL LACY. *A village with timbered buildings in the notable Herefordshire group which includes King's Pyon, Weobley, Pembridge, and Eardisland.*

wool, prompted glorious memorials in the Cotswolds and elsewhere, the country's later epoch of greater worldly prosperity that developed under the rule of King Coal, steam, and the steam engine created its own monuments, of which Birmingham obviously is one. When coal ousted wood for smelting iron, and consequently shifted the centre of the iron industry from Sussex and Kent to the Midlands, Birmingham rose on the swelling tide of fortune. Its long record of ceaseless industry, busy workshops, alertness, and spirit of advancement marked the point for a meeting-place of ideas, invention, scientific discovery, and a certain brilliance of intellectualism. Statues of James Watt and Joseph Priestley in the squares, reminders of such men as Matthew Boulton, William Murdock, John Baskerville, and Francis Eginton recall shining lights that fired minor revolutions and affected kingdoms.

"The toy-shop of Europe," so named by Edmund Burke (and called "Brum" by the vulgar), has projected the fangs of industry far and wide, both within and outside Warwickshire. Manufacturing "toys" of steel and iron not intended for children's playthings, ramifications of a long-established armoury, and a thousand trades ever expanding have wiped out fields, farms, woodlands, villages, changed them into things quite different. If the builder of a Jacobean Aston Hall, Sir Thomas Holte, Lloyd the banker, Squire Taylor of Moseley Hall, David Cox of Harborne, or even Joseph Chamberlain returned again to look round their former haunts they might blink and rub their eyes more than twice at the sight of the widespread agglomeration.

As years count in a superhuman world, it is not long since the glitter of iron, steel, and brass outshone the jewels of nature's providing in and around Birmingham. Cherries grew in Walker's orchard in the eighteenth century on the site of Cherry Street, and less than 200 years ago the present fine thoroughfare of New Street was bordered with farmlands and barns. Nevertheless Birmingham is old enough though it may not look so to-day. First a Saxon settlement, the Bermingeha of Domesday Book early developed the long main street from Deritend to Dale End. For reasons on which history is silent the town undoubtedly rose in wealth and importance through the medieval years, had markets by royal charter from 1166, fairs from 1250, a considerable Gothic church with a spire and chantry chapels, religious guilds, and a priory founded in the thirteenth century. One significant record of growing status was a permission to pave the streets granted by Edward III, evidentally a beginning of the ways cobbled with the "petrified kidneys" that generated ill fame, odium, and bad language for centuries afterwards. Subsequent to the Conquest the family of de Byrmyngham held the manor. The manorial home stood at Smithfield Market, where cattle and cabbages now change hands for cash within the limits of Moat Lane and Moat Row, names of course derived from the de Byrmyngham's moat. Next door to the cabbages knightly effigies repose inside the rebuilt church of St. Martin, the supposed memorials of the Edwardian lords of the manor. More names recorded, of esquires and persons of local consequence, emphasize that the town got on well in the world, first trading principally in leather and later in metals. Nobody thought of trading in pen and paper to tell us what their early habitations and hovels looked like. Certainly they must have been of the traditional kind determined by the use of Warwickshire timber, wattle and daub, and sandstone. Leland, who arrived in the reign of Henry VIII and so wrote the earliest description, saw these buildings or their successors when he noted "a mansion house of tymber" at the end of "Dirtey (Deritend), a praty street as ever I entered." The "smithes and cutlers" observed on the same occasion were sure signs of the flourishing metal industry. "Anvils" and "great numbers of smiths" impressed Camden when he followed in the 1580's, and at that time he must have noticed the timbered houses which I sketched years ago in this same street. The growth and success of the town in the early years wholly depended on a self-reliant population. Here existed no castle or powerful monastic constitution with people inside to meddle and dominate outside. Neither were there trade guilds or a corporation, local government being done in the usual manorial way by a high bailiff, low bailiff, two constables, meat conners, bread weighers, ale tasters, and odd-jobbers. Sadly deficient in controls and limitations imposed by wicked feudal capitalists, ecclesiastical overlords, or guild ranters on labour, the town was one of freedom in which, to use the words of my old friend Howard Pearson, "any man might work at any trade at any time," produce high quality like that of Benedict the Cutler, and live laborious days and nights without hindrance from jealous rivals or the scum of the earth. Therein lay chances for prosperity. The local circumstances, then different from those at the greater centres of trade like Coventry, naturally spurred effort among the natives and attracted free and skilled artisans from elsewhere. Thus it is quite easy to understand how and why the inhabitants acquired their traditions, their sterling human qualities, and the independence of thought and action that early and late landed them into all sorts of scrapes, riots, and tremendous successes.

Following the visits of Leland and Camden, time swinging along brought one of the rows and planted its mark at a spot still called Camp Hill. There Prince Rupert squatted on Easter Monday, 1643. With him were 2,000 horse and foot, 4 drakes, 2 sakers (small cannons). The townsfolk with muskets numbered only about 140, but decided "to stand it out, stay and trie the issues rather than be so perpetually reproacht." Twice they beat off the invaders, called them "Cursed doggs, develish Cavaliers, Papist Traytors." Then numbers told. The Royalists broke through, murdered, burnt about 80 houses to ashes, thieved, raped, got drunk, did all the correct things that victorious warriors usually did, and generally delivered unpleasant medicine to the enthusiastic

Parliamentarians and Puritans who had forged 15,000 swords for the Earl of Essex but refused to make one for their King.

The wonderful increase of trade after the Restoration expanded the town over the top of the hill. There, early in the eighteenth century, dignified lay-outs developed, charming and spacious effects that now, alas, can be gleaned only from copper-plate prints and "prospects." Sedate house fronts, the Bluecoat School (1724), and avenues of trees lined the square about St. Philip's Church, consecrated in 1715. Shorn of all but one or two of its original frontages, the square at least remains, and the church continues to show the tower, dome, and cupola, a most original and masterly composition designed by Thomas Archer, uncle of Lord Archer of Umberslade (195). The Old Square, an open space still, developed in similar style with Queen Anne and Georgian houses all round and lawns in the middle, pleasant features long since engulfed by commerce. Here the earliest houses, due to William Wesley, a forgotten architect, were occupied by 1713. The last of them to stand, the demolition of which I witnessed from the site of the priory, made a home for Hector, Samuel Johnson's lifelong friend and brother of Ann, the wordy master's first love; there in 1733 the Doctor produced his first book, the translation of Lobo's *Voyage to Abyssinia*.

Carried onward by the Industrial Revolution, the splendid and tragic event that brought so much and spoiled so much, the town grew bigger and bigger. Fame spread out, wealth poured in. The eighteenth-century increase of inhabitants from 15,000 to 73,000, made Birmingham one of the foremost places in the kingdom. Trade advancement and multitudes of people meant more streets and more and more buildings—premises and workshops for little and big manufacturers, artisans and merchants; homes for masters, homes for men, homes for inventors and thinkers; a place for Joseph Priestley's laboratory and one for the library of William Hutton, the historian (both burnt down by rioters in 1791); an establishment at Easy Hill for John Baskerville after he had risen from teaching writing in the Bull Ring to be a very prince of typographers, friend of Shenstone, Dodsley, Benjamin Franklin, and Horace Walpole. Substantial houses with classic doorways approached from iron gates and forecourts made comfortable and elegant residences for the men and women who helped to forward the great centre that sold "what all the world desires to have—Power," as Boulton told Boswell in 1776. Some of these roomy abodes continued a chequered existence into this present century in shabby surroundings, then gave up the ghost as their former prosperous owners had done. The de Byrmyngham's moat was filled up in 1816; it's a long time since Mrs. Gillott called orders to the workshop upstairs "Another pen, Jo"; and many a year has passed since the town developed into the colossus that offered a sure mark for German raiders. But the city with a Royal Charter, and ever marching forward, keeps a sentimental thought for its early days by stimulating crotchety old ages for the timbered Golden Lion Inn and for Sir Thomas Holte's Aston Hall, built in the full Jacobean style of mullions, curved gables, long gallery, elaborate staircase, and fine interiors, nowadays sadly rattled by the yelling and cheering from the Aston Villa football ground.

New triumphs in the nineteenth century brought new faces of people and buildings. Among them were George Borrow to see "the greatest workshop of England," Cardinal Newman at the Oratory, J. Henry Shorthouse to weave the romance of Rome into *John Inglesant* at Edgbaston. Peculiar things of a peculiar architectural period developed. Now they are particularly remembered by Francis Goodwyn's 1823 Gothic at Holy Trinity Church, the Roman Catholic cathedral known as one of Pugin's "spiky 'uns," Barry's rebuilt Grammar School of King Edward VI (recently destroyed), which enabled Archbishop Benson, Burne-Jones, and other celebrated and ordinary mortals to swot up their first Latin pronouns and verbs. The Town Hall made an effective display with the imitative classicalism of the 1830's; it was all ready for Mendelssohn to go inside in 1846 and first produce *Elijah* at one of the Musical Festivals, the celebrated events to which sensitive early Victorian ladies arrived from miles around and took their pleasures in the manner indicated by these words written to my grandmother

I never heard anything so splendid as the music, it was overpowering. One of the Miss Cliffords fainted and was taken out, and her sister soon followed in strong Hysteria from which she fell into an Epilepsy and continued insensible for three hours.

The writer, Lady Boyne, added, "I could not bear the excitement every day but to-morrow I will go to the *Messiah*"; evidently she was one of the brave women of the period. This classic hall on an island site, designed by Hansom, producer of the Hansom cab, brings to an end my slight notes on the Midland metropolis, my one sample of a great industrial city offered in this book.

EAST AND WEST OF THE MALVERN HILLS

When days are bright and clear you may stand on the Worcestershire Beacon above Great Malvern Priory, one foot in Worcestershire, the other in Herefordshire, look eastward over the great Severn-Avon plain, spy over a grand cathedral tower and across Worcestershire bounded by the Clent Hills, Lickey Hills, and the Cotswolds (132), then turn eyes west to see the rich green vale of Herefordshire with another cathedral tower, broken configurations, courses of the Rivers Wye and Lugg, and distances of hills and mountains that lead into Wales. Doubtless Will Langland had looked both these ways when he slumbered and "dreamed—marvellously," saw in a vision *Piers Plowman*, the "fair felde ful of folke," kings, nobles, bishops, monks, squires, merchants,

BRAMPTON BRYAN. *De Harley's ancient stronghold,
stubbornly defended in the Civil War, aligns with Richard's
Castle and Wigmore in the castled country of the Marches.*

STOKESAY CASTLE. *This rare survival of a fortified home was
erected by the de Ludlow family in the thirteenth century. Later
builders added the overhanging timbering and an Elizabethan gatehouse.*

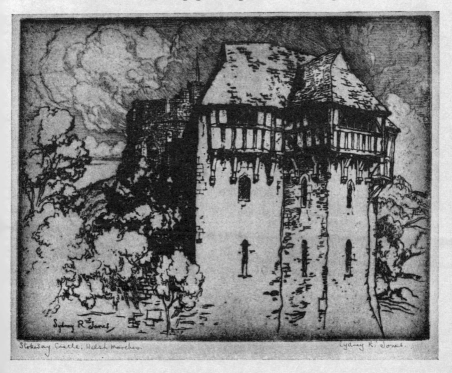

Stokesay Castle, Welsh Marches.   Sydney R. Jones.

CLUN. *Lofty ruins of Fitz-Alan's Norman keep in the gaunt little town near Offa's Dyke and entrenchments ascribed to Caractacus. The castle probably figures in "The Betrothed"; Scott stayed at the local inn, The Buffalo, when writing the novel.*

freemen, and serfs, the society of his own time in the reigns of Edward III and Richard II. At this beacon top of 1395 feet, showing more than a dozen counties, anyone still can see visions, dream dreams, in the reign of King George VI. Spread out below are many of God's own fair scenes not yet spoiled by man, cathedrals and churches of old faith, Evesham, Worcester and Mortimer's Cross where battles were fought, time-honoured houses, country towns, secluded villages, and particular homelands to be pried at, if desired, for reminders of Richard Baxter (Kidderminster), David Garrick (Hereford), Walter Savage Landor (Ipsley), Elizabeth Barrett Browning (Hope End), Edward Elgar (Broadheath), A. E. Housman (Bromsgrove), John Masefield (Ledbury), and other gifted folk about whom much or little is known.

First of Worcestershire. Wanderings through the county have given me excitements now best recalled by things of this sort—glorious trees and orchards everywhere; masses of yellow plums here and there; loveliest reaches of the Avon through the vale in sight of Bredon Hill (113); a sequence of two centuries beautifully shown by the towers at Pershore, Worcester (108–109), Malvern (132) and Evesham (114); Tenbury, Bewdley, Upton-on-Severn, Pershore and Evesham for representatives of country towns with old pasts; half-timbered houses and historic homes (118, 124); tithe barns at Littleton and Bredon; dozens of pigeon houses from Avon to Teme (129); the general prettiness of the villages (116, 118); Croome D'Abitot, Naunton Beauchamp, Grafton Flyford, Chaddesley Corbett, and Hanley William for samples of the good-sounding, double-barrelled place-names; Green Hill, where Simon de Montfort tragically ended his fight for English freedom; Worcester's standing reminders of Charles's getaway from Cromwell, which enabled England to continue with a King later on; the Gunpowder Plotters' route of flight after a mad bid for religious liberty; the kindness of a lady met at Hampton Lovett, who suggested the possibility of meeting Sir Roger de Coverley's ghost at Sir John Pakington's tomb if I waited in the church until midnight—a prank I didn't fancy; facial and phychological studies offered by natives under the royal sign of the *Queen Elizabeth* inn at the most precious of villages, Elmley Castle, on a night after a Boxing Day meet of foxhounds on Bredon Hill; an anchorage from a night of deluge inside the *Union* inn, Flyford Flavell, when more human impressions were accumulated from local patrons, who spoke the speech of their fathers and did not wear Worcester gloves while mixing Worcestershire sauce with their stories.

Signs of the quiet life and nature's luxuriance pure and undiluted might not be considered the particular attractions for visiting the Worcestershire regions of Dudley, Oldbury, and the outliers of Birmingham. But once clear of industrial bulwarks and urban sprawls a good deal is visible that cannot have greatly changed since the Papist historian of Hindlip, Thomas Habington (1560–1647), made his observations while captive in his own county after being involved in the Babington plot. Through Worcestershire, and onwards into Herefordshire and Shropshire, the farther west you go the better are the chances of finding the things that some people think made and make England. Stanley Baldwin, Earl Baldwin of Bewdley, evidently found them and thought so. Hereabout it is appropriate to recall the statesman's words spoken in 1924. "To me, England is the country, and the country is England," he said; no doubt memories of a native Worcestershire were in his thoughts then voiced on an England known through the various senses—sounds of the corncrake, the scythe against the whetstone, the hammer on the anvil, sights of wild anemones in April, the plough team, the last load of hay,

"and above all, most subtle, most penetrating and most moving, the smell of wood smoke coming up in an autumn evening, or the smell of the scutch fires: that wood smoke that our ancestors, tens of thousands of years ago, must have caught on the air when they were coming home. . . . These things strike down into the very depths of our nature, and touch chords that go back to the beginning of time and the human race. . . . These are the things that make England."

Or, I humbly beg to add, the things that did make England before the tractors and combine harvesters arrived, before the last few generations converted fields into towns to engulf the bulk of the population without day by day chances of seeing wild anemones, hearing corncrakes, or sniffing wood smoke.

Except at the northern tip, verging on the Black Country, Worcestershire is blest with the kind of ground and scenes that did and do make the best of England, real English in essence and on hand-shaking terms with Herefordshire, a county known to knowing ones as the most beautiful of all. Without extravagant scheming for startling effects nature showered her gifts with a loving hand over the Worcestershire plain, and man has been working hard at it ever since William of Malmesbury found the Vale of Evesham fruitful and lovely in the twelfth century. Landscape forms, far extended, mark the variegated mixtures of pastures and ploughlands, miles of orchards, trim patterns of market gardens. Strings and poles train green avenues of hops westward from Worcester into Herefordshire. Trees in abundance add full and rich colours, bright, deep green, and golden in changing seasons, gracious with trunks and branches in their winter garb. Elms ranked like standing sentinals or trusty warriors on parade, the elms which I adore, give to the county a special character. The River Severn traces a strong and bold line from north to south, from Wyre Forest to Tewkesbury's meadows, an immemorial line of strife and fighting when wars swayed to and fro over the Marches, and a water-line of thriving trade in the later days of the prows and busy wharves, now grass-grown, at Bewdley. The Avon, river of peace, curves and winds below Bredon Hill, where, long ago, the soft valley air rang with melodies of abbey chimes from Evesham and Pershore, and monks passed over the four bridges at Offenham (now gone), Evesham (replaced 1856). Pershore (*c.* 1413), and Eckington (rebuilt 1729). The Teme hurries down from the high lands of romance; rippling along from Tenbury to Powick old bridge, it is nice to fancy the eddies circling to a haunted strain of *Comus* caught from Ludlow,

> Sweet Echo, sweetest nymph, that liv'st unseen
> Within thy airy shell.

Rivers, little streams, rich leafiness, haunts of quiet, lands of diligent labour, church spires and embattled towers, towns and villages of black and white and brickwork, old manorial homes—all the wealth of the plain is set out like a green bowl of golden promise sheltered below the ring of hills. It can be looked into all round, from the Malverns, Bredon Hill and Broadway Beacon, from the Ridge Way used by ancients laden with Droitwich salt, from the Lickey Hills above Bromsgrove's Gothic steeple, from Woodbury Hill, where Owen Glundwr mustered his forces against Henry IV and a future Henry V.

Though not an exceptional group, most of the Worcestershire old parish churches are interesting and many occupy very rural situations. Developed in the usual medieval styles onward from Norman, a sprinkling of Georgian effects rounded off the periods. Lowish and embattled towers of the fifteenth century are characteristic and plentiful (as at Alvechurch, Astley, Bretforton and Berrow) and Bredon, Halesowen, and Bromsgrove have the less frequent spires. This wooded county gained uncommon features with the five towers constructed of sixteenth-century timbers, two of which sparkle in black and white at Pirton and Dormston. Eighteenth-century modes are well illustrated in several places and notably at Worcester. The church on the hill at Tardebigge, produced by Francis Hiorn of Warwick and sat in by the Earls of Plymouth, followed the classic fashion of 1777 and mounted one of the most graceful spires of the period. Some years earlier, in 1763, the Earl of Coventry fancied and paid for an essay of "the Gothick" at Croome d'Abitot. Prettily placed on the edge of "Capability" Brown's park, the goodish tower, the outside of the church and its amusing interior may have been designed by Robert Adam. Sanderson Miller, both, or neither. That's a secret. These two churches keep a stock of Coventry and Plymouth monuments. In other directions there is no lack of display in reminders of pride departed. Samples are offered by the tombs of the sixteenth-century Blounts at Astley, Talbots at Bromsgrove, sixteenth- and seventeenth-century Biggs at Norton, Savages at Elmley Castle. Impressive Sheldon monuments at Beoley recall originators of the celebrated tapestry weaving begun at Barcheston in the middle of the sixteenth century. The Russells assembled a large family party at Strensham. First arrivals turned up in armour and brass onward from 1375 and so provided Worcestershire with its oldest memorial brass; Sir Thomas (1618) and Sir Francis (1704) appeared later with sculpture most cunning, but eventually the line wore thin, went feminine, and the gathering tamely ended at a wall tablet of 1774. During four centuries, however, this party made up a remarkable display of costume, heraldry, and craft expression. Earlier members observed the traditional solemnity of their occasions, reposed flat, with hands at prayer in hope and expectation. Not so Sir Francis. He lived through the Restoration, had known the disillusions of experience. He kept to his curled periwig, cravat and breeches, lolled comfortably on a cushion, figured in a kind of conversation piece with his wife under the eyes of plump heavenly cherubs instead of a neighbour ancestor's skulls, with as much as to say that even a tomb, while symbolic of vanity, virtue, and joyous immortality, can be quite a human and sociable affair if properly schemed in the round to the many dimensions of earthly life. Sir Joshua Reynolds did not think this sort of thing seemly. Others may agree with him. Yet this figure represented in a wig, reclining, and talking perhaps can be just as allusive for immortality as one portrayed lying flat and silent, particularly if it is reckoned that some people at least will go on talking for ever.

On the right days for scent very good scenes were made by the Croome Hunt; fox, hounds, master, huntsman, and riders extended in a swift line from the fox's nose tip, with Besford church for a static and secondary accent in the background, gave me one of the best hunting pictures I ever saw, a proper Herring or Crawhall effect only, being the real thing, much better. The memory of it also reminds me that the secular rather than the ecclesiastical department of life had the best architectural run in Worcestershire. Pursuit in that direction brings plentiful rewards. Manor and country homes, villages, hamlets and towns, offer in total a well-defined expression of vernacular building conspicuous for timber construction and brickwork and bearing a family likeness to similar work in Warwickshire, features of which I have tried to indicate in the previous section.

Neither my space nor the need exist for enlarging on words already written by experts and others on the great houses of Worcestershire, mansions which include the Lyttleton's home of Hagley Hall, lively inside with Vessali's plaster decorations and Chippendale's fittings; Witley Court, produced out of the iron industry by the Foleys; Croome Court, standing in the park created out of a swamp by Lancelot Brown; Hanbury Hall, correct to the year 1701 with angle quoins, eaves cornices and dormers; and best of all, Westwood House, made vivacious by Pakington owners, Elizabethan four-square in plan with Restoration additions set diagonally at each corner, and containing elaborate oak interiors and the best of late seventeenth-century plasterwork. These big effects are not for everybody to see. Soon they may be widely available. At Croome, for instance, delinquent juveniles were to follow the earls; they did not arrive, so now sub-normal boys will inherit the works made in a noble past by Robert

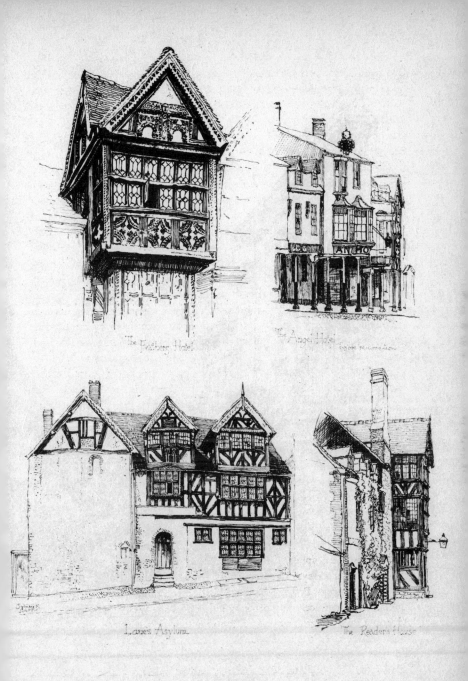

The Feathers Hotel

The Angel Hotel before restoration

Lane's Asylum

The Reader's House

NOTES IN LUDLOW

SHREWSBURY. *Wyle Cop, the ancient and picturesque street leading down to*
when travelling to Bosworth Field in 1485. Apartments occupied by Charles Dick
stayed at this famous coaching establishment, De Quincey slept in the elegant eightee

English Bridge and the Abbey church. The central timbered house lodged Henry Tudor
out beyond the main frontage of the Lion Hotel. Disraeli and a host of celebrities
century ballroom, and Paganini played in the musicians' gallery.

CAER CARADOC FROM SHARPSTONES. *The reputed fort of Caractacus, entrenched on the height of 1506 feet, commands Church Stretton and Mary Webb's country.*

Adam and "Capability" Brown for the sixth Earl of Coventry and Maria Gunning, the famous beauty painted by Reynolds.

Ordinary mortals, in possession of their senses and out of the peerage, are better suited with the lesser sights to be seen at close quarters or spied at from respectful distances. Village streets at Cleeve Prior (116), Ombersley, Rous Lench, and Ripple; villages like Abbot's Morton, Himbleton, Naunton Beauchamp, or Broughton Hackett (129) away from beaten tracks; adorable villages spread below Bredon Hill from Offenham (118), Cropthorne, Hinton-on-the-Green and Great Comberton; very many old family houses that offer such pictures as an early hall and screen at Eastington, a moated Birtsmorton known to chaplain "Thomas Wulsey" before he was a cardinal, Talbot's sixteenth-century oak and bargeboards at Salwarpe, Mere and Middle Beanhall both conspicuous for black and white gables, the Washington's home at Wickhamford (118), Kyre Wyard joining the work of earlier and eighteenth centuries (129); these, with more and more similar sights, give the truest architectural pattern of Worcestershire. Aspects of past day to day life are accurately set out by the plentiful sixteenth- and seventeenth-century timber construction, brickwork made to the fancies of late Tudor and Stuart builders, the more formal arrangements that served in Georgian and Regency times. Rarely out of sight is the prevalent black and white. It happily blends in landscapes and brightly groups in villages and country towns.

In this prosaic age, with little better than B.B.C. voices on the air or red traffic lights winking in the dead of night to give a body shudders and creeps, the old sort of phantoms, ghosts, hobgoblins and night fears shrouded in dim halos of the past may seem to be interesting and even sprightly. Worcestershire acres and houses had a good share in accommodating such spectral visions. No doubt ghosts as well as history were supplied by King Charles bolting from the battle of Worcester and Simon de Montfort trapped at Evesham; in quite early days the Conqueror's cousin, Urso the Bear, over from St. Jean d'Abbetot in Normandy, planted something more than the village names of Croome d'Abitot and Redmarley d'Abitot with his harryings, cruelty, and rapacity that earned the curse of the Saxon Archbishop of York,

> Highest thou, Urse,
> Have thou God's curse.

The district was long a centre for dissent, religious and political upheavals. Sins of Catholics, Protestants, and Puritans in the space of a hundred years from the time of Queen Mary to the Cromwellian interlude made life very uncomfortable for a great many people. Foxy houses developed, spooky places with mysterious insides hidden behind innocent oak and plaster, picturesque brickwork and big chimney-stacks. In one of them my body slid under movable stairs down a black bogey-hole, but hit neither fire, brimstone, nor clanging chains. That happened at Harvington Hall near Chaddesley Corbett, moated, timbered, reconstructed with brickwork in the seventeenth century, and successively lived in by the Pakingtons and the Throckmortons. At Huddington Court, 5 miles from Droitwich, I disappeared behind a wainscot into a secret gloomy recess, only to come out unharmed and make a drawing of the old walls from the edge of the moat. Tricks like these once could be performed all about Worcestershire, and nowhere better than at John Talbot's Grafton Manor and Thomas Habington's Hindlip House, monuments to the Jesuit archpriest of bogey-hole construction, Nicholas Owen, alias "Little John." Nobody used to get into these places for fun. They were risky necessities in the daily lives of most of the important local families who, after the close of Queen Mary's reign in 1558, clung to the old faith—sincere and devout men and women who worshipped in secret, suffered the religious persecutions under Queen Elizabeth and James I, were styled "Popish recusant convicts" and fined £20 a month for their belief, or endured, as Sir Thomas Tresham did, years of imprisonment and a fine of £2,080 annually for not attending the particular kind of church service dictated by the ruling power in control of the rationed religion. From these conditions, intimately connected with Worcestershire, grew the historical event now celebrated by juveniles with much hilarity, guys, and blacked faces. Of all the flights, escapes, captures and hidings that made nights shimmer with spectres for years afterwards none had more dramatic incident or even now offers better matter for hair-raising, none ever made more rubbish and fireworks to burn and explode than the one historic occasion remembered by the wild stampede of desperate fugitives galloping across the counties after the London news had spread on the fifth of November, 1605, "There is treason discovered! The King and the Lords should have been blown up."

Quickly the drama developed. Guy Fawkes, captured almost at midnight, went to the Tower. Soldiers guarded the 3,000 billets of wood, 500 faggots, 36 barrels of gunpowder. Catesby and John Wright, followed by Christopher Wright, Percy, Keyes, and Rookwood rode with haste and more haste from London on the relays of horses earlier placed by Rookwood at certain hostelries along the Holyhead Road. Travelling furiously in the wind and the rain of that November day, they reached the *Lion* inn, yet standing at Dunchurch, early in the evening, met the large company of Catholic gentry assembled there, told of the failure of the plot to proclaim the Princess Elizabeth queen. Ill news and forebodings dispersed the company. Forty members that remained by ten o'clock determined on flight westward, took horse, disappeared into the night.

Modern conspirators who disappear from Dunchurch in daylight to follow the tracks of the Gunpowder Plotters can cover their ground and find properties to fit this exciting old story; also, not being chased, more than once I have known there are opportunities for enjoying rural scenes and the sights of a very attractive locality. Even the charms of Warwick may suggest the fugitives helping themselves at midnight to remounts from the stables of Benock, the horse-dealer. Four miles on, at Northbrook below Sherbourne Hill, the early Victorian farmhouse locates the home of John Grant, brother-in-law of Robert Winter, at which arms and ammunition were collected; the moated grange of this wealthy squire long since shared the doom of its owner. The Plotters' route onward, started before dawn and laboriously followed during a wild wet day, lay through Snitterfield, the swollen ford of the river near Great Alne, Alcester's picturesque streets, and along the pretty Worcestershire lanes around Dormston to Huddington Court (124), a timbered house with a fine Tudor chimney, the home of Robert Winter, ardent Catholic and large landowner, Catesby's cousin, and married to the daughter of John Talbot of Grafton. Moated and forlorn, this manor-house as I first found it on a damp autumn day years ago seemed the most melancholy yet intact reminder or the beliefs, hopes, and crime that made the Gunpowder Plot. Though in need of repair the house kept the general look it had in 1605. Rain teemed into the moat. A kind country woman asked me inside out of the wet and also to see interiors fitted with contrivances for concealing Papists. A decayed window in the east gable, called, she said, Lady Winter's Window and originally made for lighting the hall, no doubt had been looked through by Robert Winter's wife when she saw her husband and the weary, travel-stained fugitives arrive in the afternoon of that Wednesday, November 6, later to be joined by the fearless Thomas Winter, the last in flight from London. A stone fireplace showed the arms of Edward III, the Huddingtons and the Cromleys carved on the mantel. Round it had gathered and dined together for the last time the thirty brave Englishmen who had risked all and lost all in the cause they believed to be right, conscious of the impending fate earlier voiced by Catesby to Winter at Warwick, "What, hast thou any hope, Robin? I assure thee there is none that knowest of this action but shall perish." At three o'clock the next morning Mass was celebrated in the house. The conspirators confessed, re-armed, rode away in the darkness before dawn. Meanwhile an armed force prepared for pursuit, commanded by the Sheriff of Worcestershire, Sir Richard Walsh, over from his timbered Court House at Shelsley Walsh, where motorists now meet for car trials.

"It's a pity the old place is in such a bad state," a friend said to me at Huddington.

"Yes," I replied. "Whether you like the Plot or not it did cause the annual search and spring-cleaning of the Parliament cellars, besides suggesting a possible good way for posterity to deal with redundant politicians. This house has a niche in our history. Also, it is very pretty to look at. Something ought to be done about it."

An appeal in a responsible quarter to save the house brought the reply, "Let the damned thing perish," evidently sent by an unbeliever in Gunpowder Plots or Plotters! I did not see Huddington again. It suits me best to picture the scene through the eye of memory, particularly after reading this news in John Russell's *Shakespeare's Country*, "a house whose restoration is more than usually to be deplored . . . uniform Trust House black-and-white, walls being broken and extra gables inserted in existing bays."

The desperate ride of the Plotters continued. Dumpy hills, green vistas and the elms, thatched roofs, brick cottages, the black and white of houses mark their route past Hanbury, Tardebigge, Hewell Grange (here arms and gunpowder were stolen from Lord Windsor), Burcot to Clent in sight of the Lickey and Clent Hills, onward through Hagley and Stourbridge (where the ford in flood damped the stolen gunpowder) and lastly to Holbeach, five miles within Staffordshire, Stephen Littleton's home, in which the gunpowder exploded while being dried and burnt Catesby and Rookwood. Soon the Sheriff appeared, set fire to the house, captured prisoners; before Catesby was shot dead he said to Thomas Winter, "Stand by me, Tom, and wee will dye together." Only relics of the original house and two hiding-holes survive from that final scene on November 8, 1605. Apart from the London executions of the conspirators, including Thomas and Robert Winter, and also of the celebrated Father Garnet, the Jesuit, who was captured at Hindlip after hiding in a hole for eleven days, the end of this sad, eventful history in Worcestershire leads us to the county town where John Winter and Humphrey Littleton met their end at the scaffold on Red Hill.

Less than fifty years after these executions, when Cromwellians had murdered a king and accomplished a deed that plotters failed to do, Parliamentarians at the Battle of Worcester crowded the cathedral with 6,000 prisoners, wrecked "Popish" imagery, plundered and damaged the interior of the fabric. Hardly less destructive were the onslaughts of restorers. From the middle of the eighteenth century until 1874 they attacked and transformed the exterior, but did earn thanks for keeping the building upright. In spite of these varied attentions, gifts from the golden age are visible in the grandeur of immense expanse, length and height, the noble proportions created in the rebuilding begun in 1224 and culminated in 1374 with the completion of the glorious tower, the earliest of their great Perpendicular masterpieces. Beauty and craftsmanship tell of the bygone time in the long nave, double transepts, the Norman crypt, clustered shafting in the thirteenth-century choir, Prince Arthur's magnificent chantry, the cloister complete, and a fourteenth-century refectory now part of the school. Great church and tower dominate the famous views seen from the Severn bank (108–109). Possibly they did not attract the plotters of ugliness, who usefully could have applied gunpowder on completing their power

BRIDGNORTH. *The up-and-down town on the River Severn has queer stepped byways and the leaning tower of a Norman keep. Good examples of timbered houses include the birthplace of Bishop Percy, famed for his poetical "Reliques."*

COALBROOKDALE. *The early iron industry settled here, marred beauty on one of the finest stretches of the River Severn. A mile away the ruins of Buildwas Abbey in a glorious setting offer one of the sights of England.*

THE WREKIN *from Grinshill. This volcanic mountain, isolated 1335 feet over the Severn plain, stands for the Shropshire toast, "To all friends round the Wrekin."*

NORTH SHROPSHIRE PLAIN *from Clive, near Wem, and backed by the Welsh mountains beyond Ellesmere. Clive was the birthplace of William Wycherley, the Restoration dramatist.*

station with four circular vomit pipes alongside the bridge. These utilitarian objects belched forth like hell upon earth during my sketching operations, sent filthy vapour towards the grand symbol of faith stronger than kilowatts, emitted smoke over the cricket ground where the Fosters merrily knocked up centuries in the summer suns of yesterdays.

Though smoke and manufacture exist elsewhere in this active county capital, no lack of pleasant things remain left over from candlelight years. Eighteenth-century houses in the close, a good collection, have the proper calm and cultured outside demeanour for their situation, whatever may happen inside them to-day. The Edgar gateway of a destroyed castle opening into the court of the King's School, buildings extending to the cloister and spread below the grand cathedral tower, give scenes gracious enough to make anyone wish to live school days there for ever. Conspicuous among the early churches is the fifteenth-century spire of St. Andrew's, notably visible above the bridge and the houses in one of the river views. For those who like the idea of Christian worship without soaring Gothic vaults and mysticism there are the Georgian churches of St. Nicholas (1730), St. Swithun (1736), All Saints (1742), and St. Martin (1772). These add particular character to the city's skylines. Most impressive is the steeple of St. Nicholas, obviously adapted from a design by James Gibbs for St. Mary-le-Strand, London. St. Swithun's interior, delightfully intact as completed in 1736, mounts a *tour de force* in the imposing three-decker with pulpit perched high under a sounding-board, the dove above, an eagle below, and enough carved devices and etceteras all round to illustrate any parson's texts and thirdlys. Inns abound; before visiting all of them an explorer might first sample the timbering of the *Farrier's Arms* in Fish Street, effects reminiscent of a Cecil Aldin at the *Crown* yard in Broad Street, the big and solid front of the *Star* that used to intrigue me inside for sirloin in the merry decades when Englishmen could enjoy real roast beef. New Street, Friar Street, and Silver Street show off the old fancies for black timbers, white panels and overhanging beams. The Commandery, a rare English treasure, stands at the site of the Saxon Bishop Wulfstan's charitable foundation; history's tales are told with Tudor hall and oriel, hammer-beams and wall paintings, an Elizabethan staircase and the room in which a Royalist duke went to die after the fighting at Fort Royal. In this "Faithful City" you appropriately read carved on an old beam in Cornmarket, LOVE GOD—WB 1577 RD—HONOUR YE KING, and perhaps at the same time think that Charles bolted from a back door behind the said beam en route for the Boscobel Oak. Round about ancient streets are mazes of narrow passages and courts unaltered in plan from early centuries, the death-traps in the hand-to-hand fighting and the carnage of that awful September day in 1651, proudly called by Cromwell his "crowning mercy." But merrily rang the bells of Worcester on May 29, 1660. The Stuart had come back to roost to be merry. "FLOREAT SEMPER FIDELIS CIVITAS" blazed resplendent from the Guildhall in 1724, when Thomas White, designer and stone-carver, completed the brightest and most loyal of civic buildings. Arms, trophies, cupids blowing trumpets, urns, and a lantern high up aloft join in the felicitous, even giddy, display behind the railings and gates made by the famous smith, Robert Bakewell. Royal with figures of Charles I, Charles II, and Queen Anne carved by White, the classic centrepiece also offers warnings to evil doers with the scales and sword of justice and Cromwell's head nailed up by the ears. And a warning, too, for me. We are long overdue for Herefordshire.

Particular people who know what's what, therefore not very numerous, have no doubt that Herefordshire is the most beautiful of all English counties. Some of them have told me so, and why; but with Shropshire on one side and Monmouthshire on the other, to award the laurels seems as difficult as the predicament of Paris faced with the girls and the apple. Other people, not very particular, titled M.P.s for short, and given to talking overmuch when the face of Big Ben is lit up, wish to wipe this very beautiful county clean off the map of England. To them, and all others who threaten Herefordshire's right and just place in the country's cartography and record of history, home and beauty, I say go to the — that is, go and look for themselves if they have eyes to see and vision to understand.

For Herefordshire is a comely county, friendly and kind to be in, just the place for enjoying orchards and gardens, trees magnificently grouped and shaped, great big woodlands stretching for miles, tumbled hills and high places commanding wide panoramas. Ridges, steep valleys and mountains of the Marches can lead weary souls clean out of this troubled century into the back ends of nowheres. From the fastnesses of Wales the River Wye flows down past Hay and the Edwardian castle relics of the mighty de Cliffords, Lords Marchers; tracing curve after curve and many a horseshoe bend the river crosses the county through Hereford and Ross (137), turns a romantic course below the wooded promontory capped with the Norman keep and broken towers of Goodrich, triumphantly meets the borders in the grand and famous sweeps at Welsh Bicknor and Symonds Yat. The River Lugg, fresh from the Radnor mountains, courses through Byton and Aymestrey between hill slopes verdant with the finest woodlands imaginable, then bounds the battlefield of Mortimer's Cross, handsome young Edward's victorious point for the White Rose and the Throne in 1461; the waters divide the flattish and fertile vale to and past Leominster, circle round the hill and the church of the Knights Hospitallers at Dinmore, and finally swell the Wye at Mordiford. Where the Black Mountains show in the west the little River Dore leaves the heights, the tumps, and the cromlech near Dorstone for the Golden Valley; the stream babbles through Peterchurch, gathered round the slender Decorated spire pointing over an unspoiled Norman church interior, meets Abbey Dore, rare with the Early English loveliness left by the Cistercians—and it's golden in the vale when cornfields ripen for harvest, apples colour, and beauty mellows on the hillsides showering gold, gold more precious than old-time sovereigns. Beyond the valley's eastern end is the rarest of rarities, Kilpeck church (*c.* 1150-75), standing by the Norman fragments of Hugh FitzNorman's castle; humans, beasts, birds, fishes, beak-heads, a monkey, a bull, a pig, warrior knights thought to be Welshmen, all manner of features, shapes, and grotesque, here and there looking rather paganish, show what the Romanesque carvers could do in the way of rich decoration when they really meant to show off (143). There is no suspicion of paganism over the neighbouring hill by Garren Brook at Orcop when the Christian message perpetually freshens around midnight on Old Christmas Eve and the miraculous symbol of the Holy Thorn blooms year by year, so the oldest inhabitants say.

The wide vales centred round Leominster, Hereford, and Ledbury give pastoral landscapes of the real Midland sort, softly coloured with field and hedgerow, pastures where the Herefordshires feed, climbing leaves and catkins criss-crossed in the gardens near the pointed cones and cowls of the hop-kilns. Cloud effects form and change above these green levels—I've spent hours sketching them over by Pembridge, Eardisland, and Ashperton—and the Arrow, Frome, Leadon, and smaller streams wind in and out past feathery trees, banks speckled with wild flowers, and rushes in sight of sporty trout that send rings circling through watery reflections. Wars, "grim-visaged," rather than the piping times of peace, are definitely hinted when you find Offa's Dyke above the Wye at Mansell Hill, the point at which the defensive ramparts turned north from the river in advance of the Roman line through Kenchester and Leintwardine. Not much of the Dyke is on view until Shropshire is reached. But banks, ditches, and broken-down castle relics crown height after height from de Lacy's Longtown in the south to the northern reminders of the Mortimers and the de Harleys at Wigmore and Brampton Bryan (149). These bristle up in quantities prolific enough to satisfy all romantic enthusiasts who like to ponder on warriors that faced, fought, and chased each other, raided east through Hereford to the Severn, raided west into the mountains, and regularly killed each other when English, Welsh, and Norman blood flowed through the Marches. Ravens feasted and widows wept in the "days of old," now tinted with romance only because they occurred such a long time ago.

Often it is prettier and much more romantic to find still in commission amongst peaceful green backgrounds and orchards the black and white buildings, the remarkable and conspicuous features in the Herefordshire make-up, which show how the native carpenters developed timber construction to its zenith from the trees of the woodlands. At Cradley (137), Bosbury, Church

LOWER BROCKHAMPTON HALL

Lane, Ledbury, Mansell Lacy (144), Pembridge, Luston, Dilwyn—here, there, and everywhere shine the magpie patterns on houses, market halls, cottages, farms, barns and dovecotes, lively with the particular turns the craftsmen gave to posts, braces and brackets, windows, bays, doorways, and gables (138), all held together with mortice and tenon, an invention in use from the beginnings of history. You can admire the brightness of timbers, light panels and carved fancies in manor-house after manor-house; for instance, at Wythall near Ross, Orleton Court, The Ley near Weobley, Staik House, Eardisland. Perhaps you may find Lower Brockhampton in a woody hollow near Bromyard, the fourteenth-century hall of the Brockhampton family, and the gatehouse reflected in the moat, a sight liable to make anyone gasp, as I did on first discovering this prize more than forty years ago. It is as many years since I found Weobley (10), one of the most remarkable townships in any shire. Then it was quite fantastic in black, white, and aged unrestored wobbles. Rarely visited by antique hunters of black or white intellects, meals had to be found and eaten under hoary timbers in the smelliest of bar parlours, remarkably queer for the pungent and beery atmosphere of centuries. All that remained of John Abel's town hall made a weathercock on the roof of a shop; but to wander in the old town below the perfect Decorated church spire brought a feeling of being a real Elizabethan or Jacobean prowling about in settings correct to period. Now tidied up, it's no longer

> Poor place, proud people;
> Low church, high steeple.

The *Red Lion* is delicious for more than outside appearance, and the sparkling streets and byways still constitute an English wonder. The weathercock abovementioned reminds that Herefordshire was the homeland of John Abel, "one of His Majesty's carpenters," creator of a splendid town hall framed in timber at Hereford (demolished), another one at Leominster (now Grange Court of

High St.
Ireland's
Mansion,
Elizabethan

Castle
Gate,
1601

Butcher
Row.
Abbot's
House, 15th cent.

Frankwell. 1576

School Gardens. Jacobean

SHREWSBURY DETAILS IN TIMBER

WHITCHURCH. *A Queen Anne group of old school (1708) and St. Alkmund's Church (1713). John Talbot, the great Earl of Shrewsbury who figured in Shakespeare's "Henry VI," was buried under the porch of the earlier church after he had fallen in battle near Bordeaux in 1453.*

1633), the screen at Abbey Dore church. the old school-house at Weobley, many more local halls and houses. This master constructor whose work and fame have lasted also, alas, concocted his own epitaph to commemorate a long span of ninety-seven years from 1577 to 1674. To demonstrate how the mighty may fall I quote the first two lines from the inscription at Sarnesfield church,

> This craggy stone a covering is for an Architector's bed,
> That lofty buildings raised high, yet now low lies his head.

Much more than is slightly noted on my pages does the face of Herefordshire present and suggest. While the early houses developed the ball-flower ornament flourished for the cathedral and churches in the fourteenth century. Poetry— the land has bred and inspired poets for England since Langland's summer days on Herefordshire Beacon until "Ledbury bells broke forth" for Wordsworth and chimed "sweetly, slowly" over John Masefield's birthplace. The county gave Kembles and David Garrick for the stage. It has fermented cider for centuries, grows hops, shows "Hop Pole" inn signs, breeds the white-faced cattle. This countryside of promise and delight, one that keeps beauty unalloyed and does not advertise itself, offers wealth more than enough to convince any- one, even M.Ps., that Herefordshire should be treasured, kept intact on the map of England, preserved from robbers just as the unique world map, the Mappa Mundi, has been guarded at the cathedral since about 1290.

While Adam and Eve and the Ark on Richard of Haldingham's map in the cathedral concern a time somewhat earlier than the beginning of Hereford's long past, a great deal of history belongs to this ancient town of King Offa, its see claimed to be one of the oldest, its shrine famed in the Middle Ages, its sieges, Border strife, and burnings, its buildings that once made streets of black and white, and the generations of men and women who did deeds remembered onward from the days when Ethelbert, King of East Anglia, made love to Offa's daughter, Altrida, lost his heart followed by the loss of his head, consequently expired in 794, caused a shrine to be erected and the cathedral to be dedicated to St. Ethelbert as well as to St. Mary. It is not for me to enlarge on such matters of general knowledge, nor to resurrect the Norman keep and great stone towers demolished by Cromwellians at Castle Green, medieval town walls reminded by Wall Street, the lost six gates, John Abel's large, timbered and departed town hall, all now invisible, merely notable for remembrance, possible lamentation, and rosemary. Rather do I put down quickly a few im- pressions likely to be gained in this city now busy, flourishing and attractive on the banks of the Wye plumb in the middle of the county.

The cathedral precincts, the fifteenth-century bridge, and the river walks afford the prime viewpoints (130-131). Byways and the quieter thoroughfares best show the timbered and Georgian brick frontages; survivors in High Town, and conspicuously the capital black and white of the former Butchers'

Guild House constructed in 1621, indicate the earlier pattern in this central and generous space. Widemarsh Street has the Coningsby Hospital with the Black-friars ruins adjacent. Interesting woodwork and misericords belong to St. Peter's Church, and to All Saints; the latter also possesses 313 chained books. The *Green Dragon*, the *Mitre* with a gay sign, the *Tabard*, the *Hop Pole*, and a crop of significant inn names aptly commemorate various happenings and blessings bestowed on this centre of holiness and knightly deeds where cider has been on draught since the fourteenth century.

Human departments of life in various ages and stages are available for observation and speculation. Contemporary natives and country folk in the streets, at the race meetings, adorned for Three Choirs Festivals, in juxtaposition with animals at the celebrated livestock markets; famous singers visible every third year over breakfast bacon and/or one egg each at the *Green Dragon*; men, women, innumerable brats, their bundles, meat pies, and speech, arrived at the railway station for the hop-picking; these and other effects regularly or periodically in view naturally suggest earlier celebrities who, though not on view, probably at midnight haunt certain places that are obvious in daylight. One of the latter is or was, David Garrick, born in Widemarsh Street; here, while Captain Peter Garrick looked for army recruits, Mrs. Garrick produced her own recruit for the stage in 1717. Four years later Mrs. Kemble continued the good work by presenting Roger; and he, conscious of duty, fathered twelve more lights for the footlights, including John, Philip, Stephen (baptized at Kington), Charles, and the divine Sarah (Mrs. Siddons). Corinthian capitals, frieze, and pediment at the Kemble Theatre in Broad Street classically stand for the classic name—but I wept to find the movies featuring in the place of Sarah's Desdemona. Not so classic, yet not void, is the long blank wall beyond the west end of the cathedral. There, years ago, an old, old man of whom I sought knowledge about this wall merely said he was very deaf, felt very middling; and a grubby young angler carrying a jam-jar by a string brightly answered my questioning by asking, "Say, mister, have you got any cigarette cards?"—two encounters which proved that prophets, even shady ones, are not without some sort of honour save in their own country. Unaided I found the expected object, the lettered tablet prophetic of oranges in Old Drury, red coats in Chelsea, bar-sinister babies, all dependent on "The site of the birthplace of Nell Gwynne, founder of Chelsea Hospital and Mother of the first Duke of St. Albans. Born 1650. Died 1691." Nice it was to think that "pretty witty Nell" did infantile capers and practised on this wall in preparation for King Charles over the garden wall in Pall Mall; nice to stand at the very spot, while also careful to forget that perhaps she never did, didn't found Chelsea Hospital, didn't even die in 1691, because the funeral happened in 1687!

A matter of boiled bones of a much earlier date rounds off my meditations on the human species in Hereford. Thomas de Cantilupe, the good bishop with the long nose and red hair, went to see the Pope in 1282, died on the way back, was promptly boiled down by his chaplain, Richard of Swinfield, afterwards bishop, and the bones reached Hereford Cathedral for burial. Very soon things began to happen. Miracles of healing occurred. Pilgrims consequently arrived from far and wide. In the medieval period the abode of the bones achieved a popularity and knack of gathering gold, silver, jewels, and cash only excelled by the shrine of St. Thomas at Canterbury. The shrine's base, now in the north transept, richly carved and unrestored, is one of the very few examples existing in England. More valued to-day than old bones are the jewels and treasures in stone left after severe maulings and restorations at this small cathedral. It remains intact with strong Norman masonry, and is proudly marked on Wye bank with the broad and sturdy tower, rebuilt about 1310, a premier specimen of ball-flower enrichment. Perhaps the most precious possession of all is the largest and most wonderful library of chained books in the world. Now, having just come out of it filled with admiration and despair at the sight of superb lettering, illumination, and printing, and without hope of bursting the chains to pinch even one book, I must away from Hereford, its beautiful county of vales, hills, timbering and castles, to continue my own inferior work.

IN SHROPSHIRE

Here again, beautiful to see and explore, is another claimant for England's most beautiful county; those like myself, with Shropshire ancestry and blood in their veins, of course rank it first, A1, nonpareil. Hills and mountains for grandeur, solitude, and wide-swept panoramas, miles of wooded banks, exquisite dales and rich vegetation fill the south from the Severn to Offa's Dyke where successively mount the heights of Clun Forest, Stiperstones, Caer Caradoc (158), Wenlock Edge, the Brown and Titterstone Clee Hills, grand viewpoints all for spying far and wide from camps and trackways made by early ancestors. The Marches in the west, scarred from old wars but dreamlands now in the quietest places under the sun, bristle with earthworks and ruined castles from Hopton Castle keep and Fitz Alan's Norman tower at Clun to Oswestry and Peverel's Whittington (175); over these scrapping grounds of vanished Lords Marchers and the fiery Welshmen who rarely disgraced their condition of birth by dying in their beds,

> The vanquished eve, as night prevails,
> Bleeds upon the road to Wales.

Northward from the Severn the big plain stretches in level miles and little rises to the lakes round Ellesmere and the Cheshire border; true pastoral country is this, patchworked with pasture, ploughland, and farms, the parks and the places, timbered and brick homesteads in the villages, pleasant towns old with streets for marketing and country folk to meet in at Newport, Hodnet, Wem, Whitchurch, and round the butter cross at Market Drayton. You can stand on Grinshill Hill above Clive (William Wycherley's birthplace) to see the vistas, the bird's-eye views over this plain, east and west from the aged volcanic Wrekin to the mountains of Wales, expanses from the Stretton hills in the south to the northern levels fading away in blue distances (164).

This county of mountain and hill, dale and plain, with heights for wide panoramas and shades for high romancing, has all sorts of wonderful things there for the finding. You can speed along Watling Street, Telford's Holyhead Road below the oldest English rock, Shropshire's very own Wrekin, enter and look round Roman *Uriconium* at Wroxeter, then with map handy, spirits up, and promise ahead follow on the tracks of the Fourteenth Legion along their route controlling the frontier, stopping on the way to look over many a fine view, remarkable half-timbering at Pitchford Hall, ruins of Edward I's council hall for the Statute of Acton Burnell, Caradoc oval camp and double ditches, black and white at Little Stretton, a Jacobean Sibdon castle, the rare fortified home of the thirteenth century at Stokesay (149), and Clungunford in the Clun valley. Ruined castles and signs of wars, though very plentiful, are matched by the works of men of faith and sometimes of peace who made the abbeys, now beautiful in decay and showing their Norman beginnings at Lilleshall, Haughmond, Much Wenlock, and loveliest of all, Buildwas, where the Severn swings round between the woods in a scene rarely equalled in England. Churches of all periods tempt church-hunters. Diddlebury has one of more than a dozen churches with Saxon masonry and herringbone work. Lydbury North, Edstaston, and frequent hill and valley places keep their Norman features of characteristic sturdy towers, Romanesque arches and carving. Of Gothic churches visited and remembered I can only mention the beauty, dignity, and sculpture at Tong and Shifnal, a fourteenth-century rebuilding at Chelmarsh, Battlefield Church commemorating the victory of 1403 (and Shakepeare's *Henry IV*), the spire at Worfield, Tudor roofs at Selattyn, a fifteenth-century screen and roof at Bettys y Crwyn high and remote by the Black Mountain; and of churches built in the classical period. St. Alkmund's in the eighteenth-century group at Whitchurch is one of the best (170).

Churches are not for everybody now we no longer expect to be Saxons, Normans, medievals, Georgians or Christians, but for travellers all on wheels or hiking, good to discover, nice to be in, and often difficult to leave are the villages, old houses, and country towns about which Salopians have lived since Saxon and Norman times and in which they continue to thrive. There are the villages of the plain, cosy groups of black and white, red walls, tiled and thatched roofs, not particularly distinctive or spectacular, but quiet, rural, and

OSWESTRY. *Timber window, Lloyd Mansion.*

WHITTINGTON CASTLE *between Oswestry and Ellesmere. The Plantagenet gatehouse to the ruined Norman stronghold, rebuilt after the Conquest by Peverell, kinsman of Peverel of the Peak.*

HAMSTALL RIDWARE. *The Hall Farm, once part of the manor-house with a watch tower. The farm contains linen panelling and carved roundels of the Tudor period.*

KING'S BROMLEY. *The green and the fifteenth-century church tower. The village, a royal possession in Norman years, stands on the River Trent within reach of the parks and oak-trees of Needwood Forest.*

fitting the wide landscapes broken by sundry bumps, the Hawkstone ridge, and the abrupt sandstone at Grinshill. More exciting, especially for those who carry fly-rods in addition to sketch-books or cameras, are the villages partly stone-built in the Clun valley, Corve Dale, Ape Dale, and more dales and vales, never far away from quick streams chattering along for sporty trout—and for you and me. In out-of-the-way villages high up and sometimes bleak—Clee St. Margaret, Easthope, and Ratlinghope are three—the summer air is as stimulating as the great ranges of scene offered; draughty seasons there and keen wintry days may bring an idea of Mary Webb's Deborah gazing out from John Arden's stone cottage "when grey rainstorms raced across from far Cader Idris," or can suggest Old Thomas Parr lustily thriving on good Shropshire air to the age of 152 years at Glyn. Practically every parish has its larger houses or a manor-house. Either built of native sandstone, patterned with black timbers and white panels in the west Midland style, or schemed to the local ideas of the early and late Renaissance, they stand all about Shropshire, often beautiful, always interesting, mostly dating from the easy sixteenth- to eighteenth-century times when prosperous people then knew that to have was to hold without being unduly skinned by harebrained politicians and ubiquitous tax-gatherers. Scores of these emblems of hearth and home can be tracked far and wide; some of my favourites are the sixteenth-century Wilderhope grim and high on Wenlock Edge, Elizabethan stone and broad bays at Shipton Hall in Corve Dale, Elsich very picturesque and moated a mile from Culmington, the Tudor hall at Willey south of Broseley, Whitton Court's fourteenth-century, Elizabethan, and Stuart features, Richard Baxter's timbered house at Eaton Constantine, many gables and high chimneys at Minsterley, a stately eighteenth-century brick and stone front at Halston Hall, Whittington. Numerous homes famed for associations, architecture, or the charms of noble situations can urge a leisurely wanderer to the Walcots' Walcot Park, the Plowdens' Elizabethan and Jacobean Plowden Hall, brave Viscount Hill's Hawkstone Park where the Red Castle (1232), the rocks, and the caves awed Dr. Johnson, Styche Hall of the Clives, the Corbetts' Longnor Hall perfectly preserved from 1670, Apley with the terrace and hanging woods, an eighteenth-century Attingham Hall, splendid Elizabethan stonework at Condover Hall (1586–1598), and one of the timbered gems of England, E-shaped, at Pitchford Hall. Within such houses, great and small, of course toasts have been drunk from generation to generation "To all friends round the Wrekin," ceremonies at which in my own time I have joined. The sight of these old homes, their smooth lawns, flower borders, roses, and topiary trees can send one's thoughts rambling back a bit. Easy it is to imagine successions of country squires settled on ancestral acres; their progeny, like Robert Clive and Rowland Hill, going out into the world to brighten the country's fame; bookish gents in panelled

177

libraries; ladies furbishing by candlelight in powdering closets; original sitters for family portraits I have discovered here and there painted by Thomas Hudson, Gainsborough, and lesser lights—to say nothing of cellars of canary, old port, and cobwebs that I never discovered, and their departed patrons, rakish, horsy, and hard-drinking sportsmen who may have bullied their wives, frightened their children, and possibly ended with poisoned pottage, as the *Gentleman's Magazine*, dated March 31, 1773, reported of my ancestor, Edward Fleming, lord of the manors of Westhope, Sibdon, and Shadwell.

Memories of Shropshire towns make me wish for the dozens of pages I cannot have to praise them. Shrewsbury, friendly rare Shrewsbury, shines like the jewel it is amongst English county capitals. Ludlow leads the country towns (page 18, 155). Almost matchless, it has the great castle ruined yet rich in pictorial motives to reanimate past glory, historic deeds, young Philip Sidney and Milton's *Comus*; grouped around are treasures of beauty at St. Lawrence's Church, the *Feathers* and the *Angel* for looking at and going inside, timbered buildings, Georgian houses, Broad Street and Broad Gate, every joyful sight imaginable mounted on, and in view from the rock above Ludford and opposite Whitcliff where the Teme circles round, running fresh and clear from the rugged steeps of Bringewood Chase and Downton. Towns on the Welsh border, peaceful now, keep a grim suggestiveness of stormy pasts in this tilting-ground of old feuds. Oswestry, where Penda of Mercia killed Oswald of Northumbria and nailed the body to a tree years before I can remember, even now looks crouched and ready for anything that might threaten from the mountains and Offa's Dyke; but the castle used for battles by Henry II, John, and Richard II has fallen to pieces, the presence of a lady mayoress on my last visit (1948) ensured no fighting in the streets between the friendly English and Welsh, and from the comfortable *Wynnstay* hotel you can safely emerge to see the few sights at the Lloyd mansion (175), Holbache's old school gables facing the churchyard, the Griddle Gate (1631), the great tower dating from about 1200, survivor of the church mostly demolished in the Civil War battle of 1644. Southward and beautifully set near the lonely Welsh border ridges lies Bishop's Castle with town hall Georgian, church tower ancient, and for the inevitable signs of fighting the scant relics of the Norman fortress of the mighty bishops and their outwork keep at Lea. South again, beyond wooded slopes and the high entrenchments of Bury Ditches, Clun fits its own wild valley: sleepy old Clun, hoary to summon the romantic mood and make you not wonder a bit that Walter Scott stayed in the *Buffalo* inn to write chapters of *The Betrothed*. Interesting for the church, a fine timbered lych-gate, the stone bridge, and charitably graced with the court-yard Trinity Hospital of 1614, its inmates and the kind master parson who used to give me nice teas, the grey little town has quite forgotten the turbu-

CLUN

lent years of fighting round the Norman keep (150) and the fortress-like church tower begun by the Saxons. You can sally forth westward without need of helm or armour for battling fiery warriors, climb heights studded with camps and tumuli, see from Hergan's 1342 feet the great Dyke of Offa still on guard facing the Caer Din Ring, idle away hours in the solitude and silence brooding over Clun Forest; if the tinkling bells of the Clun sheep tumble you to sleep on a grassy bank you may dream of the Fitz Alans, De Says, Prince Rhys, ghosts of hosts of raiders and fighters who used to prance about dangerously—even revivify old Caractacus himself in his camp of Caer Ditches, or perhaps at Coxall Knoll, making the last stand against the Romans, when the blood of the three days' battle dyed the stream that flows down from Llanvair Hill and to this day is called Redlake. Away from these borderlands of bloodthirsty fame captivating points abound in more historic towns. The wrought-iron bird of the *Raven* inn sign at Much Wenlock welcomes you to streets of old houses, the timbered guildhall, the Cluniac abbey ruins, the lovely prior's house. Queer stepped byways at Bridgnorth mount up from the Severn bridge to pretty and queer sights on the hilltop, handy to the black and white frontage of the *Swan* (163). Shifnal retains the "old houses crossed and recrossed in a great many directions with black beams" that Charles Dickens found useful for *The Old Curiosity Shop*, and not far away are more black beams at Boscobel, where King Charles hid in the oak tree (189). The pleasant and wide main street of Newport leads to the big fourteenth-century church tower and the school founded in 1657 by William Adams, the haberdasher (189). Another High Street, in Whitchurch, has one of those rare and curious shops called "penthouse-like" by Shakespeare, and at St. Alkmund's Church, rebuilt by Smith of Warwick in 1713 for £4,287 4s. 2d., all who enter by the porch must pass over the relics of John Talbot, thus obeying the dying wish of this Earl of

Shrewsbury, the foe of Joan of Arc that strides, fights, and dies across the pages of Shakespeare's *Henry VI.*

You may come to Shrewsbury from Shropshire's northern plain or the western hills, along Watling Street, or very attractively by following the Severn's course from Wyre Forest through Bridgnorth, Coalbrookdale (163) and Wroxeter, the lost Romano-British *Uriconium*, once a walled city of 170 acres for a highly developed civilization that vanished after thriving through four centuries, yet one of the most thrilling places in England when I saw Bushe Fox excavating this station of the Fourteenth Legion called Gemina. Six miles from these ashes of the dead the river curves to greet *Uriconium's* rival in age. Past the abbey church and stone relics of Roger de Montgomery's monastic foundation you reach the English Bridge, and lo! alive, thriving, lovely in features, steeped in old dreams stands the goal promised in A. E. Housman's lines,

> High the vanes of Shrewsbury gleam
> Islanded by Severn stream;
> The bridges from the steepled crest
> Cross the water east and west.

Worthily crowning its own delectable shire, here present delight joins with beauty, history and legend to yield everything that any respectable heart could desire for looking at, probing into, finding out. About the two immemorial hills almost encircled by the river, at every turn the past springs to life.

Shrewsbury pictures and stories could fill volumes of a long and full record. Early times developed in the Pengwern of the British, Scrobbesbyrig of the Mercian Saxons, Edward the Confessor's town recorded with 252 dwellings of wood and thatch. Middle and later ages are marked by the Norman castled stronghold of the Conqueror's kinsman, Roger de Montgomery; existing town walls of *circa* 1220; visible reminders of Austin, Black and Grey Friars; colours in windows and sermons in stones at churches founded by Saxons at St. Mary's, St. Julian's, St. Alkmund's, St. Chad's (classically rebuilt in 1790); Wyle Cop, High Street, Mardol, Frankwell, and more streets rarely equalled, and nowhere bettered for the timbered mansions, halls and houses of Tudor, Elizabethan, and Stuart years (156–157, 169); dignified homes erected with brickwork in Belmont, College Hill, The Crescent and elsewhere when Charles, William and Mary, Anne, and the four Georges sat on royal perches; the lodging in Wyle Cop for Harry Richmond before the Battle of Bosworth, the old school of Philip Sidney and Fulke Greville, the departed place for Pailin's Shrewsbury Cakes in Castle Street, Charles Darwin's birthplace at The Mount, the great market in which Mary Webb sold carrots; and, most wonderful, a dive out of Pride Hill under the sign of "The Fifty Shilling Tailors" into the medieval and Elizabethan atmosphere of Butcher Row, Fish Street, and Grope Lane, where it would seem most natural to meet an abbot of Lilleshall

PILLATON HALL, *near Penkridge, below the wooded uplands of Cannock Chase. The chapel (c. 1480) and the Tudor gatehouse are relics of the moated mansion lived in by the Lyttleton family for 300 years. Numerous Lyttleton monuments are in Penkridge church.*

THE FOUR CROSSES, *dating from 1630, an inn on Watling Street patronized in the coaching days by the London–Chester coaches. Tradition credits Dean Swift with a rude couplet scratched on a window-pane after spending a night here.*

LICHFIELD, *the city of Dr. Johnson's birth and Joseph Addison's child*
English and Decorated architecture. It was commenced in the twelfth cen

he cathedral with the only group of triple spires in England is notable for Early
mpleted in the fourteenth, wrecked by Cromwellians, and restored by Victorians.

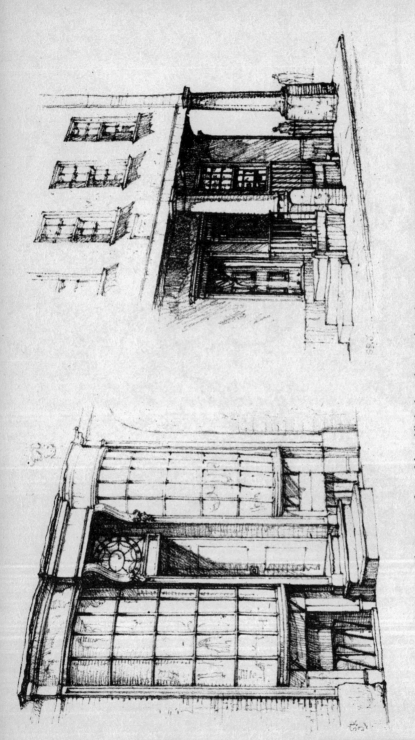

LICHFIELD. *The Georgian front of the saddler's shop adjoining the archway to " The George" hotel (left).*
LICHFIELD. *Entrance to Michael Johnson's house and the place of Dr. Johnson's birth in 1709 (right).*

lolling against his own angle-post or spy Falstaff in for a drink at the *Bear* after his alarums and excursions at Battlefield. But words, mere words, never will do for this treasured town. It is one to be seen, explored, and inevitably loved.

To end my deficient babblings on one of the most fascinating large centres left in England, and for you, kind readers, and travellers all who merrily refresh and gratefully rest on their journeyings, I conclude by mentioning that Shrewsbury's remarkable, interesting, and historic inns include miniature forests of timber at the early *Golden Cross*, *Trumpet*, and *King's Head*, the *Old Post Office* grouped round a courtyard, the *Cross Keys* highly ornamented, a late Elizabethan *Nag's Head*, and the restored *Unicorn* of 1603. The *Lion* (157), a prince of its race, rebuilt over ancient cellars late in the eighteenth century by a prince of landlords, Robert Lawrence, has one of the rarest ballrooms on earth choicely decorated in the Adam style, a room in which Paganini played, De Quincey slept, Prince William Frederick (later William IV) danced, followed by generations of the fair and the brave twirling round and round on the oak floor until this present year of grace. "The strangest little rooms" upstairs, numbered 27 and 27a, were occupied by Charles Dickens; and the drive-in through which you now steer your car served the mighty coachman, Sam Hayward, in his supreme moments when townsfolk kept out of bed o' nights to see this artist of the ribbons spring 'em up Wyle Cop, majestically circle his team at the top, shoot the opening with bare inches to spare, and deliver the speedy "Wonder" coach into the inn yard at 10.30 p.m., Shrewsbury time, to complete the 158 miles from London in 16 hours. Lastly the *Raven*, where I write these words. Not an architectural masterpiece is this hotel. Though the black bird has perched there since the fifteenth century, his plumes were plucked and curled afresh in Victorian style, accompanied by a sad laying of those ghosts that make chains rattle and teeth chatter at midnight. No longer is visible the room of Dr. Sacheverell's explosions on local parsons in 1709. But above the chatter and pleasant tinkle of coffee cups in the lounge I seem to fancy hearing an old strain—surely it must be Captain Plume singing,

> I still will complain
> Of your frowns and disdain,
> Though I revel through all your charms:
> The world shall declare,
> That I die with despair,
> When I only die in your arms.

The notion sets me thinking of Justice Balance, Justice Scruple, Mr. Worthy, beloved Melinda, loving Silvia, all the jolly puppets that George Farquhar romped round the Market Place, in the streets and by the Severn when he wrote *The Recruiting Officer* in 1706 "at the sign of the Raven in this good town of Shrewsbury" and properly dedicated the Restoration concoction of wit and naughtiness "To all friends round the Wrekin."

4. CENTRAL AND NORTH MIDLANDS

STAFFORDSHIRE, DERBYSHIRE, CHESHIRE

The sandstone of the Central and Cheshire Plains meets the limestone and millstone grit of the hilly districts in north Staffordshire, east Cheshire, and about the end of the Pennine Range in Derbyshire. Clear rivers, including the Dove and Derwent, flow fast from the heights to swell the winding Trent; other streams go west from the moors to the Mersey. The Dee curves in from Wales, bound for Chester and the sandy estuary. Scenery is varied. It offers wide vales and plains richly cultivated, the celebrated dales and highlands leading up to The Peak. There are quiet rural expanses, grand trees of the old woodlands and forests, river landscapes placid and charming or beautifully wild, long views from high points, and gloomy sprawls of brickwork, factories, coalpits, ironworks, and sundry allied effects contributed in mining and industrial areas. Local stone made the interesting series of sandstone churches, and the grey towns, villages and boundary walls in the dales and the hills. Oak trees, once very plentiful from Needwood Forest in Staffordshire to Delamere Forest in Cheshire, framed the black-and-white buildings and famous timbered halls.

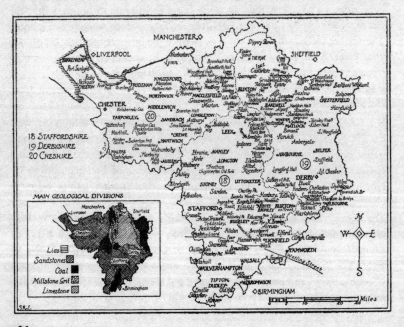

186

THROUGH STAFFORDSHIRE AND TRENT VALE

If all my readers carefully followed the instructions and routes to Shrewsbury given at the end of the last chapter—and of course they have done so—certain peculiarities of scene may have been noticed. These include smokiness round Oakengates on Watling Street, a cast-iron grave slab facing the west end of the dull Georgian church at Wellington, ironworks in Coalbrookdale, the pioneer bridge built of cast-iron by Abraham Darby in 1777 at Ironbridge. Adjacent in South Staffordshire lies the Black Country, an area well supplied with arid ground, mean streets, blue bricks, chimney stacks, slag heaps, and other contributions made by the Industrial Revolution and its developments. These topographical features denote that in the Midlands and over many murky miles in the North things exist to scare even the bravest modern Doctor Syntax in search of the picturesque. Splendid though the scenic effects may be for those who like beauty decked drab, ugly, plain or 2d. coloured, my modest pages never would do them justice. Therefore, now casting my mental eye over particular regions in Staffordshire, among many omissions of products made by the peculiar human arrangements known as civilization and economic progress I do not illustrate (1) the view from Hanley church tower ("Indian-red architecture, tall chimneys, rounded ovens, scarves of smoke," *vide* Arnold Bennett); (2) monuments dedicated to Bass, Allsop, and the Burton-on-Trent brotherhood; (3) gloomy Brownhills in which I first saw Joseph Chamberlain and heard about Karl Marx; (4) scenes in Swan Village.

The Black Country lies mostly to the south of the line made by Watling Street from Fazeley to Weston-under-Lizard. You can observe its scenes from afar and hurry on, look into them at close quarters, admire or condemn; for myself I incline to a remark Shakespeare might have quoted from his own play if he had hopped over from Warwickshire into Staffordshire later than actually happened, "We are not the first who, with best meaning, have incurred the worst." Nevertheless sundry articles merit inspection in many places. St. Peter's Church, Wolverhampton, for example, has the fine interior with double clerestory windows, chapels, tombs, and a remarkable fifteenth-century pulpit on the first column of the nave. The high mound of Dudley castle retains the ruined keep of 1264 and extensive relics of buildings begun by Normans. Other objects of interest include overhanging gables below a black-and-white lantern of the Oak House, West Bromwich; crow-stepped gables and brickwork at the Old Hall, Old Hill; the *White Hart* inn, Walsall, in which Charles I's queen stayed before the battle of Edge Hill in 1642; an Elizabethan Moseley Old Hall that obliged Charles junior with a couple of nights hiding after the battle of Worcester; and it pains me to mention the first steam engine sold by James Watt on view at Tipton, to recall one of the causes for urging to full blast the catastrophe of the Industrial Revolution.

Beyond the smoky pall nice country opens out, particularly towards the Shropshire borders. Kinver Edge commands miles of views over Wyre Forest, Enville Chase, and the Stour valley. Hilton mound, near Shareshill, is another good viewpoint for countless acres farther north. Here are eighteenth-century Patshull, Sir John Soane's design at Chillington reached by grand avenues, lordly Weston Park, the Vernons' home at Hilton, Stourton castle, birthplace in 1500 of Reginald Pole, the Archbishop of Canterbury during the martyrdoms in Mary Tudor's reign. These stately homes in private parks give promise of many more to follow, built by the ancient families on their broad lands in Staffordshire. Countrified villages begin to appear. They show features common throughout the lower regions of the county—timbering and brickwork of the larger houses, tiled roofs, thatching here and there, cottage walls of brick or oak timbers divided by panels of light plaster, churches made of the local sandstone and often dating from the fourteenth and fifteenth centuries. A number of hoary inns with black beams continue to distribute liquids. They are fitly represented by the *Whittington*, Kinver, and the *Four Crosses*, dated 1636, at Hatherton, near Cannock (181), an historic centre of roadside hospitality claiming a couplet attributed to Dean Swift. In happy past years I used to imagine the rev. gent posting along the straight miles of Watling Street bound for the deanery of St. Patrick, spending an uncomfortable night, fuming over breakfast, and scratching on a window pane with a diamond this expression of regard for his hostess,

> Thou fool ! to hang Four Crosses at thy door ;
> Hang up thy wife, there needs not any more.

From the Dean's years to those of Nero means a jaunt of only a few miles along the Roman highway to Wall, once the busy township and posting station of *Letocetum*. Traces of the walls or barricades of oak trees, remained until the eighteenth century. More recently the busy spade has turned up many things for inquisitive people to see and remember—pots and tiles and hypocausts— why the baths were hot or cold—where the bones and ashes went—in the glory that was Rome.

Near to these lifeless curiosities of a lost empire living reminders of the medieval golden age shine in beauty. Clear of the Black Country's gloom, and to the north of Watling Street, the remark made to Boswell hereabout in 1776 might yet be appropriate, "Now we are getting out of a state of death." The air is salubrious. Ridges of Cannock Chase show beyond flattish fields and woods. A trio of spires stand out. Sandstone coloured and graceful, they beckon to the shrines of St. Chad and of Dr. Johnson, to the homes of

> the most sober, decent people in England, the genteelist in proportion to their wealth. "Sir," said Johnson, "we are a city of philosophers ; we work with our heads, and make the boobies of Birmingham work for us with their hands."

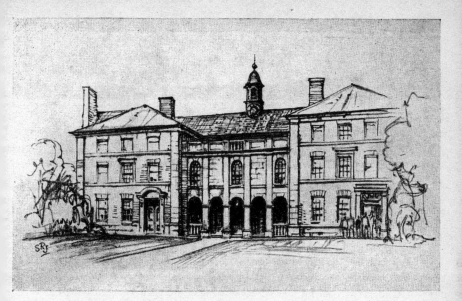

NEWPORT. *The pleasing front of the grammar school situated near to the interesting church in this Shropshire market town. The school was founded in the seventeenth century; famous scholars included Sir Oliver Lodge and "Tom" Brown, the Restoration wit and satirist.*

BOSCOBEL. *Home of William Penderel, one of the family that sheltered Charles II in September 1651. The house contains the hiding-hole used by the King, and near is the descendant of the original oak-tree in which the King hid.*

MOW COP *in the Staffordshire high-*
lands overlooking the Cheshire plain.

CANNOCK CHASE *at Milford Hill.*

Lichfield has the tranquil and comfortable aspect common to most of our major cathedral cities. Streets and pavements are narrow enough to give fellowship with yesterdays; their frontages of Midland brick and timbering, here and there notable, can flit the instant and proximo down Georgian, Restoration, and earlier years. A number of shop windows, bowed and bulging, emphasize the unloveliness of adjacent plate glass; so attractive in this wise is the establishment of Mr. Mercer, the saddler, that any enthusiast, albeit horseless, could hardly resist going inside to buy a bridle (184). Behind the streets are gardens and green stretches for those who fancy action, peace, or meditation in sunlight and under shady trees. Stow Pool bounds a graceful town scene, and the Minster Pool perpetually reflects the spires locally called the Ladies of the Vale. With many attractions and charms Lichfield must be pleasant to live in; no doubt environment partly accounted for Dr. Johnson's praise and high opinion of the inhabitants. Certainly it is a nice spot for a temporary anchorage, for pottering about to look at this and at that. Modernization has not achieved spoliation so well here as elsewhere. The gasworks hardly show, and though bars for fish, chips, milk, and similar contrivances exist for those who esteem them, the modest appearances of these present necessaries do not especially offend the senses of sight, smell, and gentility. Modern times have not dimmed all the freshness and purity of the city's heart. This is remarkable when one reflects that Lichfield for many years past has stood near to the gates of money-getting beyond the dreams of avarice and grime beyond the imagination of chimney-sweeps; it has managed to continue placid and aloof outside the very portals of the mechanical industrialism which made England great, glorious—and in vast areas, ghastly.

If a middle point can be found in the irregular shape of England, the three spires must very nearly mark it. This particular situation, adjacent to Wall at the junction of two important Roman roads pointing east, west, north and south, and the city's position on the old coach route from London to Holyhead via Chester, made Lichfield a centre of travel onward from dim ages. Saintly Chad, settled in a cell by a well that sparkles to-day as it did in A.D. 669, planted the banner of faith; he sanctified the ground for the line of Mercian bishops and Offa's archbishop. Norman and successive prelates devised the beauty of arch, vault, and soaring masonry. They surrounded the city with a moat to keep nasty people out, and a gate near St. John's Hospital served for entry and exit until it disappeared in the eighteenth century. While the cathedral grew in dignity and magnificence, buildings and homesteads rose round about it. A piece of walling now preserved marks the place of a friary founded in 1229. Tudor brickwork and eight gallant chimneys all in a row stand over the thirteenth-century site of St. John's Hospital. Gables and timbers, and pleasant seventeenth- and eighteenth-century houses, still attractive and worth finding, took shape and place on old foundations as the years passed on. Within their walls lived churchmen and laymen, tradesmen who flourished well on the old-established market days, and prosperous men renowned for brewing very good beer. "I remember," said Johnson, "when all the decent people in Lichfield got drunk every night, and were none the worse thought of"; and Boniface in *The Beaux' Strategem* recommended the local tipple with eloquent jollity. Some of the buildings acquired the nameplates of fame. The grammar school, founded soon after those at Eton and Winchester, nurtured bishops, judges, Addison and Garrick. At Priests Hall, now quartered with an auctioneer rampant, Elias Ashmole took preliminary breathers before being Windsor Herald to Charles II and founding the Ashmolean at Oxford. Almost next door Mrs. Michael Johnson (*née* Sarah Ford) produced the infant Hercules of Toryism (184). The presence of extraordinary powers of mind at that corner of Breadmarket Street soon placed the possessor at the head of a juvenile kingdom. Down those steps the youthful genius went, to receive the homage of his schoolfellows and be borne shoulder high in triumph to school. The original bookshop and birthplace, lit by ample windows, white-faced up to the late seventeenth-century cornice, and rich inside with personal relics handy to the immortal teapot, is the premier milestone in the Johnsonian pilgrimage. Statues of Johnson and Boswell outside in the market place rise silent and curiously over animated scenes and buses loading up. Further afield ways lead by Stow Pool to the descendant of the Doctor's beloved willow tree, to Michael Johnson's ill-fated parchment factory, Dame Oliver's school, and various reminders of Lichfield's and England's illustrious son, Samuel Johnson.

This city of age and fame, centrally placed and served by ancient routes as I have stated, must have known a medley of arrivers and departers that popped in and out or halted for high business, ordinary business, or with no business to be there at all. Monks and clergy, the mighty and the lowly, pilgrims to St. Chad's Well, country folk amarketing, packmen and waggoners, martyrs doomed to be burned outside St. Mary's, Lord Brooke at the head of fanatical Cromwellians mad for the destruction of the cathedral, and all sorts and conditions of men and women came and went. Some of them brightened and others darkened the scenes in the watered vale. The late 1600's opened the reign of the coaching years. Teams of horses and the merry toot of horns enlivened the Holyhead and other tracks that led to Lichfield. Coachmen, delivered their passengers. One day Captain George Farquhar alighted in search of recruits and chanced to find *dramatis personæ* for the Haymarket stage. A few years later Captain and Mrs. Garrick drove in from Hereford and deposited the infant David for a twenty years' stay. An actress arrived, and played under the name of Mrs. Siddons for the first time. Some travellers, like young Samuel Johnson and younger David Garrick, set out for London and conquest by coach (3rd class). And some, including the celebrated Doctor Johnson and the Honourable James Boswell, sped down from the metropolis by post-chaise at 2s. a mile (1st class).

These evolutions of trafficking on the roads naturally caused an adequate supply of inns, just as motoring does to-day. Here then, in Lichfield, are numerous old established and coaching inns built in a variety of fashions. Only to look under archways and down long yards can rouse up all sorts of fancies. Remembrances develop. In the dim shades riders trot out, coaches swing in, leaders start off, horses reach journey's end; and the merry, merry years and the dreadful past years yield up once again their stocks of coachmen, guards and passengers scrambling down; pretty chambermaids by candlelight and feather beds up aloft; highwaymen off duty looking bland; snug quarters bursting with old English plenty; and possessors of frost-bitten or sunburnt noses stoking up copiously with the local home-brewed to warm or cool the cockles of their hearts. There stands the *Swan* with an archway and a spacious cobbled yard leading to the boots only knows where, the establishment that provided a breakfast for Johnson when he flared into satire at the sight of Mrs. Thrale's riding-habit and delivered a lecture on "propriety of dress." Next door a drive-in leads to the *King's Head;* and another opening at the *Three Crowns* in Bread-market Street accommodated the bulky Doctor and Boswell on their visits to greet and stay with mine host Wilkins.

And there is the *George*, a saintly and royal George, Georgian fronted on an ancient hospitable site, with an archway and yard of its own, passages to get lost in, and lo! a ballroom too, with mirrors to reflect beauty, and a frieze giddy with demure cupids that must have winked over sentimental sights and nights by the score during their perpetual young years. If you stay in this comfortable haven, treat with propriety its joyful provision, retire to room No. 47 or thereabouts, repose sweetly, rival the lark in her waking, you can leap out of bed to behold a vision fit for the upper place promised to some of us later on. Soon after the sun begins his day's work the cathedral can be seen glittering in brightness and shade high over trees and roofs (182–183). Should the night mood develop a bit more shifty than above-mentioned you may or may not in the small hours dream of queer happenings, Landlord Boniface shuffling about with his three wicked conspirators Highwaymen Gibbet, Hounslow and Bagshot, or even Archer warbling to Cherry,

> But you look so bright,
> And are dress'd so tight,
> That a man would swear you're right,
> As arm was e'er laid over.
> Such an air
> You freely wear
> To ensnare,
> As makes each guest a lover!

For George Farquhar, rambling about this very inn and through Lichfield, discovered more than a landlord, his daughter, and the fleshy beings of common life. His creative mind conceived phantoms and pageants to flit airily through *The Beaux' Stratagem*, the sprightly Restoration comedy that delighted audiences throughout the eighteenth century and in later years made Charles Lamb the gayer for reading it. Cruel fate intervened after the author's best and most successful work was first produced at the Haymarket theatre on March 8th, 1707. "Poor, nature-loving, cheerful, melancholy Farquhar!" wrote Leigh Hunt. "He took to his sick chair; retained enough of the blissful abstraction of genius to write the 'Beaux Stratagem' in six weeks; and died during the height of its success, before he had attained his thirtieth year." How many more visitors of fame have halted at the *George* since Farquhar's years and the appearance of Boswell and Colonel Stuart in 1779? When a Prime Minister arrived during my sketching operations in 1947 I recalled Dr. Johnson over the way at the *Swan* in 1774 and then almost shuddered to think of the explosion that might have burst if the Hercules of Toryism had come to life again, crossed the street, and bumped into the Achilles of Labour!

My last Lichfield sight, the cathedral, of course ranks first in the order of spectacular appeal. But the central monument of the diocese, a magnificent heirloom of England, already has worthy champions wiser than myself to relate all of the history, beauty and falsities of this warm-coloured creation in sandstone, survivor of one of the loveliest of our smaller cathedrals and unique in the grouping of triple spires. It represents man's virtues and vices, is symbolic of inspired creation, worship, destruction, restoration, and hope perpetual.

The cathedral's ages, briefly stated, fall into a number of periods. The Saxon church or churches appeared after the death of St. Chad at Stowe on 672. A cathedral of the first Norman bishop followed. The present form of the structure began to develop late in the twelfth century and was finished about 150 years later. Building thus progressed through the times of Early English and Decorated architecture, both of which styles are well represented. A hint of the Perpendicular style came in 1337, when William of Ramsey, King's Master Mason to Edward III, started the four bays of the presbytery to complete the edifice; these four bays connected the superb Lady Chapel of *circa* 1330 to the original three western bays of the choir. A costly shrine to St. Chad and an embattled wall to fortify the close were provided by Bishop Langton (1296–1321) of splendid memory.

One of the thirteen cathedrals served by secular clergy, Lichfield escaped the grabbing propensities of Henry VIII. Similar good fortune did not happen in 1643. Cromwell and his minions then met to plan foul deeds in the Tudor house at Mavesyn Ridware, six miles from the city. Lord Brooke, zealous to abolish "all decent order in the service of God," determined to destroy the cathedral

TWO MIDLAND CATHEDRAL TOWERS. *St. Philip, Birmingham (left), a masterly design of 1710 by Thomas Archer, courtier, architect, and uncle of Lord Archer of Umberslade. All Saints, Derby (right), the finest Perpendicular tower in the district, designed early in the reign of Henry VIII.*

STAFFORD. *The College, founded in the middle of the seventeenth century by Sir Martin Noel, built of local stone and well preserved.*

STAFFORD. *Chetwynd House, a dignified example of Renaissance building in brickwork and stone, and formerly the town house of the Chetwynd family. Richard Brinsley Sheridan used to stay here when M.P. for Stafford.*

held for the King by the Royalists. With his forces outside the close he set about the work in grim earnest. A sniper, however, perched on the parapet of the central tower, spotted my lord and shot him dead; the site of this fall from grace can be inspected in the street suitably named Dam. Nothing daunted, the Roundheads continued to bombard the building and close. After three days the besiegers conquered. They advanced in fanatical triumph to do devilish work in their customary way, wrought havoc unthinkable, chased cats with hounds through the vaulted aisles. Battered, roofless almost everywhere, treasures smashed, archives and historical documents burnt, the close walls down, the central spire gone, the once glorious pile was reduced to the worst of all the cathedral wrecks made by Puritanical madmen.

With King Charles safely restored to home sweet home, the cathedral obviously needed a restoration too. Those gayer years brought along Bishop Hacket—all hail to thee, excellent Hacket! For the glory of God and the honour of man he determined to revive the cathedral of his see, then standing gaunt and ruined in 1662. With right good will he collected vast sums for the enterprise; and if the pretty story of the prelate's own coach and horses bearing away rubbish and hauling in stone may be no more than a fable of good intent, a likeness of the original Gothic splendour and ancient dignity had been recaptured after seven years of great labour. Again the central spire completed the trio, reconstructed it is thought by Sir Christopher Wren. A lapse followed. Long periods of neglect caused masonry to decay. More restorers arrived in the 1850's to undertake tasks long overdue. Doubtless their intentions were good. But these Victorian architects and craftsmen represented the spirit of their own time, a hard, mechanical time dead to the true meaning of medieval thought and inspiration. Not only was the building rescued and strengthened; it suffered such a dose of inharmonious reconstruction, furbishing and touching up that the results, only too obvious at present, and the names of the gentlemen responsible for them need not be dwelt on by me.

Yet Lichfield cathedral continues glorious. It has triumphed over destruction, restoration, and other deadly sins, is of the noble things on this earth, permanent in appeal. The grand medieval masses and compositions captivate beholders to-day as they did in the old time. The grouped spires, lovely from every angle, point heavenwards above lengths of roofs and clerestories, geometrical traceries in the nave, tall choir lights and the long windows of the Lady Chapel. The majestic west front, finished early in the fourteenth century, keeps its original scheme of surface decoration, gable, beautiful doorways, the spire-capped towers concealing the ends of the aisles. A hundred memorable sights are presented within. Arches and ribbed vaults spread from west to east; they emphasize the full design of the nave (*circa* 1250–1280) and grandeur at the crossing where the transepts open out. The choir, remodelled onward from 1337, terminates in the east with the cathedral's great treasure, the Lady Chapel (*circa* 1320–1330), aglow with exquisite colours of sixteenth-century Flemish glass. Where so much that is fine remains, inharmonious restorations and falsifications need not be noticed.

Time and again during visits to Lichfield I have experienced the thrill of turning from the main street between pretty brick and timbered houses to see the cathedral's western front, rich, warm-coloured, and with symbolic beauty leading the eye and mind upward. Round the great church extends the close, bordered with Restoration and Georgian houses and, tucked away in a retired quadrangle, the little Vicars' close patterned with timbers, flowers and greenery. Wandering here and there you can easily imagine Dr. Johnson shambling along his favourite Dean's Walk or picture pale young Joseph Addison, son of the Dean, making his way to the grammar school. This close charms at all times and never more than at the end of a spring or summer day. Then it is very quiet. The sightseers have gone. The spires catch the late evening glow as the sun goes down. Lights begin to twinkle from casements and window panes. Night deepens. One by one some of the lights pop out. Lively cherubs, angelic choristers of the *Magnificat*, have finished their larks and gone to roost. The big bell booms. The last loiterers in the walks depart. The shade of Johnson has gone home and Addison's ghost is tucked up in the Deanery. The cathedral spires and the great western front loom in silhouette from a darkened sky. You seek your host or inn and, grateful for impressions stored in memory, sleep in peace. Dawn and sunshine light another day. Ways lead to pastures new. The spires lessen in the distance. As they fade from sight I say "Amen" to Lichfield—until the next time of asking!

Enthusiasts for Mercians or for coal are both suited with routes from the seat of Offa's defunct archbishop at Lichfield. The Mercian-minded can travel east to Tamworth, the place of Mercian kings more than a thousand years ago; then, as now, handy for Watling Street, and now, but not then, valued by archaeologists, with whom I have climbed the high castle mound to inspect Saxon, Norman and later masonry. More than once Shakespeare found the old stones useful for Act scenes and war's "noises off." In the town below may be noticed good fourteenth- and fifteenth-century work at the church, the glass windows by William Morris, Ford Madox Brown and Burne-Jones, a William-and-Mary town hall, St. James's Hospital in an incongruous hiding-place. From the castle mound you look over the champaign country. Little streams wind down to the green meadows of the Tame valley. The fertile earth, garnished with woodlands, sets off villages, hamlets, churches, Clifton Campville's slender spire, and Elford, worth a day's pilgrimage to see the carved alabaster effigies of the Ardernes, Stanleys, and more knights and ladies of the 1400's and 1500's.

Westerly routes from Lichfield are satisfactory for those interested in coal and the defilements on land achieved since economists set out to plan the labours of man. Travellers not so minded and content with God's free air and nature's bounties can still find plenty of both on the undulating plateau of Cannock Chase. This ground accommodated myself and legs on the longest day's walk of my life, more than forty miles of it and egged along by an athletic young man down from Oxford who nearly hobbled me to premature doom. I mention this exploit merely to indicate a few points we then saw and which yet may remain unspoiled and worth finding: Hammerwich overlooking miles of Chase scenery; Farewell, once a priory of Lichfield, quiet in the meadows by the stream and Georgian hall; Castle Hill earthworks and acres of bracken round the early Renaissance hall of Beaudesert (now *ichabod*); the pleasant placing of Rugeley and the town's unpleasant reminders of William Palmer, the poisoner; lovely woods and parks, in parts dating from Domesday, stretching in fine succession at Hagley, Wolseley, Oakedge, Brockton, Milford and Shugborough; views of the Chase presented from Milford Hill (190); timbered cottages at Acton Trussell; wooded slopes of Teddesley Park; black-and-white houses and Littleton monuments at Penkridge; St. Modwena's chapel and Pillaton Hall gatehouse (181), survivors of the "antique mansion residence of the respectable family of Littleton Baronets . . . standing marks of convivial mirth and good old cheer" (*Gentlemen's Magazine* 1789).

West of the Chase the country to the Shropshire boundary is pretty and pleasant, true to the Midland character. Quiet lanes and footpaths wind among meadows, rushy streams, woods, lowly heights. Railroads are few. Villages and hamlets, often marked with the local brickwork in cottages and houses, keep prime and secluded. Adbaston is one good specimen; "Dear native Adbaston, remote from care," wrote Bowker Ash, the poet whose verses pleased Coleridge. Lands of the flattish south lead northward to the broken tracts of hills and extensive woods about Whitmore, Ashley, and Blore Heath, where Richard Neville's White Roses defeated the Lancastrian Red Roses in 1459. The sandstone churches continue. Gnosall tower stands out conspicuously; it marks a notable building of the centuries dated from the Norman to the fifteenth. Norbury and other church interiors have more monuments of the old gentry on view. Great parks are not so frequent here as in the county's centre and east; those at Keele and Swynnerton make good in quality, and a once ducal Trentham now has risen to the heights of democratic sociability.

Stafford, the county capital in the middle of the shire, lives on the Sow, a tributary of the Trent, whose name does not properly advertise the town's raw material of leather. Here we meet sniffs of industry again. But the smells of tanned hides of the horse or the cow are grateful, even comforting, when compared with the odours compounded in the Black Country or the Potteries. That peculiarity I noticed with a degree of pleasure on the spot during endeavours to cobble my own offerings of art with the local products. The reason for the hides, shoemaking, also seems to be an historic craft. According to *Exodus* Moses wore shoes and according to Webster Anglo-Saxons had *sceóhs;* without dwelling particularly on feet so ancient as theirs or who fitted them, it is evident that shoemaking has benefited all sexes throughout all ages. Long after the Industrial Revolutionists rode their iron horses shoes continued to be made by hand; they enabled Stafford's M.P., Richard Brinsley Sheridan, to invent the neat toast, "May the trade of Stafford be trod underfoot by all the world." To-day, though mechanized, shoemaking is a clean job not unduly burdened with smoke, fumes and smuts. That is why it is not in the least unpleasant to walk about Stafford and to track more scents than those of leather by following in the shoeprints of Saxons, Normans, Tudors, and staunch Royalists.

The castle mound leads back to the Norman years of Lord Robert, who settled himself on the Conqueror's reward for accomplishments. The existing masonry is a nineteenth-century reconstruction made on the foundations of the Edwardian keep, a square structure of 1348 with octagonal corner towers, duly blown up by Cromwell. Two notable churches have weathered centuries. St. Chad's interior is magnificently Norman; St. Mary's remains impressive throughout from its Saxon beginnings to the nave arches, Tudor clerestories, and the noble octagonal lantern erected over a spacious cruciform plan. Numerous gabled and timbered houses tell of times from 1475 to Elizabeth's reign and the seventeenth century. One of the casements first lighted the infancy of the valiant Cavalier and saintly brother of the angle, Izaak Walton; thus undying fame came to the town in 1593. A show-piece for black-and-white, the High House in Greengate Street, made a lodging for King Charles and his friends in 1642; Prince Rupert, always looking for sport, then fired a couple of bullets over the garden wall into the weathercock's tail on St. Mary's. Later days brought Chetwynd House, town quarters of the Chetwynd family, a Renaissance effect of much dignity and charm schemed in brick walling, stone features and pilasters (196). This home and other Georgian houses fronting the streets remind of little seasons in the county town, elegant gossip, scandal over port by candlelight, and occasions made brilliant through the presence of Sheridan, the local M.P. from 1780 to 1812. More lowly inhabitants whose bottles were few settled in the Old College in Mill Street (196); the almshouses have been well preserved since Sir Martin Noel in the mid-seventeenth century provided the doles, the stone gablets, and armorial embellishments.

The town, busy enough now and busy for centuries past, accumulated a good supply of inns and coaching establishments. They continue visible and serving. A

CHATSWORTH. *Ducal, classic and renowned, the stately palace is beautifully set above the River Derwent. Designed for the first Duke of Devonshire by William Talman, the Restoration architect, it dates from 1687–1700 on the site of Bess of Hardwick's Tudor house.*

HADDON HALL. *The seat of the Vernon and Manners families is just*
famed for picturesqueness, beautiful situation and romantic suggestio
Always planned for domestic use rather than for war, this home of lovel
buildings stands round two courtyards. It was begun in 1070 and finishe
during 555 years.

few, like the *Vine*, are very ancient. Dickens knew the *Swan*, called it dowdy as
"the Dodo," thereby implying extinction. George Borrow thought otherwise,
brightened it for ever in *The Romany Rye*.

> Truly a very great place for life and bustle. was this inn. And often in after life,
> when lonely and melancholy, I have called up the time I spent there, and never
> failed to become cheerful from the recollection.

My exact sentiments, dear George! During my past artistic and leathery
adventures in Stafford the shoemakers often entertained me at this inn. Full of
life, bustle, plenty, and good fellowship it was then. At the long table in the
dining-room talk bandied round—of shoes—and ships—and sealing-wax—over
cabbages and English sirloin. Then I gleaned two weighty secrets. They are now
exposed to the world as I bow adieu to the town: (1) Tanning with the bark of
oak, a method possibly dating back to the year when Queen Nefertiti donned
her first pair of "Lotus" shoes, is still the most satisfactory way of converting
hides into leather. (2) A tip to reimburse my readers for the money spent on
buying this book. New soles of shoes wear best if the wearer first walks through
grit or fine gravel. The grit works into the leather. Soles thus last longer.
There's nothing like leather! so they say in Stafford.

The near "Trent, by Tixall graced"—that's how Michael Drayton put it—is
also graced with more fine parklands at Ingestre and Sandon. Admirers of
Wren's City churches should not fail to visit the church at Ingestre. While
examining the interior screen and pulpit made of Flanders oak, the general
richness of work in stone, wood, metal, and plaster, I certainly felt transported
from Staffordshire to my *London Triumphant* days. Often attributed to Sir
Christopher, the building is the most finished and elaborate country example
of his period. It was due to Walter Chetwynd, the lord of the manor whose
Stafford house we have seen in Greengate Street; after the consecration of the
church this squire gave a "splendid dinner for the Nobilitie, Clergy, and
Gentry, both men and women." Everything, except the dinner, remains much
as it was on that August day in 1677. Thrice historical Chartley and its old
woodlands lie a mile or two from the river. Upstream is Stone, abode of more
shoemakers, and bright with the halos of a painter and a poet, Peter de Wint,
born there in 1784, and Richard Barnefield, the Elizabethan, who sang,

> As it fell upon a day
> In the merry month of May.

Beyond more parks and Trentham neither merry months of May, June, or
July will conceal Industrial Revolutionary features and charms, nor dispel the
gloom and vapours diffused over the concentrated and packed five towns of
the Potteries. Of them Arnold Bennett wrote, "Beauty was achieved and none
saw it," and noted "the chequered sky," a "scarlet market-place." And if
artistic history was made by William Littler of Longton Hall, Josiah Wedgwood

at Etruria, Spode, Minton, Copeland, and other giants in transforming clay, the landscapes have been considerably upset in providing for the uses, washing and peculiar needs of man. Therefore I hastily retreat and pass onward.

The Staffordshire highlands spread from the Potteries to the county borders. Ah! it is clear and fresh up there. Nature offers beauty and wise people from the towns take care to see it. You meet broad open spaces, moors, rocky shapes, woody gorges, miles of distances; you can trace the lapwings' rapid flight overhead and the flash of trout in clear pools of valley streams. Hills fill the area. High elevations are broadly marked by the Weaver Hills, Ipston Edge, Morridge, Merryton Low (1603 feet), and the fantastic outlines of The Roaches, all spectacular points to be on and to look from. Moorlands extend to Flash, quaint little Longnor, and to Mow Cop (190), where the eyes at least seem to be in possession of all Cheshire. New patterns of England open out. Grey stone churches and villages climb the slopes or nestle in glades and dingles. Native stone colours field boundaries and the walls and roofs of cottages and farms. Leek, the capital of the district and famed for the silk manufacture first introduced by the Huguenots, stands out on its slopes facing the heights. Here the Young Pretender came in the advance and the retreat of 1745, but probably had no time to admire the pinnacled Gothic church tower or the interesting seventeenth- and eighteenth-century houses and domestic architecture.

Infant waters flow down. The Trent begins a long course from Biddulph Moor, near to the Elizabethan hall ruins wrecked when a Royalist Brereton faced a Parliamentary Brereton. The Manifold, Hamps and Churnet, lovely rivers all, leave the heights. They descend to green borderlands and woods, swish below crags in deep valleys. Circling and rippling melodiously, the clear streams perform remarkably well in amplifying the stuff of picturesqueness, romance, history, and memories. At Beeston Tor nature's towers crown a memorable scene at the meeting of the Hamps and the Manifold. The Churnet's divine loveliness at Alton is piled with the Talbot turrets, battlements and dogs rampant, Pugin's chapels, de Verdun's ruined Norman keep, immense and singular effects that might do for a fabled vision, castles on the Rhine, or a nightmare in fairyland. Apart from prehistoric finds in Thor's Cave, high on the bold rocks above the Manifold, and remains left by Saxons and Danes in the cave at the base of Beeston Tor, previous distinguished arrivals and their places are remembered. Copper miners, for example, delved enough cash value out of Ecton Hill to enable Carr of York to design and build the fine eighteenth-century Crescent at Buxton for a Duke of Devonshire. The Manifold's disappearing trick below ground at Ilam completely mystified Dr. Johnson in 1774; many years earlier underground rivers probably had no effect on William Congreve sitting in the grotto writing *The Old Bachelor*, the play that delighted London, shocked the Jeremiah's, and made the author's name when produced at the Theatre Royal in 1693. Mary Howitt liked to climb and write on "the top of Caldon-Low" above the River Hamp, and Ellastone, between the Rivers Churnet and Dove, gave George Eliot "Hayslope" for *Adam Bede*.

The River Dove, a joint possession of Staffordshire and Derbyshire, hurries down from Dove Head to Beresford Dale, a beautiful combination of stream, green slopes, woods and rocks. Here, on Staffordshire soil, is just the place to dip into *The Compleat Angler* and pay homage at the little stone Fishing House dedicated to "I W—C C—Piscatoribus Sacrum—1674," to visit the hiding-hole used by Charles Cotton for dodging creditors, and amble over his deserted bowling-green on the height above. Experts perhaps may succeed in catching trout; seekers for less elusive prey will be quite content to follow Cotton's example,

> Oh, my belovèd nymph, fair Dove,
> Princess of rivers, how I love
> Upon thy flowery banks to lie,
> And view thy silvery stream
> When gilded by a summer's beam.

Past the "Pike Pool" and lower downstream is the wild scenery of Wolfscote Dale. Mill Dale comes next. Then begins Dove Dale, the sylvan and precious jewel of nation-wide fame needing no poor words of mine to sing its praises. The waters flow on in sight of the Weaver Hills. They circle past a Roman camp and Norman abbey foundations at Rocester, just miss Uttoxeter, once Roman, but better known for ancient markets and the present contents of the *White Hart*; at the carved panel on the conduit in the market place tears may be deposited for the sad story told by a penitent old man, Dr. Johnson:

> "Once I was disobedient; I refused to attend my father to Uttoxeter market. . . .
> A few years ago I desired to atone for this fault; I went to Uttoxeter in very
> bad weather, and stood for a considerable time bareheaded in the rain, on the
> spot where my father's stall used to stand."

Gliding along, curving endlessly through its lower wide vale, the river offers rapture here, joyous scenes there, and meets romance and history at Tutbury. Norman arches and rich carvings of the church remain from the priory founded by Earl Ferrers soon after the Conquest. John of Gaunt's castle, grim and ruined, crowns the height dominating the stream, the follower of two earlier strongholds destroyed in the years of the Normans and Simon de Montfort. Here was Mary Stuart's prison; ill, her beauty faded, the Queen of the Scots left through the gateway for the last time in 1585. King Charles came in 1645, hid after the disaster at Naseby. A year later General Brereton arrived and Cromwellians achieved the wreck now to be seen—proud Lancaster's two stately halls, window traceries, carved fireplaces, vaulted undercrofts, the stone gateway, buildings round the tilt-yard, all shattered and mouldy relics. Latterly the yard

Sydney
R. Jones
Reynard's Cave DOVEDALE

has staged only tilts, arguments, and a fight or two between antiquaries who mediate on mounds, stones, usually disagree on everything, and retire to the *Dog and Partridge*, an inn with black timbers intact after centuries of wear.

South of the River Dove lowish hills stretch around Marchington Woodlands and Hanbury. You spy over the Trent vale and far across Derbyshire. Near trees beautify the uplands. Names locate Bagot's Wood and Park, Woodend, Holly Bush, Abbot's Bromley, and Bagot's Bromley, where Bagots lived before Domesday Book was made. Trees and names remind of a pre-Conquest Needwood Forest, with 24 miles of it left in Queen Elizabeth's reign and recorded for 47,150 oaks in the time of Charles II. Oaks as big round as any number of men's bodies, and antique holly bushes here and there may be discovered and admired; but many of God's high standards have gone the way of other beautiful things that are slaughtered in man's quest for low standards of high living. Ancient families, settled hereabout almost as long as the oaks, are remembered by their effigies in the churches. At Blithfield in the Blythe valley, for instance, memorials to the Bagots portray members of the line that figured all down the pages of English history; on Hanbury hilltop repose carved monuments of the Hanburys, Adderleys, Agardes, and the Egertons. In the early days, when sport was state controlled, kings hunted deer through the Forest. To enable them to do so men were deprived of their homes and means of livelihood, even lost eyes, hands, life itself under the cruel Forest Law rigidly enforced before *Magna Charta* was sealed and Henry III reigned in King

DRONFIELD WOODHOUSE. *A farmhouse example of the stone tradition in east Derbyshire, a local style of building that is not widely known.*

STANTON-IN-THE-PEAK, *a stone-built village with cottages and three halls high above the Lathkill Dale. Many prehistoric remains in the neighbourhood include those on Stanton Moor and the great stone circle of Arbor Low.*

WATERGATE STREET, CHESTER, *has the best preserved sections of the Ror*
originated in the thirteenth or fourteenth century, were erected on the top of Rom

se unusual arrangements in streets are unique in England. They probably
dations, and have been continually transformed in succeeding centuries.

CARTLEDGE HALL on the heights between Chesterfield and Sheffield probably dates from the early 1500's. Inside are panelled interiors and enriched plaster ceilings. It was a manor-house of the Wolstenholme family and thus is linked with Canada by the name of Cape Wolstenholme at the head of Hudson Bay. The author Robert Murray Gilchrist lived here in the present century.

EYAM HALL in the Derbyshire dale country. The manor dates back to Saxon years. This hall was erected 10 years after the Plague had spread from London in 1665 and devastated the village.

John's stead. That is why inquisitive people, including myself, have gone to see a type of larking which originated in those misty years of Merrie England. Pranks are presented in the venerable little town of the abbots of Burton, Abbot's Bromley, on the Monday of the September Wakes. Then the deer-skulls with antlers, bows and arrows, and the hobby-horse come out of store from the church tower and the Horn Dance is performed. Now the dance is an amusing and lively caper through the streets in front of the black-and-white gables and spectators gladly pay tribute into a funny old bowl. But in the reign of Edward I the buffoonery had a real meaning. The natives danced with joy to celebrate their grant of the *Charta de Foresta*, which mitigated the severities of the Forest Law and restored their freedom.

Below the uplands of Needwood the Trent vale opens out wide. The river bends remarkably through level miles and winds out of Staffordshire and across south Derbyshire, reinforced first by the Dove and then by the Derwent. Landscapes are homely rather than spectacular. Flattish, with rises here and there, and far extended to distant low hills, this unmistakable Midland tract of pastoral country offers just the effects that might be expected. Scenes and features make pretty pictures of old villages, shady greens, halls amongst trees, church towers like the one at King's Bromley, a spire or two as at Repton, fields divided by hedgerows, quiet buttercup meadows, the wide deep Trent flowing between low banks, and the cows I saw lazily paddling in the stream on a hot summer day near the hermit's Anchor Church at Ingleby—pictures all very nice and very English. They can be sampled in pottering about the three Ridwares—Mavesyn, Hamstall, and Pipe—Yoxall, King's Bromley, and Alrewas, Staffordshire villages in the pastures watered by brooks and little streams running into the Trent. Mavesyn Ridware has a Tudor gatehouse, a dovecote, and carved armoured knights in the church, well worth finding and meaning that a Malvoisin left France in 1066, fought at the Battle of Hastings, and then settled his family in the parish. A quarrelsome lot were these Mal-voisins; some of them continued to live up to their French name for "evil neighbours," one derived from the movable engines used by old-time warriors for battering down walls, anything, and anybody standing in their way. To me this ominous tinge in the sweet air also seemed suitable for the place selected by Oliver Cromwell for hatching his plans to destroy a cathedral, mentioned previously in my note on Lichfield. If asked very politely the kind farmer at Hamstall Ridware manor-house (176) may show a visitor the good panelling and carvings of Henry VIII period, and the lofty watchtower too, relics of the departed mansion of the Leighs, whose Warwickshire home we round at Stoneleigh. Perhaps nicest of all in this part of the river vale is King's Bromley, once a home spot of Leofric, Earl of Mercia, husband of the celebrated naked lady of Coventry. The Trent glides past trees behind the fifteenth-century church tower and churchyard cross, and the prettiness of the village is emphasized with cottages, farmhouses, long barns and thatched roofs (176).

Past Alrewas the river turns north-east and sends along its gypsum waters to tickle up the beers at Burton-on-Trent. Without dwelling on blots added to landscapes through compounding beneficent products of hop-gardens and Trent water, it is better to contemplate an emblem of peace, the Dove, meeting the Trent, or to look across the broad vale to distant hills, visible from the Derbyshire soil at Newton Solney, centuries ago lived on by the de Solneys, now silent in stone and alabaster at the church. The characteristic scenes continue. There are the wide meadows, villages near the ever-winding stream, a charming group of church, rectory, and hall at Aston-on-Trent, a hall at Shardlow built of stone in 1684. Particular points for calling a halt include Repton, its medieval buildings at the school, the remarkable Saxon crypt in the church at this old capital of Mercia; the Georgian Cavendish Bridge put up in 1758, a gay spot in the coaching days on the route from London to the North; the medieval bridge at Swarkeston, a dismal spot in 1745 when the Young Pretender's advance petered out there, still a mile long, but a good deal altered since the thirteenth century and now without its chapel that used to stand at Stanton-by-Bridge; Melbourne, mentioned in Domesday Book, picturesque to-day, and noted for the Queen Anne gardens at the hall and the cruciform Norman church, one of the most interesting parish churches in England. Southward the woods and uplands rise from Ticknall, Calke and Hartshorne to the Leicestershire borders.

North of the Trent the sandstone plain is broken by patches of higher ground. Quiet villages, old-fashioned dreamy places like Findern, Etwall, and Sutton-on-the-Hill group round hilltops and hollows. Fine halls stand at Sudbury and Longford. Fame of the Middle Ages belongs to Chellaston and its hill. Alabaster from the quarries, artists, and the local craft workshops enriched the golden age of English handiwork. Particularly in the fourteenth and fifteenth centuries beauty spread from Chellaston to all parts of England, often abroad; it penetrated far and wide through the genius and skill of the men who created famous sculptured reredoses for altars, images, canopies, patterned tombs, and representations of armour and dress carefully rendered. Though many of these works met their doom from Cromwellians and other destroyers, numbers still remain fresh and vital to enthrall lovers of things stately and beautiful. In its prime years this busy centre, near medieval Derby and the ancient Trent crossing at Swarkeston, knew much coming and going while patrons and craftsmen flocked in and out; thus in 1414 the King's master mason of Rouen, de Berneval, visited Thomas Prentys "the alabasterman," the designer of the angel weepers with shields yet to be seen on a tomb in Lowick church, Northamptonshire.

To go across the stretches of productive land from Chellaston to Derby may seem like a jump of sorts from the golden age of English handiwork into the splendid epoch of genius for mechanical invention; a transition from carved alabaster that has lasted in beauty to locomotives with steam boilers, the finest petrol engines in the world, and other things for utility that eventually will end on Time's scrap-heap. If Derby is not one of my ideal towns for dreaming in, and is vitally remembered for platforms and sheds at a big railway centre, it has travelled through many stages and changes since Romans and Danes arrived and departed on roads and trackways now polished by motor cars. Normans built churches where five churches now stand. The chapel of St. Mary-on-the-Bridge, the timbered *Dolphin* in Queen Street, William Deusbury's Crown Derby porcelain, Joseph Wright the painter, and Samuel Johnson's marriage, all originated here in their various periods. Historical events happened, not to be detailed on these pages beyond a mention of the Young Pretender in and out of the town in December 1745, and whose whereabouts in that adventure we may find again on our way to Carlisle. Earlier years brought the Gothic church of All Saints with one of the finest Midland towers, completed in the sixteenth century shortly before the Reformation (195). The body of this church, demolished to the order of a turbulent parson, was replaced in 1723-25 by the graceful classic interior designed by James Gibbs. Splendid screens and gates, magnificently hand-wrought by Robert Bakewell, show this celebrated Derby smith's masterpiece, in its way and for its day quite comparable to the Derby mechanical feats in metal by Rolls-Royce in this present time o' day.

DERBYSHIRE HIGHLANDS AND THE CHESHIRE PLAIN

After Staffordshire, whose poor reputation for beauty I have endeavoured to raise a notch or two, northern Derbyshire presents me with an area of Dale and Peak country that still merits all the words of admiration showered by enthusiasts for many years past. Here are moors covered with heather, desolate heights, limestone cliffs, bold crags, ravines, rocky glens, caverns, waterfalls, luxuriant woods and verdure, fast clear streams, the Derwent, Wye, and Dove for rivers, deep gorges from Matlock and Dove Dales to Edale, Peak Forest leading up to the Peak at the end of the Pennines. Combinations of these natural features, the strong masses, varied groupings, the panoramas and distances where great clouds ride above untarnished glory offer exquisite landscape effects. Early natives left stone circles, many "lows," and Arbor Low, Derbyshire's competitor of Stonehenge. Romans used existing routes for conveying lead. At Castleton Peverel erected his Norman stronghold in a position most dramatic. Vernons settled down at Haddon Hall to create romantic picturesqueness that is hardly matched in all England. Dukes of Devonshire built the grand Renaissance mansion at Chatsworth (201) and the notable Crescent at Buxton. Stanton-in-the-Peak, Bakewell, Eyam, Sparrowpit, and more villages, remote hamlets, and towns made from the native stone, developed in wooded valleys and on hillsides. Dr. Johnson talked to Boswell of and in Dove Dale, declared that no one who had seen it need visit Scotland. John Ruskin remembered that in Monsal Dale,

> "You might have seen the gods there morning and evening, walking in fair procession on the lawns, and to and fro among the pinnacles of its crags."

The Derwent, a most beautiful river, bisects the county. Its course from south to north, which can be followed by road, gives the scenic transition complete. Pastoral landscapes of wide Trent–Derwent meadows extend at little more than 100 feet elevations around Cavendish Bridge and Wilne. Upward from Derby's railways and the Roman point of Little Chester the stream changes sandstone borderlands for the millstone grit and mountain limestone. From Duffield, prettily settled in its green hollow below slopes and the mound of Ferrers's huge Norman keep, banks and hills become higher and steeper. Belper and Ambergate passed, the characteristic and impressive groupings of limestone scenery mount up. Precipitous rocks, pinnacles, cliffs, and woods rise high from the waterside. Harmonies of cool stone tints and foliage colour bold shapes and varied arrangements. These fanciful designs piled by nature give effects of extraordinary beauty to which light, shade, and distance add brilliance and mystery. The vertical rifts of High Tor dominate the

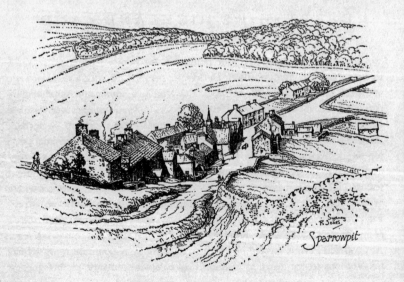

Sparrowpit

KNUTSFORD, *1906. King Street in Mrs. Gaskell's "Cranford."*

MALPAS. *One of Cheshire's pleasant smaller towns in the pastoral countryside. Here are timbered buildings in black and white, a good church with sculptured monuments to the Cholmondeleys and Breretons, and the mound on the hill recalls a border castle.*

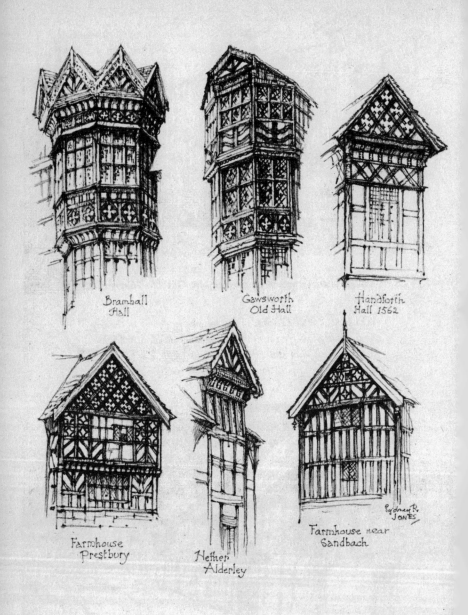

Bramhall
Hall

Gawsworth
Old Hall

Handforth
Hall 1562

Farmhouse
Prestbury

Hefner
Alderley

Farmhouse near
Sandbach

Sydney R.
Jones

CHESHIRE DETAILS *of patterns from the half-timber houses.*

setting of peculiar magnificence in Matlock Dale; from 800 feet high on Masson I have seen wonderful views of the river winding through the rocky gorge, with Tansley Knoll and Matlock Moor for backgrounds. At Oaker Hill —Wordsworth's "yon fair hill"—Darley Dale opens out in pastures and woods that continue to the old bridge of Rowsley. Here the Wye joins its parent stream after leaving Wye Dale and Topley Pike, circling round Chee Tor, shooting under the pointed arches of Bakewell Bridge, and passing Haddon Hall, one of the most romantic courses made by any river. It is an aristocratic Derwent in Chatsworth Park and looks so. The river, meeting the bridge ornamented with Cibber's carved figures, exactly fits the famed ducal scene of Talman's architecture (1687–1700) set in noble surroundings; whoever may have walked over the moor from Haddon to Chatsworth never will forget the first impression of the spectacle presented by "The Palace of the Peak," acres of lawns and gardens, parklands, continuous woods mounting to East Moor, the silver stream winding below, a perfect union of natural grouping enriched by man. Outside the park the three-arched bridge and stone cottages of Baslow have woods and steep hillsides to set them off, and the tree-clad slopes continue to Grindleford Bridge and Hathersage. The scenery rises higher and wilder, stretching up to the moors. The Hope valley opens out, directing to Castleton and Peverel's castle. Road and river traverse Derwent Dale between the Bamford Edge and Win Hill (1523 feet). The real Peakland heights are near. Years ago the Ashop river swept down from the solitudes of Kinderscout to its tryst with the Derwent under Crook Hill and Ladybower. The hills at present remain, but a spice of the romantic meeting has gone. Huge reservoirs have swamped most of Ashop Dale and extend for miles to the Slippery Stones on the Derwent at the Yorkshire border. They are dedicated to Sheffield and other centres of manufacture so that the inhabitants thereof can refresh and wash themselves.

Splendour of rocks, stream, foliage, and colouring are repeated along the course of the Dove at the western boundary of Derbyshire and obviously this river merits all the fame it owns; its paces and graces have been located in my previous Staffordshire notes. On and between the Dove, Wye, and Derwent are the dales, the Derbyshire Dales of Beresford and Dove, Ashwood, Miller's and Monsal on the Wye, Middleton (Eyam), Hope (Castleton) and others of renown, each abounding in exquisite pictures. One only do I particularize, the view of Monsal Dale and the sweep of the Wye seen from Little Longstone. On summer evenings I have watched the light flood this dale, trace patterns brilliant and dark over verdure and banks of trees, brighten exposed rocks and the tops of the heights, send lengthening shadows across the green floor and pick out the winding stream; there, and in other dales too, reality and suggestion can stimulate mental visions, gods in procession among the lawns, the pinnacles and crags such as Ruskin imagined, and much more than writer or artist ever set down on paper.

It is exhilarating to go from Ashford-in-the-Water up Kirk Dale, over Bole Hill, strike below the old marble quarries of Ricklow into Lathkill Dale, and thus sample specimens of the smaller wild dales that occur from Hartington and Winster up to the High Peak. The Lathkill stream hurries down through the steep and wooded glen, a true enchanted valley. Past picturesque banks the waters leap along to Conksbury bridge, Alport village and Alport Dale—enchanting waters all the way, pure and transparent as Charles Cotton saw them when he said they bred "the best trouts in England." Alport is one of my favourite villages, charmingly placed at the meeting of streams and dales. Stone cottages and gables stand high, low, and at quaint angles. Little waterfalls splash below rocks. Trout dart through pools by the bridge and round the mill. Natives welcome a stranger with the time o' day, and one kind soul used to tickle my appetite with strong tea and girdle cakes hot from her cottage hearth to help along my sketching—for here in Derbyshire, be it remembered, begins the north country famed throughout for girdle and tea-cakes. Apart from the joys of Lathkill Dale the surroundings are good. The stream joins the Wye near Haddon Hall. A big fifteenth-century tower at Youlgreave marks one of the best local churches. Stanton-in-the-Peak (207) is mounted high with its stone cottages, houses, and owns the three interesting halls of Stanton Old Hall, the eighteenth-century Hall in a deer park, and an Elizabethan Stanton Wood-house facing Darley Dale. Searchers for fine views or reminders of prehistoric ancestors can find all they may wish from Stanton Moor to the stone circle at Arbor Low.

The above-mentioned places, with towns, villages, and hamlets up and down this district, introduce the native architecture developed with stone quarried from the hillsides, an expression in traditional building that is seen with local variations all along the northern stone belt, the great Pennine backbone of England directing through Lancashire and Yorkshire to the Border. In Derbyshire the characteristics begin to show. Homes and domestic buildings have a sturdy look, appear strong and workmanlike. Wall surfaces, heavy surrounds to doorways and windows, roofs of stone slates often large in size, exhibit the nature and texture of the millstone grit and limestone. Details are bold rather than finely wrought, made in simple and straightforward ways without any show of affectation. Masonry from foundations to chimneys and also the roofs illustrate traditional methods in construction and usage. Thus built up, this distinctive stonework is significant and suggestive. It reflects the spirit of locality and the life it served. Determined largely by physical and climatic conditions and based on practices accumulated by experience from generation to generation, these buildings of Derbyshire and further north do in a manner make known the way of life, the character, and temperament of the native people who looked no farther than near quarries for resources and used the stone to meet their needs of hearth and home. These stone houses in towns and villages, the cottages and the farmsteads group and combine well together, and boundary walls of stone carry the prevailing theme into the fields and over hillsides to the mountains. But the northern grey stone-work sinks into the landscapes rather than stands out from them; it takes a secondary and right place in the scenes, as it should do where nature reigns predominant and has worked in fine creative mood to mount grand sweeping lines and big effects.

Explorers with eyes now and again off the scenery will notice the most finished examples of the native architecture in the south and east parts of this stone district. Interesting features and pictures are visible at manor-houses, farms, village groups, and town streets in leading up from Ashbourne through Parwich, Bonsall, and Winster to Rowsley, Bakewell, Baslow, and Eyam. Gabled cottages with worked mullions to the windows in Alport might be mistaken for Cotswold examples by the unobservant. The *Peacock* inn at Rowsley is a capital specimen of developed 1652 stonework; being a place of delight for fishermen, you know the kind of fare to be expected inside behind the carved bird of the Manners family. An Elizabethan school-house with six gables, the *Green Man*, houses, and almshouses add distinction to Ashbourne. Perhaps Dr. Johnson did not notice how nice they looked on his frequent visits, after his mental reflection on the Staffordshire canal and " the great efforts of human labour and human contrivance," and not all people find lowly architecture much in their line. But for those that do, well worth exploration are the parts of Derbyshire beyond East Moor and Owler Bar in the direction of Holmesfield, Unthank, Dronfield Woodhouse (207), Dronfield town, and on again past Chesterfield's crooked leaden steeple to Barlborough and Whitwell near the county boundary. Here are houses built centuries ago in a local style very fitting for the local scene. A very good style it was, developed in stone throughout for walls, roofs, chimneys, doorways, and mullions, and not widely known to-day because coal-mining progressed after these buildings were made and George Stephenson arrived to bring that kind of prosperity concerned with making money, spoiling landscapes, and frightening searchers for beauty. Northward, under the flanks of the Peak where the scenery mounts up, observation proves that the finish of the rural architecture went down. Sparrowpit, for one instance, shows very rough rubble walling and heavy stone roofs (214); and through the Peak Forest and high lands round Castleton the cottages and farms generally, dotted here and there over the open expanses, are structures of extreme simplicity built to withstand the severities of climate. Nevertheless, they look right in their locations, accord with the natural backgrounds, seem to be growths of the moors and the mountains.

Hardy folk who were born and bred in these Derbyshire dales, uplands, and moors, set their stamp on the manor-houses and roomy homes which they built for themselves and their followers, particularly during the sixteenth, seventeenth, and eighteenth centuries. They constructed solidly, usually achieved the strong and severe individuality common to the traditional masonry. Nearly all the villages show one or more of these houses. Two are Unthank Hall and Hallows Hall on the hill at Dronfield; and Elizabethan Wolleys, Milwards, and Batemans built their halls at Riber, Snitterton, and Hartington. Often they stand in view, to be spied at beyond entrance gates and piers, lawns and gardens; fortunate wanderers may penetrate inside to see the panelling, oak staircases, the frequent plaster ceilings, adjuncts of a past day-to-day life lived comfortably by squires and country people who generally kept on good terms with their neighbours, looked after dependants, served their country well, and filled a social niche in the antiquated system developed before tax grabbers and land grabbers ruled the English roost. I illustrate two examples. Eyam Hall (210), built by the Wrights and their home ever since, dates from 1676, some years after the terrible visitation of the Plague had devastated the village, and the heroic devotion of the Mompessons and Thomas Stanley had given Derbyshire one of its most moving stories. Cartledge Hall (210) sits squat and four-square to the wind and the weather on the moor a few miles south of Sheffield. A home of the old Derbyshire family of Wolstenholme, it probably began early in the 1500's. From here in the reign of Edward VI John Wolstenholme went to London, and it was his son John (1562–1639) who became the rich merchant adventurer, and after whom Henry Hudson and William Baffin named Wolstenholme Cape (1610), Island, and Sound (1615) during their adventures in the North-west Passage and Hudson Strait. Long ago the Wolstenholmes left their home, but inside you can see how nicely they did for themselves with oak-panelled walls, deep-set windows, ceilings of ribbed and modelled plaster, a carved fireplace representing the temptation of Adam and Eve to serve for a warning, and a fret to show the hours on a clock-face cunningly contrived in the panelling.

At this house in my own years lived the author of *The Gentle Thespians*, Robert Murray Gilchrist, true artist in words, a humble student and storyteller of the lives, lore, and home places of the Derbyshire hill folk. Huge in build, his frame held a big heart and a nature lovable and humorous. By the wide fireplace do I remember him with his bosom crony, George Garfitt, and lecturing me with impish delight on the sins of extreme youth, a reflection on the success of my first book published at the time by *The Studio*.

"Jones is only sixteen," he said to George. "Dreadful. He ought to be

CHESTER CATHEDRAL and St. Werburgh Street from Eastgate Street Row.
The Perpendicular tower crowns the former Benedictine abbey. It was converted
into a cathedral in 1541 and contains monastic features of great interest.

RABY. *A characteristic village group on the levels of the Wirral Peninsula near to the sands of Dee.*

SMALLWOOD. *A black and white farm-house of the type common in the Vale Royal.*

confined in a perambulator instead of cycling about to rob responsible workers of good bread and butter. And oh! the hairy butter he must consume for breakfasts at obscure pubs in prowling round out-of-the-way places! The thought makes me shudder. Much too young to be allowed off the lead."

"Have mercy, sir," I appealed. "I cannot help my looks and twenty-odd years. But what have you to say of your own efforts made in your teens?"

"That's the point," he gravely added. "You look on a warning, not an example."

Then he chuckled, ended leg-pulling, went to the old pianette by the window, played air after air charmingly and his tenor voice filled the room. Only a time or two more did I hear that voice or see those strong hands tinkling soft melodies. The gods winged the author away in his prime. The scenes that he loved and showed me in the High Peak to the west knew him no longer. His grave is in Holmesfield churchyard. Farewell.

Great families built the great houses. At Haddon and Chatsworth they gave to Derbyshire two of England's most famed and historic mansions. The manor-house at South Wingfield might have made a third if it had not come to grief in the Civil War. This home of Lord Treasurer Cromwell, dating from about 1440 and later a prison of Mary Queen of Scots in 1584, when the Babington plot was hatched, remains an extensive and interesting ruin of two courtyards, gatehouses, beautiful late Perpendicular windows, and one of the finest vaulted undercrofts in the country. Bess of Hardwick, proud collector of husbands, mansions, and vast wealth, made the immense windowed frontage of Hardwick Hall; the pierced parapets ornamented with the initials E S to flatter herself, and the Elizabethan showiness are retained unaltered to-day. Equally Elizabethan undiluted, but on a smaller scale, is Barlborough Hall, with its glassy bays and busy turrets erected to suit Judge Rodes in 1583. Where Peverel had ruled in Norman years at Bolsover, Cavendishs set up the early Renaissance walls, turrets, terraces, and long ranges of unfinished rooms, now grouped in dramatic skylines above the high rock on which, in 1634, courtiers performed Ben Jonson's masque of "Love's Welcome" before King Charles I. But for me Haddon is the prize. Occupying the slope above the Wye and banked in high trees of the upper ground, the setting is rare, perfect (202). The stonework blends, glints from the massed greenery in a fantasy of turrets, towers and chapel, bays and oriels, battlements of the upper and lower courtyards, gardens terraced towards the river. On outer walls and inside the great hall, state rooms, long gallery, and domestic apartments, the accumulations of craftsmanship in stone, wood, plaster, metals, and sixteenth-century leadwork tell the long story, adorn the tale of building, reconstruction, and enlargement successively advanced from the eleventh to the seventeenth centuries as Vernon followed Vernon and Manners followed Manners. Never a house for defence nor disturbed by wars, slowly developed during more than five hundred years and not altered since, it is an epitome of a way of thought and peaceful, cultivated life that gave lustre to a past England and beautified the scenes. That past is dead. Haddon expresses it, and nothing more captivating of the kind does any county show. The buildings continue lovely, cared for, rare and secluded. lived in by descendants of those who made them—for which, it seems to me, we ought to be thankful when the purpose, meaning, spirit, and charm of England's heritages are being shattered.

Up from Haddon and Bakewell through Taddington, Buxton, and Goyt's Moss to Macclesfield Forest, and there the Peakland heights soon drop to the levels. It is a bleak region, one in which travellers often have been glad to find the *Cat and Fiddle* at 1,690 feet above sea-level. The stone-built look is brought into Cheshire at Rainow and infrequent villages and hamlets. Stone field walls make sinuous lines over the slopes. Shuttlings Low (1,659 feet), Shining Tor (1,833 feet), and points all the way northward from Mow Cop (190) to Sponds Hill above Kettleshulme, well reward anybody in search of fine air and widespread views. You obtain overlooks swept from south, north, and westwards across the great plain of Cheshire. Distances blend with the outlines of Welsh mountains, where the River Dee winds from Llangollen bound for Chester and the sandy estuary at the Wirral Peninsula.

This Cheshire plain, widely viewed as stated above in remarkable prospects from the elevations above Lyme Park, Macclesfield and Congleton, also brings us to a gateway of the industrial North. Here the busy manufacturing centres of Merseyside face those in Lancashire. The tunnel connects Birkenhead with Liverpool. "People from Manchester and other big towns overflow into the country to grow bricks and mortar instead of crops," the agent of a large estate told me. Port Sunlight, the inspiration of its founder, William Lever, represents a splendid and pioneer effort in trying to make modern labour palatable to those who pursue it. Crewe, great and useful railway centre though it is, generally gives the impression of being dismal. Getting salt out of the earth from Nantwich to Northwich and Marston has produced peculiar streets and toppling houses settled out of the perpendicular; Boswell, bound for north Wales and evidently not interested in salt, summarily dismissed Middlewich as "a mean town, without any manufacture, but I think, a corporation"! Advantages and deficiencies such as these and the general flatness of the landscapes have caused observers now and again to dismiss Cheshire as being too busy and too level for real picturesqueness; it is not for me to direct my readers to the Vale Royal with the expectation of finding English scenery in its most exciting and spectacular mood.

But outside the industrial areas miles of real countryside spread far and wide.

There are many parks. Woodlands and meres denote a primeval character of forest and marsh. The rich agricultural land is coloured with pastoral greens and fertile surface textures. Prosperous farms and market gardens, the pastures, cattle, and cornfields make the rural scenes appear all the more friendly. A few isolated sandstone ridges break into the plain. The hill group at Alderley Edge, rocky and clad with fir trees, commands wide distances towards the Peak, Lancashire, and Wales; standing at the Armada beacon-stone in the evening I have seen fascinating effects of the lights twinkling five miles away at the hill town of Macclesfield. In the south another grouping is marked by Bickerton Hill, Harthill ridge, the Peckforton Hills, with a bold finish made at Beeston rock on which you can feel like a prophet viewing promised lands that seem to comprise half England. Strongholds of all ages on these wooded escarpments give a suspicion of romance, of "castles in the air." Though modern, the large castles of Peckforton and Bickerton stand out formidably from green backgrounds; poised on its cliff the thirteenth-century ruined walls and gatehouse of Beeston survive from Civil War batterings and Prince Rupert's escapades; far back in the Iron Age natives made the ramparts of Maiden Castle; and down below in Cholmondeley Park the towers and embattled walls would do very well for an excursion into the Middle Ages if they had not been erected in the eighteenth century by the ancient Cholmondeley family. The stretches of sandstone highlands from Tarporley to Frodsham are luxuriant with survivals of the great Forest of Delamere; here the British had their camp of Kelsborrow, and over the hills and through the forest Romans drove the route that still connects Chester and Manchester.

Across the plain are scattered attractive villages. The usual make-up is a good church built of the local sandstone, warm-coloured, often notable for a big tower finished with battlements and pinnacles; round about group old houses and cottages schemed in black timbers and white facings, a proportion of stonework, and eighteenth-century brick frontages. As likely as not the big house is one of the timbered manor halls for which the county is famous. Occasionally, as at Marton and Warburton, the timbered patterning is repeated by the ancient oak of the churches. Along the lanes and down in the fields the farmhouses add sparkle to the scenes with walls and gables of black and white; the effects they give are suggested by my examples sketched at Smallwood (222), Sandbach (216), Prestbury (216), and it is many years since I discovered the capital timbered cottages with overhanging dormers at Nether Alderley (216) and Artists' Lane, Alderley Edge. A number of the villages have particular interest and beauty to rank them as minor show-pieces; of these my space only permits a mention of Gawsworth, Lower Peover, Prestbury, Wybunbury, and Astbury completed at the corner of its green with a noble church and spire. Far afield in the deep rural country these pleasant places continue to Tushingham and Marbury near the Shropshire border and through the wide levels sloping down to the River Dee. Often a pretty out-of-the-way spot can bring to mind and fit a page out of *Cranford* :

"The aspect of the country was quiet and pastoral. Woodley stood among fields; and there was an old-fashioned garden where roses and currant-bushes touched each other, and where the feathery asparagus formed a pretty background to the pinks and gilly-flowers."

Cheshire's good examples of old English country towns resemble the villages for possessing sandstone churches and streets of black and white, brickwork, and stone buildings. Two worth finding are Audlem and Malpas in the country-side near Shropshire. Malpas, on a hillock facing Wales, and with a castle mound to recall the old border fighting, particularly attracted me for street pictures and Tudor details in the fine church containing the Cholmondeley and Brereton monuments (215). Progressing northward more pleasant town sights are offered in the long street of Tarporley; round the cross built on the rock at Lymm; at Parkgate and Neston on Wirral overlooking Dee sands and Welsh mountains; in the curious street with quaint houses and the stone gabled *Bear's Paw* inn at Frodsham, the home town and pastorate of Parson Gastrell, the scoundrel who pulled down Shakespeare's New Place at Stratford. Knutsford of course has literary and wide fame for being the original of *Cranford* and the place of Mrs. Gaskell's childhood (215). Popularity, modernism, and tea-shops have not dispelled all the qualities Miss Matty and Captain Brown knew; houses, streets, the seventeenth-century chapel, and little features help to add depths in the perspectives which still mirror a something of the fragrance and charm diffused by the gifted creator of the early Victorian ladies. My own and mundane reminiscences are liable to fix on the old *Angel* inn and the real Cheshire cheese it used to provide to aid me in my wanderings through this district.

Cheshire's most striking feats of architecture, the timbered buildings, are abundant in these small towns, in the larger towns among which Sandbach, Nantwich, Congleton, and Macclesfield may be cited, and throughout the countryside and the villages. Here, and in south Lancashire, we meet a culmina-tion of the native style in home construction that has shown brightly along our routes through Warwickshire, Worcestershire, Herefordshire, and Shropshire: the great domestic building style of the West, indigenous to and developed from the wooded and forest lands until it was superseded by the widespread use of brickwork in the seventeenth and eighteenth centuries. The timbering in Cheshire has ornate arrangements of black woodwork and white panels, storeys overhanging one above another, bays of extraordinary shapes, elaborate carv-ings on bargeboards, beams and brackets, combinations which border on the bizarre and fantastic. These may be thought either startling, masterpieces of late

RIBCHESTER, *at the site of the large Roman fortress on the River Ribble. The porch of the White Bull inn is supported on four Roman columns.*

HALL I' TH' WOOD, TONGE. *Tudor post and plaster in black and white. This fine example was presented to the Bolton Corporation by Lord Leverhulme. Here in 1779 Samuel Crompton invented and worked the Mule for spinning.*

BORWICK

CLAUGHTON
Old Hall

TURTON
TOWER

THURLAND
CASTLE

TOWERED HALLS IN LANCASHIRE

Tudor, Elizabethan, and early seventeenth-century carpentry, or like nothing on earth; and indeed the manor-houses and halls, led by the incomparable Moreton, certainly are unique in England for their variety and exuberant patterning. They stand in all directions; in line from Little Moreton Hall towards Manchester at Brereton, Gawsworth (216), Chorley Hall (Alderley), Adlington, Woodford, Handforth (216), and Bramhall (216), at Moss Hall (Audlem), Holford, Tattenhall, Poole on Wirral, and village after village presents particular specimens. They are standing reminders of the old Cheshire families, the Warburtons, Fittons, Stanleys, Breretons, Leghs, Davenports, Mainwarings, and their like, many of whose monuments are to be found in the neighbouring churches.

The half-timbered style of these homes, one dear to the hearts of latter-day English people and sometimes sniffed at by innocents who see no more in it than antique combinations of the pretty-pretty, has suffered in repute from overmuch enthusiasm by admirers and because modern producers of fakes plastered town and country with cheap effects in black and white. Though the style is dead and could have no place in the life of to-day, it was true and real when it flourished, a logical expression of ideas in materials, construction, and workmanship. The inheritance from Gothic times dictated general principles and influenced the shapes of overhanging projections, gables, oriels, wood mullions, angle posts, and enrichments, all of which took new forms of detail as fashions moved with the impulses brought by the Renaissance. These Cheshire halls and houses, with those in south Lancashire, framed in timbers pegged together with oak pins and faced in panels of wattle and daub, reached their prime development and complexity in the 1500's and the early part of the following century, a period in which men's craniums and homes were not so exposed to summary cracks and dangers as in earlier years. Times had become more settled. Life could be lived comfortably, prosperously, even luxuriously. Provision might safely be made for generations to come. Scantlings of the timbers and the richness of effects show that the creators of these homes spared neither materials nor workmanship. They built with pride and in oak to last. Their work, tied with beam, mortise and tenon, became truly indicative of human character and an English way of life. Exteriors, and interiors now existing at Bramhall and elsewhere, with panelled walls, rich chimney-pieces, massive staircases, and carved fittings, illustrate the vivid domestic interlude of the sixteenth and seventeenth centuries. They show how and where men and women lived who saw the beacons on Overton Hill and Alderley Edge flash news of the Armada. Timbers and patterns call to mind adventurous days in which the wide world was sighted by Drake and Raleigh, days when the nation reached out to fuller expression in the flush of hope and expectation while poets and dramatists tuned exquisite numbers to the rhythm of brilliant years. In these present times, conspicuous for planning, controlling, and docketing inanimate things and human objects as economic units in a system notable for prefabricated miseries, it can be quite refreshing to ponder on such an old stalwart as Uryan Brereton contemplating with just pride the finishing touches on his fine entrance porch at Handforth, complete with uneconomic enrichment, arms, crest, and the inscription that still testifies,

"This haulle was buylded In the yeare of oure Lord God M. CCCCC. LXH by Uryan Breretoun Knight Whom maryed Margaret daughter and heyre of Wyllyam Handforth of Handforth Esquyer and had Issue VI sonnes and II daughters."

Original builders of timbered houses also knew a thing or two about prefabrication. It was customary to prepare the oak at "framing-places" before erecting on actual sites. Posts, vertical and horizontal timbers, beams and joists, were assembled together, the position of each piece being marked with a number, many of which are still visible lightly cut on the timbers. The structures then went to their sites for final erection. These mobile houses thus could be taken to pieces and fitted together elsewhere. One house I know of departed to Kent, where it now stands. In Shropshire, at Shrewsbury, the house at the castle gate originally stood in Castle Street, and a number of the Cheshire homes have been carefully pulled down, packed up, and exported to begin life anew in America. A good deal might be said in favour of these dwellings nowadays. Nasty neighbours or unpleasant conditions in general can be changed any time by moving house, bed, and hope for experiments in fresh directions. I live in a timber-framed house myself!

More timbered buildings attract us to Chester, the historic gateway to Wales for nearly 2,000 years, and also a pointer to the North, whither our tracks next lead. In this English show-town the large quantities of famous black-and-white decorate the streets in the gayest possible fashion and brightly animate scenes bustling with shoppers, tourists, traffic, antiques for sale, trippers in chars-à-bancs, and battalions from neighbouring industrial conglomerations invading to win the beaches, sea, and breezes of the Welsh resorts. It cannot be denied that Chester gives the impression of being a very lively and busy place, brilliant with high lights and the blackest of blacks when the sun shines. Jostled by crowds in the Rows, running up and down little stairways, and quizzing here and there, you find timberwork both genuinely ancient and obviously recent. It needs sorting out by those on the lookout for old patterns. Things have been erected in the newer antiquated manner that might make even the builders of Little Moreton Hall turn in their graves, and it is possible to enjoy tea and bread and butter under timbers hoary with stain and not age. But in this grand old city one need not carp overmuch on articles genuine and imitative standing in juxtaposition. They impel both admiration and amusement and can offer much for exhilaration. That is the right spirit for setting out to see and do Chester.

Centuries before the timbering arrived in bulk Chester began its crowded history which carries the English story far back and might fill volumes. Roman *Deva*, settled by the Twentieth Legion on the Dee estuary, successively fell to the Northumbrians, the Danes, and the Mercians. Before the Conquest it was important enough to have its own mint and royal palace. Conquering William made Chester one of the castled key-points for the dual purpose of defending the Welsh border and keeping his own turbulent companions in order. Here Hugh de Avranches spied out his chances, just as Roger de Montgomery did at Shrewsbury and William FitzOsborn at Hereford. When the last Norman earl died the earldom passed to the Crown and ever since has given the title of Earl of Chester to the eldest son of the King. An early church, by tradition founded in Roman times, developed into the powerful Benedictine Abbey of St. Werburgh. Kings arrived and departed both for warlike and peaceful deeds. One, Henry III, strengthened the castle with stone walls and towers; another, Richard II, mounted on a "nagge not worth 40 francs," got locked up there on his way to be deposed.

After early disturbances and unpleasant occasions Chester prospered and grew splendid. It did so in spite of fires, plagues, floods, and constant attacks by fierce Welshmen. The walls, first built by the Romans, were kept in order and further extended to the west and to the south in line with the river and the bridge. At various points towers rose above them. Strong gateways, replete with the contrivances of welcome for intruders usual in the Middle Ages, guarded entrances from the east and west, the north and the south. The port, outside the Watergate and defended by the Water Tower, brought wealth and prosperity with trade over the seas.

These walls, gates and towers enclosed the varied aspects of beauty, sparkle and gloom common to a medieval city of first rank. The castle made a base for war expeditions. Under the Norman earl, Hugh Lupus, Lord of the Welsh Marches, the Mercian church became the abbey of the Benedictines in 1093. It gained landed possessions far and wide and riches flowed in to the shrine of St. Werburgh. Black, Grey, and White Friars had their own establishments. Mansions served for town quarters of the county families. Sheriffs from Norman times, mayors onward from 1238, and the guilds all played their important and customary rôles. Groups of tradesmen and craftsmen banded together, kept to their own particular quarters mostly in sections of the curious Rows built on Roman foundations. Lines of buildings then newish, and here and there now remaining to show the old and worn faces of age, made backgrounds for movement and brave colouring as civic ceremonial, mystery plays, and pageants wound from street to street. These added liveliness to the regular scenes; a wonderful "Deluge" performed by the Water-leaders and Drawers of the Dee, "St. George and the Dragon," and the "Devil very boisterous" gained high favour. The mills near the end of the bridge ground corn for the whole population and at least one "jolly miller . . . sung from morn till night." The bridge itself, almost certainly first built by the Romans, mentioned in Domesday, rebuilt in the late 1200's, and arched to its present form in 1347, gave Chester particular importance by affording the strategic crossing into north Wales at the head of the Dee estuary. Unpleasant circumstances also developed behind the outward show. Raiding Welshmen, fires, plagues, and floods aforementioned did not add lustre to the city's most glorious years; and dungeons, one of them thirty feet deep in the rock, were only seen by certain people. But, all in all, medieval Chester with its walls and buildings, life, activities and diversions must have presented a shining example of a thriving centre in the old days, one very nice to think of and picture in bright trappings, especially if you prefer to forget, the smudges, the sanitation, and the dungeon chains.

Tangible reminders of the medieval brilliance, of the earlier phases, and of Tudor and succeeding centuries help to make Chester the great place it is for absorbing strong doses of historical suggestion and preserved beauty in circumstances that offer explorers no perils, and every comfort and discomfort of this age. Even the beams in the Rows, at *Ye Olde King's Head*, the *Grosvenor Hotel*, and the cafés do not administer bumps on the heads of the unwary, as sometimes happens in less sophisticated and more barbarous directions. The city's early beginnings in *Deva*, the fortress and Romano-British settlement with a port outside the Watergate, can be traced at many points and under the houses within the original rectangular area bounded by the north and east town walls. The crowded traffic in Eastgate Street, Northgate Street, Watergate Street, and Bridge Street follows the exact directions trodden by the Twentieth Legion. After the departure of the Romans and a gloomy period of which little is known, Chester brightened up and gained in status during late Saxon, Norman, and medieval years. Little of the once-important castle is visible. Embattled walls and the apparatus of war and chivalry were removed in 1789. A thirteenth-century tower with a chapel is the chief sustainer of glory and crime departed. A thriving port, source of great prosperity in the Middle Ages, is merely suggested by the landlocked Water Tower, built in 1322 for £100. In the fifteenth century the Dee decided to silt up. The port ran short of water. Consequently fame and fortune washed round to a lowly neighbour that eventually achieved celebrity under the name of Liverpool. Long ago, too, the monks ceased to chant over against the eastern town wall. But their abbey, converted into a cathedral of the new foundation by Henry VIII in 1541, is a perpetual and beautiful reminder of them. There are preserved the emblems of their faith, their times and life—the cloisters where they walked, meditated, and studied; the lavatory at which they washed; a noble refectory for meals below the

LANCASTER, *eighteenth-century and medieval. The Judge's lodgings below the castle built on the site of a Roman station.*

LANCASTER. *The ancient stone-built town on the River Lune is ca[*
fortress, of which the great keep remains. The church interior is

...ae castle and parish church. John of Gaunt restored the Norman
...urteenth-century stallwork of tracery patterns and foliage carving.

OLD LANCASHIRE COTTON MILL on the River Lune. The valley near this point below the Pennines made the subject for Turner's "Crook of Lune," and Ruskin described the view at Kirby Lonsdale as "one of the loveliest scenes in England—therefore in the world."

reader's rare stone pulpit; the great church of their praise and worship; remains of the fourteenth-century shrine of St. Werburgh that once was so gorgeous (and profitable); and most exquisite of all, the choir stalls and misericords of 1380 where Benedictines continuously performed acts of devotion amidst carved work and canopies, whose glory is hardly matched on earth nor probably in heaven.

In addition to the much-restored cathedral, old churches are well represented by St. Peter's, St. Mary-on-the-Hill, and St. John's. The last-named, probably founded under the Mercian rule, once a cathedral and now partly ruined, is an architectural prize, wonderfully impressive with Norman arcades and transitional upper work. In streets and byways the famed timbered houses and inns display the Cheshire black-and-white in its liveliest showing of contrasts and enrichment. Wide windows of many mullions extend across complete frontages. Elaboration reaches a climax at Bishop Lloyd's early seventeenth-century house in Watergate Street and at the *Bear and Billet*, dated 1664, in Lower Bridge Street, a former town house of the Earls of Shrewsbury. A good sprinkling of houses indicate late seventeenth- and eighteenth-century years. These make prim groups in Abbey Square, Bridge Place, and elsewhere; but their classical features and Georgian suggestiveness are not enhanced by the dull-coloured brickwork common in the north of England.

Of all Chester's weathered and still useful possessions the Rows and the walls are the oddest and most remarkable. No other English town retains a complete line of walled fortifications and nowhere else can be seen anything just like the Rows (208–209). How the Rows came into being nobody can say with certainty. Most likely the medieval builders did the obvious thing to do. Faced with extensive Roman ruins along the main streets, they made shops in front of the debris at street level, erected higher shops actually on the top of the ruins, and the flat roofs of the lower shops gave the walks, or rows, for access to the upper shops. This is certain. The Rows, which are first mentioned in early fourteenth-century records, only occur within the limits of the Roman settlement. Roman remains exist beneath them, Gothic crypts too, and fine old rooms are screened behind dark timbers. These strange ways, medieval leavings much touched up, permit one to look out over balusters to see how the world wags and keep dry when it rains (221). At any time you can walk or sit down on the top of the bits and pieces of centuries and centuries and wonder whether the shadows may shape into phantoms of Elizabethans, Plantagenets, or even Romans! Certainly the Rows of Chester, their curiosities and quantities of old curiosity shops, are unique.

Doubts and theories do not shroud the walls, their origin in Roman times and the subsequent extensions to the river frontage. Almost two thousand years meet at these walls. They have endured through wars, raids, sieges, bombardments, and fruitful times of peace bright with high hope, piety, and endeavour. What an excitement it is to walk round these walls! The footway leads for nearly two miles abreast of stone parapets. It goes by five towers from Thimbleby's to Bonewaldesthorne's, over seven gates, up and down steps, skirts the cathedral and the castle, and gives views of streets and buildings below, the river coursing over the weir to the bridge, and the distant mountains. Here, without twists of imagination, you really may feel like an Elizabethan, a Plantagenet, or a Roman, King Henry on the lookout for who might be coming from Wales, King Charles in the blues while seeing the defeat of his army from the Phœnix Tower in 1645; or you can just waddle along like an ancient duck stuck in the tracks of old time until roused into the day before yesterday at the recent Newgate, finely designed by Sir Walter Tapper.

Remembering all that the fortifications were made for and have been through, they may not be deemed especially economic, useful, or valuable to this age of paper currency. But since the walls were put up in stone they have accommodated all sorts of social and domestic incidents. In the early days no doubt other ranks of the Twentieth Legion chased British damsels round the parapets just as warriors off duty recently did flirting duties there with females. Miss Aldersey eloped down into the arms of her lover in 1573. Hopeful souls have been wishing while running up and down the Wishing Steps since 1785. George Borrow, out to conquer *Wild Wales*, met the ragged beggar, and the black man who lied, said work did not agree with him and "spat with considerable force in the direction of the river." This stonework, after maintaining an equilibrium for centuries and centuries, now keeps quite up to date by serving for pedestrian airings, lovers' meetings, somewhere to go for trippers off chars-à-bancs, and quite remarkably, for planned and unexpected encounters. Time and again I have been hailed and stopped with the exclamation, "Whoever would have thought of seeing you here!" and that is because people of all counties, nations, and languages go to see these unique fortifications of England. Of course all my readers have done so, will do so again; then perhaps—you never can tell—we all may meet, stand, look, admire the views and each other, and finally descend the steps to celebrate the occasion at somewhere or other in the treasured city gathered round the ancient walls of Chester.

5. NORTHWARD BOUND

LANCASHIRE, WEST YORKSHIRE BORDER, WESTMORLAND, CUMBERLAND

The scenery in this chapter's district is notable for mountains, moors, the Lakes, rivers of exceptional loveliness, signs of Border fighting, and England's greatest industrial concentrations. The Limestone heights of the Pennines strike northward to Cumberland; the dales run down into Yorkshire. Over the Lakes rise the peaks and dramatic outlines of the Cumbrian rocks. The Ribble, Lune, Eden, Irthing, and other rivers wind through beautiful valleys; their waters reach the low coastline broken by inlets and the tidal expanses of Morecambe Bay, Duddon Sands, and Solway Firth. Where nature's work predominates the stone-built efforts of man in villages and towns are not of much account, duly insignificant, and therefore appropriate. Elsewhere factories and smoking chimneys in Lancashire and Yorkshire tell their own tales of human enterprise and commercial prosperity. Scant relics of Hadrian's Wall, ancient towers at Skipton, Lancaster, Appleby, Carlisle, Naworth, castles in ruins, and many peel towers recall past strife in this land of ballad and story, the romantic ground in safer and later years for celebrated poets, novelists, and artists.

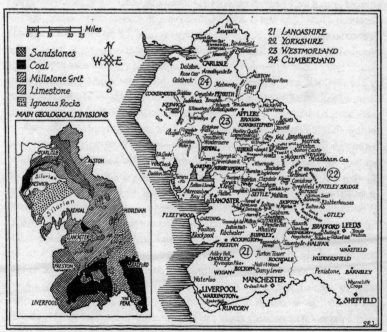

LANCASHIRE AND PENNINE COUNTRY

The obvious beginning for the next advance is to find or imagine ourselves just beyond the top ends of Cheshire and Derbyshire and prepared to face the best and the worst among a hundred manufactures in the greatest concentrations of industrial activity in England. These spread over south Lancashire and the West Riding of Yorkshire in the big and hilly area resembling a roughly-shaped parallelogram, with Runcorn and Sheffield, Leeds and Preston to mark the corners, and containing the emporium for cotton at Manchester, the centre for wool at Bradford, the home of steel at Sheffield. Just beyond this figure stands the great port of Liverpool, wonderfully placed at the end of the Mersey and facing the sea, a gateway to far countries and continents. Everybody knows of the English history made during the past century or two in this populous and busy region, and how the inhabitants set examples to the world in skilled manufacture, commercial enterprise, and speculation while they contributed to the country's material power, prosperity, wealth, and drabness. Things they thought of and did on certain days were only discovered by people elsewhere on the days following or some time afterwards, and qualities of foresight and shrewdness, highly developed locally and helped by nature's copious supplies of moist climate, soft water and bracing air, no doubt spurred onward John Kay, Hargreaves, Samuel Crompton, Arkwright, James Nasmyth, Benjamin Huntsman and a host of inventors, innovators, and astute men of business in the efforts and contributions they made to the evolution of England's commercial supremacy. The merchants of Manchester who began to run their own "Flying Coach" regularly to London as early as 1754 in order to take Time by the forelock, and the first main railway line in the country engineered by George Stephenson for much the same purpose from Liverpool to Manchester 76 years later, are but two instances of many schemes initiated for beating the clock, getting things done, and flowing on the tide that Shakespeare said leads to fortune in the affairs of men. Sightseers to-day in Warrington, Wigan, and Accrington, Huddersfield, Barnsley, Pudsey, and the crowded towns linked together for miles find ample evidence of the old progressive spirit furbished up and continuing in operation. It is still possible to learn and to realize that "You must wake up very early in the morning to get the better of a Lancastrian and to get the better of a Yorkshireman means not going to bed at all"—compliments recently told to me on the spot and which I understand are called chestnuts and also thought to be true.

If this book were in praise of commercial cities and districts, and of monuments to man's miracles in manufacture and production, I might say a good deal at this halt in our progress on the north side of the Mersey. But these present pages make no such claim; in that direction I consider my bit already

PENISTONE. *Kirkwood farmhouse with walls and roofs of local stone.
It stands between Sheffield and Huddersfield where high lands lead to the
moors and mountains of South Yorkshire.*

BOLTON ABBEY IN WHARFEDALE. A lovely combination of ruins and parish church adjacent to the seat of the Dukes of Devonshire. Built in a setting of exceptional beauty, this priory of Austin Canons formed one in the chain of great monasteries notably developed in Yorkshire. It continued at this site from 1151 until the Dissolution in 1539.

has been done with my sampling of the Black Country, Birmingham, the Industrial Revolution, and a matter of England's artistic heritage going bankrupt after Adam Smith made himself heard from Scotland. The well-known particulars, the towns, and the points of geography mentioned in the previous paragraph are given only because they relate to topography and caused re-arrangements in scenery. The area we now face offers curious contrasts for observation in the thickly populated spaces and strips of country sandwiched in between drab concentrations and smoke. Effects are varied, often unusual, sometimes impressive, yet the ground in general is not the kind that Thomas Cook would have selected for shepherding his tourists. But this cradle of industrial supremacy presents matter for meditation to inquisitive minds, and certainly has improved since Walpole considered Sheffield one of the foulest towns in a most charming situation, Blake sang of "dark satanic mills," the old saying announced, "From Hell, Hull, and Halifax, Good Lord, deliver us!", and the factory and chimney-stack system of progress proved that acceleration did not always achieve advance forward or enhance landscapes.

Writers on the English scene usually have not showered large bouquets of praise hereabout. Artists however, particularly recent ones, have found subject-matter awaiting to glorify, justify, apologize for, or present as it is the age of rationalism and scientific determination in which humanity latterly has struggled. From the back ages, too, relics have survived in the hurly-burly of making things new; they remain, grimy perhaps and strangely neighboured, yet mellow with suggestiveness of Middle Aged mysticism and of times that flourished before machinery conquered. Old houses stand, left over from the handicraft years. Hall i' th' Wood is one of them (227), a sixteenth-century home of the Brownlow family, once surrounded by great trees and facing woods as its name implies, and now facing Bolton. Inside this house, hand-made with oak framing, staircase, and carved fireplaces, it is curious to recall that Samuel Crompton lived frugal days and laborious nights in making and perfecting the "Hall i' th' Wood machine" for spinning, an innovation which hastened the change from handwork to mechanical production, brought great prosperity to the neighbourhood and England, and bestowed on the inventor little more than misfortune and poverty. This hall is but one of the examples conspicuous for timber construction and black-and-white patterns, a style of building formerly as prevalent in south Lancashire as in Cheshire. Led by Speke Hall near Liverpool, the most famous specimen completed in 1598, the timbered buildings in towns and their borderlands exist in greater numbers than is generally supposed and give Elizabethan flavours in directions where least expected. They are numerous, for instance, at and round Manchester, not infrequently hemmed in by mean surroundings. There the series includes Ordsall Hall with features of exceptional interest, and Clayton Hall, a home of

Humphrey Chetham who is ever remembered for the gracious medieval and cloistered Hospital that bears his name.

Other houses and halls show the northern type of masonry generally dating from the sixteenth and seventeenth centuries, the stone walls and heavy roofs, the low-pitched gables, the windows of many mullions. As might be expected, these are plentifully distributed in the Yorkshire section and particularly between Bradford, Wakefield, and Halifax, as at Hagstocks in Shibden Dale and Oakwell Hall, Birstall, built in 1583 and pictured by Charlotte Brontë in *Shirley*. Towns, too, preserve and care for their heirlooms—Bolling and Horton Halls at Bradford, Shibden Hall, Halifax, a splendid and historic Temple Newsam at Leeds, and more inheritances from the old families. Turton (228) introduces the peel tower, the form of defence peculiar to the northern counties and devised for the protection of hearth, home, and possessions when marauders from over the Border were almost as numerous as present-day raiders for taxes and spoliation of country. Solid and squat, Turton Tower stands near the Roman highway that led to Manchester from the great fortress now buried beneath Ribchester (227), a route used for centuries by plunderers in their descents on the Ribble valley and the fertile lands of south Lancashire. The massive tower, probably of early fifteenth-century date, with Elizabethan additions of timber and stone, came into the possession of Humphrey Chetham, the rich merchant, money-changer, and benefactor of Manchester.

Here and there old mills, in service or ruined, link with the early spinning and weaving; they modestly contrast with their successors, the giants of many windows, gaunt façades, and high chimneys. One of the older sort, though outside this big industrial area, is illustrated on page 236 to show the traditional stone architecture that served both for domestic and industrial buildings and made factories more pleasant to look at than those which followed in the nineteenth century, some of the most deplorable objects ever produced by man. More ancient and nobler buildings, the churches, are obvious in various directions, as at Wakefield, Bradford, Halifax, Rochdale, and the fine fifteenth-century work at Manchester (now the cathedral) splendidly adorned with interior woodwork. These represented the good old custom of mixing religion with business. Medieval masters and men of the crafts combined pious observance with daily labour, helped to make and support the Gothic churches inside which they went pretty often—for weavers already were settled in Wakefield in Conquest years, at Bolton in the twelfth century, and the workers in Manchester had fame for cloth as early as the thirteenth century and for cottons and woollens in the sixteenth. Wakefield became famous for its remarkable miracle plays. Once, far away at Wilburton near Ely, I immediately thought of Bradford on discovering an ancient fresco depicting St. Blaise. This bishop of Sebaste in Asia Minor appears to have lost his head after being torn with iron combs by Roman persecutors more than sixteen hundred years ago, and then passed on to become the patron saint of the wool-combers. In Yorkshire, and particularly in Leeds and Bradford, he was highly venerated and his festivals, splendid occasions celebrated with joy and pageantry, included the pretty eulogy beginning with the lines,

> Hail to the day whose kind, auspicious rays
> Deigned first to smile on famous Bishop Blaise.

In fact, more numerous than is generally appreciated are the varieties of historical association, scene, beauty amongst ugliness, and stimulating experiences offered in this kingdom of industrialism, one strangely unfamiliar to most English people because they seldom explore there. Here are natural and man-made effects for enjoyment, praise or blame, instances of tremendous gains and tremendous losses, the pointers in the country's story common throughout England and which make the miles everywhere vivid with matter to see and something to think about. These afford memories. Out of past experiences I think of the pattern and character of Liverpool from sketching the shipping, banks, busy streets, the impressive Mersey frontage viewed across the water, the interior and tower of the Mersey Tunnel; from watching the animated life on land and water at the Landing Stage, seeing the great ships pass by and the sun setting in splendour at Waterloo where Turner looked out, dreamed and painted; from exhibiting at the Walker Art Gallery, and by recollections of two cathedrals in the making, to give to the city and posterity the great conceptions of Sir Giles Gilbert Scott and Sir Edwin Lutyens. Of Manchester, superior for gloom and damp, I recall depicting the array of begrimed chapels, the late-medieval carving on beautiful stalls and the parclose screens at the cathedral, and also on one occasion sketching towels, pillow cases, pants and their feminine equivalents, and almost the complete range comprised in the term, "Manchester goods." This collection of objects, with recent art represented by the notable design of the Central Library by Vincent Harris, the Anning Bell window inside it, the Ford Maddox Brown frescoes in the town hall, and literature's pages suggested by Mrs. Gaskell's associations with the old Cross Street Chapel and De Quincey running away from the school, seemed to me to express the purpose and the soul of the ancient and the great modern city. While engaged with the mundane articles above mentioned a shining light in the cotton constellation invited me to the Reform Club, a name that made me wonder if Peterloo and politics were much in my line.

"Is this really the holy of holies," I asked on arrival, "Free Trade, John Bright, and all that?"

"Yes, this is the spot," was the curt reply. "Come and have some lunch."

We sat down at one of the long tables lined with men eating hot stew to which they had applied cold pickled red cabbage. The combination, then new to me, suggested pains inside the human apparatus. Bravely I joined in, consumed the hot and cold mixture; to do so evidently was *comme il faut* in Manchester. Immediate impressions were good, after-effects harmless. "Thus is accumulated intimate knowledge of great peoples" I muttered as I sauntered across Piccadilly to my quarters at the *Queen's* hotel. Bolton, where my early morning slumbers were sadly rattled by the clatter of clogs on the stone pavings, gave me memories of Hall i' th' Wood here illustrated, Darcy Lever Hall going to ruin, and the black-and-white *Olde Man and Scythe* inn from which James Stanley, the Royalist Earl of Derby, went to his doom after being captured at the battle of Worcester in 1651. Chorley, not quite the place for summer holidays, presents its industrial character unashamed; but I found Astley Hall in the town's possession, weathered, lovely, containing the Elizabethan long gallery 72 feet in length, and the Astley bed of about 1590, enormous, a very king of beds, wonderfully carved and inlaid, the most remarkable specimen of its period in existence and fully justifying a pilgrimage. In all directions are the concentrations of mills, factories, and chimneys, grime, gloom and vapours, unlimited in supplies for those who like to seek the emblems of work and power that truly express the spirit and functions of the locality. Yet on these I have seen the veil of romance and poetry descend where little of either might be expected; remembered by massive purposeful compositions and gaunt shapes swathed in mist, entrancing evening light shimmering on wind-swept smoke and making drabness glow, and once, at Sowerby Bridge near Halifax, brazen beauty shining from woollen-mill windows lit up at night and defying the darkness.

The hills, always near, offer compensation enough for anything. Sweeping northward from the Peak, the Pennine heights divide industrial Lancashire from industrial Yorkshire. They send out moorland masses west and east, the wide and airy open spaces handy for those whose lives are cast amidst "the busie humm of men" (and machines) in the towns thickly planted on the lower slopes and along the valleys. The town workers certainly have good cause for thanks to God and nature for these high places of wild beauty so little distant from dingy streets and ugliness, large expanses as yet unspoiled, nor very likely to be knocked down or removed at present to satisfy the money-getting propensities of man. Within a few miles of the smoke of Bolton, Horwich, and Chorley anyone can be on Smithills Moor mounted at nearly 1,500 feet, on Rivington Pike commanding land and sea and where the beacon flamed in the Armada year. It's an easy and quick change from the unloveliness of Bacup, Accrington, and Burnley to the solitudes of Rossendale and over the hills and far away into Yorkshire. You can be high up among the mills of Queensbury, look over miles and miles of moors, choose any direction for exploration without fear of being much disturbed by human beings, and wander over the lonely

KEX GILL GORGE *between Blubberhouses Moor and Brandreth Crags.*

BUTTERTUBS PASS *from Wensleydale to Swaledale.*

CARTMEL. *A quiet and ancient town with this early fourteenth-century gateway and an exceptional church, remains of the priory of Austin Canons founded about 1189.*

DENT. *The narrow street high placed in Dentdale below the Yorkshire fells and Whernside. Made of stone throughout for walls, roofs, and street paving.*

spaces of Oxenhope and Haworth Moors to scenes of the Brontë drama, to Ponden and actual places pictured in *Wuthering Heights* and *Jane Eyre*. In no time I have been away from Sheffield, past Wharncliffe Crags, up the hill at Penistone to sketch the characteristic stonework of Kirkwood farmhouse (241), and on again through the stone-walled fields and the commons, where I met a farmer one day, stockily built and tanned, who told me that on these high-lands not many really hot days are known, even in the best of summers—a chilly prospect for southerners, like Maria Brontë, born in more genial climates. Also there are the lookouts from the hills to the towns below, sometimes tuned in symphonies of smoke and sunshine, sometimes bright with industry's myriads of lights when night falls. Once, when going from Pendle Hill to the Ribble valley I spied Preston in the distance, a forest of chimneys all a-smoking and weaving changes and changes of pattern upward towards the azure, a sight wonderful enough to make a body think that after all a good deal might be said for industry's romantic moods in Lancashire.

Pendle Hill and the course of the Ribble below it, Keighley Moor above Airedale, and Rumbles Moor with the River Wharfe winding along the valley to Otley, indicate main lines of demarcation to divide landscape spoliations from scenery left much as nature intended it to be and wide acres improved by sons of the soil under clear and broad skies—that is to say, at this page we can forget all about industrialism and change over to works productive of less cash and higher standards in the real art of life, graciously presented beyond the barrier lines mentioned above in the forms of villages and country towns, farms and fields, dales and river valleys, rugged or wooded heights, untrodden ways over great silent moors, the infinite promise offered by England's best and highest mountains. These are just the places in which it is glorious to be alive, to look well around, do nothing in particular and, perched more than 2,000 feet towards heaven on Great Whernside or Ingleborough, say to hell with all politicians down at a few feet above sea-level in Westminster dictating welfare for everybody with very low standards of earthy living. It is amazing how brave and elevated you can feel, how satisfied with the world deficient in human planning when on the top of a really good mountain!

The Yorkshire Pennines can elevate our bodies and souls in remote and likely places for the purpose. They offer height and space very suitable for people fit in the legs, good with Ordnance one-inch maps, who are fond of seeing nobody about, and like unlimited draughts of bracing air coolish in temperature, for local upland dwellers have been reported to say the climate is wintry for three parts of the year and bad for the remainder—a weather depression I have found to be rather wide of the truth. Untrammelled by industry's encumbrances, this section of England's backbone is able to show off the real character and typical beauty of mountain limestone scenery, the spreading foothills, the long backs of moorlands, swelling upward curves, the outcrops and crags. The masses northward from Simon Seat, Burnsall Fell, Malham Lings and Gordale Scar, are punctuated by Great Whernside (2,245 feet), Ingleborough (2,373 feet), Whernside (2,414 feet), Baugh Fell (2,216 feet), Lovely Seat (2,213 feet), Great Shunner Fell (2,340 feet); the succession of fells, moors, and ridges mount up through Langstrothdale Chase, Abbotside, Angram and Birkdale Commons, and moors continuing to moors lead to Lune Forest and Mickle Fell (2,591 feet) at the top of Yorkshire's North Riding, a wild and solitary region that gave me the impression no human being was in residence for miles in this highest part of the county. In all these directions are the routes and no routes for discovering points and high places too good for words but true and good for the finding. They bring the feeling of being on the top of the grand world, of leaving that other spot of time and trouble far down on earth or in the bowels thereof while you see the unending panoramas, peak repeating peak, steep declivities leading to floors of valleys, the colours changing in brilliance and depth as clouds march along between the sun and mountain tops to variegate the lights and the shadows. There are the anticipated vistas you never find, those over the next hill, on the far side of that distant crag, always in the just-beyond, like the hidden treasures in the fairy tales. Here man and his works are duly insignificant; few, if any, stone buildings usually are visible among these big creations of the Master Architect.

From bleak sources—Ure Head at 2,186 feet on Lunds Fell is one good example—the becks and streams run down, growing from small beginnings to be the rivers sweeping along and ending in the River Ouse on the Plain of York. Flowing clear and fast, tumbling over rapids and waterfalls (as at Aysgarth), tuning waters' own songs against rocks, they hasten through the dales, the Yorkshire Dales loved by the dalesmen, adored by all Yorkshire folk and knowing people in every English county. Arkengarthdale, Swaledale, Wensleydate, Nidderdale, Wharfedale, and Airedale open out below the stretches of moor and fell set like the fingers of nature's hand extended from the great arm of the Pennines. Between the dales and connecting one to the other run the passes, gorges, and lesser dales, often prolific in bumps, steep gradients, twists and turns, "Paradise enow" for walkers strong on their feet but liable to be the very devil for adventurers mounted on internal-combustion engines. Typical specimens are Coverdale and Bishopdale between Wharfedale and Wensleydale; Garsdale directing west from Wensleydale below Baugh Fell to the remote market town and famous school of Sedbergh; West Stonesdale mounting to Tan Hill, to panoramas for making anybody speechless and breathless, and an inn for solace on the spot at 1,732 feet up; Stake Pass for a stiff method of progress from Buckden to Bainbridge. One way of going from Hawes and the upper reaches of the River Ure to Muker far up Swaledale is by the Buttertubs

tubs Pass (247), peculiar for limestone formations that give the pass its name; great distances show impressively, and if the route may seem forbidding and desolate in parts a certain grandeur is always piled below the upstanding peaks of Lovely Seat and Great Shunner Fell. More frequented is the way past the reservoirs, the trees, the stone farms at Blubberhouses and through Kex Gill Gorge (247). It leads to the glorious scenes of Wharfedale, and on again to Skipton commanding Airedale from its stronghold, still a great castle of massive walls, towers, fine gatehouse and Tudor buildings, a lurking-place in the good old Edwardian days for Robert Clifford who specialized in fighting the Scots and finally came to grief in the rout at Bannockburn.

Of its kind the dale scenery can give and does yield almost everything in landscape compositions and patterns schemed in nature's many moods, austere, grim, noble, buoyant, and smiling. A sombre dignity belongs to the wild places hemmed in by moors and mountains, such as you find in the upper fastnesses of Arkengarthdale, Swaledale, and Wensleydale above Langthwaite, Keld, and Hawes. Lower down the valleys open out wider, meet the slopes marked out with the stone byres and walls of fields. Variety is plentiful and well distributed. There are the cascades and waterfalls, dappled surfaces of streams running fast, ravines, wooded hollows, and distant green hills, the "rocks and crags" that Wordsworth saw, the "View of the Wharfe" painted by Girtin, the originals of dozens of subjects pictured by scores of artists. Churches, houses, and cottages harmoniously built of the native stone group in little grey towns and chains of riverside villages. Here and there particular features stand out—Grinton church, the earthworks of Maiden Castle, and Marrick priory ruins in Swaledale, the Scropes' gaunt fortress-mansion of Castle Bolton in which Mary Queen of Scots was a prisoner in Wensleydale, thick walls of the Nevilles' great stronghold and twelfth-century keep at Middleham, the old ruined church at Pateley Bridge in command of wonderful views over Nidderdale; and if it be possible to make the choice, I think best of all is Wharfedale with its wealth of natural and man-made beauty gathered at Bolton Bridge and Abbey (242), Barden Tower, Burnsall (11), Threshfield, Conistone with its bridge crossing to Kilnsey and Kilnsey Crag, and Kettlewell and Buckden crouched below the big shapes of Great Whernside, Buckden Pike, and the fells.

The Pennines face west towards Lancashire. Dominated by the long backs of Ingleborough and Whernside and cut by Dentdale, Kingsdale, and Ribblesdale, it is a part of the world full of good things. The steep heights, the streams and waterfalls, and all the features I have mentioned show the mountain scenery at its best. Typical stone villages and hamlets continue in a line from Dent (248) in its own dale to Thornton-in-Lonsdale, Ingleton, Newby, Clapham, Giggleswick, and Malham. Two in the number of family manorial homes are the Paleys' sixteenth-century hall at Langcliffe, and the Ingleby's seventeenth-

CLAPDALE
nr Ingleborough

century stone gables, mullions, and tower of Lawkland Hall. Others of the kind, and the farmhouses with rough stone or whitened walls and heavy roofs face wind and weather high up on the slopes.

The Pennines project the outlying moors and fells centred round Bowland Forest and spreading into Lancashire. The Ribble, down from the mountains, meets its lower borderlands. The lovely vale gradually widens. It gains in colour from woods, cultivated fields, parks, the lines of trees, and extends onward in broad green stretches between Harrop Fell and Pendle Hill, pointing for Whalley's splendid church and ruined abbey, and the horseshoe bend of the stream where Roman cavalry crossed the ford at Ribchester. Villages hereabout show prettily on and above the river, notably at East and West Marton, at Bolton-by-Bowland's cross on the green, Gisburn's street of stone houses, at a very attractive Downham. A picturesque landmark is made in the hilly town of Clitheroe with the castle on the rock, a battered ruin of de Lacy's Norman keep that fell to the Roundheads after their victory at Marston Moor.

One way out of Yorkshire into Lancashire is across the packhorse bridge over the River Hodder, a link between the two counties from Mitton Green to Stonyhurst College. Very graceful is the span of this bridge. It has a high central arch, smaller ones at each side, and gives a track of six feet wide as I measured it. A road bridge alongside serves for to-day now that packhorses are defunct. The country round is nicely wooded and charmingly watered by the Hodder and the Ribble flowing to and past their meeting-place. Stone buildings peep out from the greenery, seen at a restored Little Mitton Hall, New Hall of 1665, the tower and gables of Dutton Hall, and more old manor-houses and farms. Further north another and wilder connection between county and county mounts from the River Hodder at Dunsop Bridge through the Trough of Bowland, lonely and impressive, between steep declivities of moors and marked in the defile at the top with the county boundary-stone. But whichever way you enter north Lancashire from the Pennine fells, ahead lies the plain, physically and geologically an extension of the Cheshire flats continued to Fleetwood and the Lune estuary. My notes made there indicate wide landscapes generally lying low at 15 to 50 feet above sea-level; open grass country with sheep, many streams, windmills in the Fylde, copses and orchards, a sprinkling of parks, grey stone villages; Greenalgh castle in ruins near Garstang, first built in 1490 by the Stanley who crowned King Henry on Bosworth Field; a quaint market-place at Poulton-le-Fylde; and for a coastal ending, miles of sands, parades, hotels, lodging-houses, peppermint rock and—Blackpool's Tower, democracy's monument made of 2,500 tons of steel and iron!

All roads next lead to Lancaster—and also to Morecambe for those in quest of proletarian Venuses who compete as bathing beauties on dry land for silver rose bowls and free holidays. My space is running too short for praise of feminine legs and accessories observed while celebrated connoisseurs judged them in the ozone of Morecambe, but Lancaster on the Lune, by contrast meekly attractive, ancient, and meriting pages, cannot be denied a word or two. This county capital stands well on its hills and in the valley between them. Castle, church, and town group picturesquely on one eminence above the river (234–235); the other height with the Ashton Memorial on it is a wonderful viewpoint for panoramas of walls, roofs, chimney-pots, churches, two town halls, shops, houses, and streets spread out and leading to open country in a manner right and typical for an English centre that thrives on agriculture, making things, and is pleasant to live in. Of course it is historic. Being so, you naturally think of John of Gaunt in winding up the steep cobbled ways to Castle Hill. But the great stronghold, first a Roman *castrum*, then a big Norman keep with walls ten feet thick to defy Scottish raiders, and later restored and enlarged by "time-honour'd Lancaster," has been so hemmed in with conveniences for lawyers, criminals, festivities, and modern uses that it disappoints for a reminder of Edward III's son, a figure so large on history's pages. For survivals of the gatehouse, keep, towers, and particularly the cells and dungeons we may be thankful and at the same time ungrateful at not finding more. The neighbouring church with the eighteenth-century tower has fared better. It shows the Perpendicular nave and choir, and the stallwork prodigal in tracery patterns, foliage carving, canopies, pinnacles and enriched misericords, the sumptuous finery of fourteenth-century carpentry. The town, coloured cool grey with stonework built in the solid northern style, also offered me the Judge's Lodging for a picture (233), the eighteenth-century quality of Queen Anne and Georgian houses round the castle and in the streets, comfort, food and sleep at a rejuvenated *Royal King's Arms,* and a shop's sign of "Clog Repairs" to denote a local fashion. Perhaps most exciting were my discoveries of numerous yards and narrow ways lined with houses and reached through small covered entrances from main streets. These reminders of the good old days, locally called "passages" or "ginnels," served to preserve human pates and household goods when marauders from the north paid frequent visits in search of booty. Inhabitants inside a ginnel could, and did, guard and hold the narrow entrance to keep invaders out. The example illustrated on page 259 was sketched in the Market Square at the side of the *Blue Anchor* inn. Similar defensive arrangements for domestic life are obvious in Penrith, Carlisle, and elsewhere. They influenced the planning of northern towns during the sixteenth and seventeenth centuries.

North of Lancaster more signs of turbulent years are given by the towered halls, usually built round a defensive peel tower as seen at Claughton Old Hall, Borwick Hall, and Thurland Castle, originally erected in the fourteenth century and mentioned in the old ballad of "Flodden Field" (228). These stand in the neighbourhood of the Lune, the lovely river in the loveliest of valleys, pictured by Turner and praised by Ruskin. The stream ripples over weirs and shallows, flows silently through deeper pools. Sweeping along in noble bends past Tunstall (Lowood in *Jane Eyre*) and Arkholme, it traces the Crook of Lune at Caton (Turner's subject), turns a V of rare beauty between wooded banks below Halton Green, and winds round the old cotton mill (236). Rocks here, rushy banks there, line the riversides in the sylvan vale stretching away to meet the moorland hills and Pennine mountains. Churches, houses and cottages in stone-built villages—Halton, Nether and Over Kellet are three—show prettily in the valley and among bumpy hills leading towards the coast. High places above flats and the shore yield shining visions; you look over miles of golden sands gleaming in Morecambe Bay, charming estuary scenery, the distant peaks beyond Coniston Water bounding the curiously detached piece of Lancashire that promises the sights of Cartmel priory church and gatehouse (248), Duddon Sands, and the great scene at Furness Abbey.

TO THE ROMAN WALL

Pennine and Lakeland mountains, England's biggest; valleys and rivers between them, very lovely; the undulating plain around Carlisle, green and pastoral; a seaward boundary of low coast—these mainly determine the landscapes in this final peregrination through Westmorland and Cumberland. The mountain masses predominate. Man, compared with them, appears small even when six feet odd in stature. Thus it is not surprising to find that his works are not very conspicuous or notable over wide areas; earlier dwellers, short of wireless, machinery, and other devices for bridging space and removing mountains, no doubt felt an inferiority complex in living amongst surroundings so much more elevated than themselves. For centuries the region was isolated, sparsely populated with a rude and self-contained civilization. Natives followed traditional methods of primitive agriculture and building, made homespun in spinning galleries from the wool of their sheep, spent a good deal of time in rows, scraps with marauders, bull-baiting, and cock-fighting (the bishops of Carlisle even had their own cockpit at Rose Castle). The few towns where industry managed to thrive supported weavers and other workers, tradesmen, merchants. Shakespeare must have known of this in 1597 when he clothed "three misbegotten knaves in Kendal green", and records prove the existence of Hamburg merchants in Carlisle to establish woollen manufacture soon after the Young Pretender's rebellion. In due course industry expanded at both these towns, along the coast with shipping, coal and iron, and lead-mining prospered around Alston. Walter Scott met Charlotte Carpenter at Gilsland, married her in Carlisle Cathedral; consequently, instead of emigrating to Jamaica he immortalized local scenes and characters in literature. Poets arrived in Lakeland, did just the same for daffodils, shepherd boys, Kirkstone Pass, Dungeon Ghyll, and other handy objects. Old Crome painted *Brathay Bridge*, Turner produced *Morning on Coniston Fells*, both for the National Gallery. The intelligentsia followed the poets, led the processions of tourists, coaches, and cars that ever since have headed for the same direction.

Through all the changes of Time the peaks, the fells, and the moors stood unmoved, consequential and supreme. They yet rule their dominion and are likely to go on doing so unless something very dreadful happens. They remain superior in authority, influence, and pictorial motive, the district's inspiration for poets, artists, novelists, and all mankind who scan the heights from far and near, scramble over them, crawl to the tops, and on lofty points learn nature's secrets and see visions from "the everlasting hills." Scafell, Skiddaw, Helvellyn, grand shapes of Saddleback and Langdale Pikes, sharp peaks and bold outlines command the dales and watery expanses of the Lake District. The one impression I give on page 258 might be amplified by a hundred variations of the mountains and lakes, passes and tarns. But this compact and popular area needs no further pictures or words from me to explain its features or enhance its great reputation; and a visit to the rebuilt Elizabethan *Oak* inn at Keswick (now the *Royal Oak*) serves to introduce names of the celebrated Lakeland forerunners who gathered there—the Wordsworths, Sir Walter Scott, Southey, Samuel and Hartley Coleridge, Shelley, de Quincey, Tennyson, R. L. Stevenson, and John Peel. The great Pennine fells, wild, lonely, and capped by Cross Fell, face the Lakeland peaks and continue northward. The ancient Maiden Way, leading from Lancashire to Bewcastle Cross and the Border, skirts Alston, England's highest

KILLHOPE PASS

market town (12). Eastward a road directs through Killhope Pass, also England's highest. Running fast from the mountains innumerable streams grow into rivers, the Lune, Eden, and Irthing, the Kent down from Kentmere, the Duddon, Derwent, and the streams of Lakeland—names which mean that Westmorland and Cumberland river scenery is rarely equalled and nowhere excelled in England.

The vernacular buildings in town and country modestly garnished their natural settings until England developed the bad mania for industrial expansion (dreary results thereof are visible in the southward approach to Carlisle) and Victorians left examples of their handiwork now fit to make beholders weep or shudder (painfully obvious in Windermere, Keswick, and other spoilt places). In this hilly, dale and vale district the old cottages, farms, churches, town quarters, and houses were sturdily made of the native stone, built straight-forwardly, and without many fanciful or pretty bits added for the northern wet, blasts, and snows to weather off, the climate being an important influence in dic-tating appearance and style. Effects generally have a strong, plain, and serviceable look, and the homes of the statesmen and dalesmen particularly show a rugged quality in exact harmony with their surroundings. Original elements in this make-up of grey stone or whitewashed walls and slated roofs are retained in towns and villages by the score. Characteristic are Melmerby below its Pennine fell, little Whitbeck crouched facing the giant mass of Black Combe, and Troutbeck (257), with its cottages and statesmen's houses standing at the entrances to Kirkstone Pass and the Roman mountain road above Patterdale and Ullswater, in my choosing the most interesting of the Lakeland villages. Dalston, the home of the fighting cocks on the Caldew, and Temple Sowerby, once a home of the Knights Templars on the Eden, stand for two good samples of the valley villages beautifully settled along the rivers. Three other pleasant

·TROUTBECK. *One of the most characteristic stone villages in Lakeland, on the road from Kirkstone Pass.*

BOLTON-LE-SANDS. *Farmhouse, dated 1687, facing Morecambe Bay and distant Lakeland mountains.*

KESWICK, DERWENTWATER AND BORROWDALE. *Nature's architecture seen from the lower slopes of Skiddaw.*

PENRITH. One of the "yards" with houses. LANCASTER. Passage or "ginnel" at the Blue Anchor inn, formerly lined with houses. These characteristic features of the north country, reached from main streets only through narrow openings, were schemed for defence against marauders. Many of them date from the sixteenth century.

CARLISLE *keep and cathedral in the "Red City" of Border strife and ballad. The*
in 1745. Fire and war destroyed much of the cathedral and monastic buildings bu

...de a prison for Mary Queen of Scots and was captured by Bonnie Prince Charlie
...ieval choir remains with a masterpiece of Decorated tracery in the great east window.

YANWORTH, *built in the fourteenth century and subsequently altered. One of the defensive peel-towers peculiar to the counties where raids from over the Border constantly happened. It has very thick walls and look-out turrets at the top.*

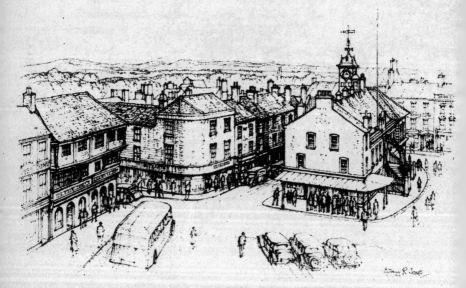

CARLISLE. *Green Market and St. Alban's Row at the junction of English Street and Scotch Street. The Guildhall, dating from the fourteenth century, is on the left and at the right is the pretty Town Hall, built in 1673.*

BIRDOSWALD. *Wreckage of a lost empire. Relics of the fort at Ambloganna, the largest station on the Roman Wall. Here the track led Roman soldiers north to Bewcastle Fells and Scotland, and the Ninth Legion never came back.*

Sidney R. Jones, Brougham Castle

BROUGHAM CASTLE in Westmorland. The gatehouse (c.1270) and the keep (c.1170) of the home of the Cliffords standing between the Pennine Range and the Lakeland mountains. A romantic story of Henry, the Shepherd Lord Clifford, inspired Wordsworth's poem, "Song at the Feast of Brougham Castle."

and noteworthy places that I liked near Penrith are Greystoke with a collegiate church, Askham embowered in greenery, and Lowther, very remarkable for its classic air, Georgian formality, and a glorious backing of the lordly park. Market squares, High Streets and byways of the towns have dignified seventeenth- and eighteenth-century houses of a local quality. Poking about, I have discovered them in Kirkby Lonsdale, Kirkby Stephen, Appleby, Penrith, Carlisle, and at Wordsworth's birthplace, Cockermouth, a sedate and balanced frontage behind the forecourt wall and pillored gateway.

In this borderland of feuds and fighting, ballad, song, and story perhaps the most exciting days and moments quickly fly in tracking reminders of man's innate desire to break the Tenth Commandment. Here, there and everywhere stand the visible signs—town lanes and back yards, castles, peel towers, ruins, some romantically poised, others draughty or looking grim, and all of them at any time liable to make one recall a line or two from Scott,

> The frightened flocks and herds were pent
> Beneath the peel's rude battlement,

or another one by Canon Rawnsley,

> Here they heard the battle cry—when the Picts and Scots swept by.

Thrilling hours have I spent in finding these relics of strife at Lammerside and Pendragon high in the Pennines, at Kentmere and Sizergh near Kendal, at Yanworth (262), Brougham (263), Penrith castle and town yards (259), Norman keeps at Appleby and Brough, Naworth most impressive and beautifully situated, and north of the Roman Wall at Triermain, Askerton, Shank, and Bewcastle. Dozens more are there for the seeking, with stones erect or tumbled down to inspire new volumes of Border ballads.

Carlisle castle (260–261) brings the story of Border fighting to the "Red City" on the red sandstone of the fertile plain, historic ground trodden by successive invaders and where Romans settled behind Hadrian's Wall that stretched from the Solway to the Tyne. Alternatively held by the English and the Scots, besieged, burnt, successfully defended, and captured more times than anybody can count, you may stand in the city to-day by the pretty town hall, admire its dainty features of 1673 painted cream and green (262), look north along Scotch Street and south down English Street without noticing any blood-thirsty marauders or moss troopers on the rampage or even dogs fighting. With so many commotions going on in the old days the cathedral was not likely to remain unharmed for long periods. After being put up by the Normans, knocked down, and put up again in bits at various times it has emerged from the past like a fighting cock shorn of its tail, or nave, but complete in headpiece, or choir, adorned with a supreme east window, a most brilliant example of Decorated tracery. Names and initials roughly cut on the fifteenth-century choir stalls show that church made a prison for Jacobite captives in 1745; reading "Richard Spenglay" and "William Monk" on the woodwork may cause one to wonder if the poor devils met their doom on Gallows Hill and left wives and children sorrowing far away in Scotland.

Thoughts and excitements about the Roman Wall naturally come uppermost in Carlisle. These can be satisfied best by visiting the splendid Roman collection excellently displayed in Tullie House, a notable building of the seventeenth century with fine spout-heads dated 1689. Out in the open air this wall can be a disappointment for those who expect to see forts, mile-castles, turrets, and ramparts bristling all over the landscapes; owing to trouble with labour, materials, and perhaps trade unionists, the Romans could only erect their fortification with turf from the Solway to the River Irthing and confined the impressive stonework to Northumberland. After miles of tramping I did find Roman stone mixed with the beautiful masonry at Lanercost Priory, at farmhouses, in the chancel arch at Denton church, and stones to draw at Birdoswald (264), the place of *Amboglanna*, the largest of the forts dramatically situated above lovely wooded banks of the Irthing. Northward from there ran the track which led Romans to Scotland. It passed their isolated fort at Bewcastle, now to be traced near the ruined castle built of Roman stones, and the Bewcastle Cross of the eighth century, one of England's great art treasures. Early in the second century the men of the Ninth Legion went that way, vanished mysteriously; probably annihilated in battle over the Border, they faded from history. But while I sought these signs of distant times, pondered, and sketched here and there, the weather was mixed, wet and fine. The wind blew down from Bewcastle Fells. The Nine Nicks of Thirlwall frowned ominously in Northumberland. Clouds lowered and threatened over the loneliness. I began to realize why Roman soldiers considered it a kind of purgatory to do duties on the Wall, decided to hasten from it myself before being drenched or blown away. Soon I reached Carlisle. While looking at the perfect east window of the cathedral from outside, a man wearing a bowler hat and a blue suit (which may have concealed a gun) advanced from the iron gateway alongside and said,

"Ya canna get in.   It's locked oop."

I fled, fearing that the ghosts of Kinmont Willie, Bold Buccleuch, and William of Cloudsley might rise up and grab me, sought refuge in the nearest peel tower, named the *Crown and Mitre*, fortified my spirits with grilled salmon (perhaps poached), roast duck (possibly decoyed), and something else (maybe smuggled), and thus completed my own raids on *England West*.

LIST OF ILLUSTRATIONS

INDEX

INDEX